D1859831

SMALL AND MEDIUM ENTERPRISES UNDER GLOBALISATION

SMALL AND MEDIUM ENTERPRISES UNDER GLOBALISATION

Challenges and Opportunities

L. RATHAKRISHNAN

KALPAZ

Small and Medium Enterprises Under Globalisation : Challenges and Opportunities

Rs. 750

© L. Rathakrishnan

ISBN: 978-81-7835-764-5

All rights reserved. No part of this book may be reproduced in any manner without written permission.

Published in 2009 in India by
Kalpaz Publications
C-30, Satyawati Nagar,
Delhi-110052
E-mail: kalpaz@hotmail.com
Phone : 9212729499

Lasser Type Setting by: Rudra Computer Graphics, Delhi
Printed at : Young Art Press, Delhi - 92

Dedicated to
My
Father

Contents

Foreword	11
Preface	13
Acknowledgements	19
List of Contributors	21

PART - I SMALL AND MEDIUM ENTERPRISES UNDER GLOBALISATION

1. **Economic Analysis of Growth and Resource Use Efficiency of Small Scale Industries in Tamil Nadu** 27
   Duraisamy, A
2. **Globalisation and Growth Prospects of Small and Medium Enterprises in India** 40
   Shashi Kumar, R
3. **Facets of Small Scale Industries in the Liberalised Regime** 60
   Sankaran, A
4. **Growth of Khadi and Village Industry Sector in India** 71
   Murugan, N. and S. Manivel
5. **Kyoto Protocol's Clean Development Mechanism and it's Feasibility to Indian Small Scale Industries under Globalisation** 87
   Dhulasi Birundha Varadarajan

PART - II EMPIRICAL STUDIES OF SMALL AND MEDIUM ENTERPRISES UNDER GLOBALISATION

6. **Benefits of Globalisation: Small and Micro Enterprises – A Case Study** 109
Ramachandran, S. and P. Narayanasamy

7. **Profitability Analysis of Select Cottage Industry – A Case Study** 121
Manivel, S. and N. Murugan

8. **Micro Enterprise in Bamboo Based Activity** 142
Rathakrishnan, L.

9. **Non-Timber Forest Products based Small and Medium Enterprises: Vehicles for Lessening Rural Poverty** 155
Vaidehi, S.

10. **Status and Achievements of Wind Power Industry in Tamil Nadu** 171
Dhulasi Birundha Varadharajan and M. Murugan

PART – III FOOD PROCESSING INDUSTRY UNDER GLOBALISATION

11. **Performance of Small Enterprises in Dairying – A Study with Reference to Madurai District** 187
Haridoss, R. and I. Jeyaraj

12. **Impact of Globalisation – Opportunities and Challenges in the Dairy Sector** 200
Seethalakshmi, M. and M. Sankar

13. **Globalisation and Cashew Processing Industry: Prospects and Problems** 208
Nehru, S.

14. **Dairy Cooperative Marketing Business Organisations in the Globalised Market Environment** 218
Samwel Kakuko Lopoyetum

PART - IV WOMEN ENTREPRENEURSHIP IN THE MIDST OF GLOBALISATION

15. **Access to Micro Finance and Women Entrepreneurship** 235
Rathakrishnan, L. and V.P. Sriraman
16. **Development of Rural Women – Role of Self Help Groups** 262
Muthaiyan, P., K. Selvanathan and James Terance Sekar
17. **Promoting Mother and Young Child Friendly Communities Through Health and Nutrition Entrepreneurs** 269
Shahin Sultana, A.
18. **An Analytical Study of Women Empowerment Through Entrepreneurship Development Policies: A Case of Chhattisgarh** 285
Sambit Kumar Mishra

PART – V SMALL AND MEDIUM ENTERPRISES: CHALLENGES AND OPPORTUNITIES

19. **Small and Medium Enterprises in India under Globalisation: Challenges and Opportunities** 311
Sabesh Manikandan, M.
20. **Challenges for Small Scale Industries in the Era of Globalisation** 332
Thiripurasundari, K. and V. Gurumoorthy

Index 347

Foreword

The process of Globalization has become irreversible in India. In a developing country like ours, Small and Medium Enterprises have a significant role to play in development process providing employment to the teeming millions. Today, the Small and Medium Enterprises are pitted against international and multinational organizations.

Globalization has offered opportunities and competitiveness. But the predicament of Small and Medium Enterprises in terms of capacity and technical know-how is a source of serious concern.

The book entitled "Small and Medium Enterprises under Globalization: Challenges and Opportunities" contains empirical studies on Small and Medium Enterprises, the status of Women Entrepreneurs and Food Processing Industries besides the challenges and opportunities ahead against the backdrop of Globalization in India.

I sincerely appreciate the efforts taken by Dr. L. Rathakrishnan, Reader, Department of Rural Industries and Management, Gandhigram Rural University, Gandhigram for bringing out this volume. The book will, I hope, awaken our conscience to look at the rural realities and work for betterment of the voiceless and the meek in our society.

Dr. M.R. KUBENDRAN
Chairman, Interim Admn. Committee
Gandhigram Rural University Gandhigram.

Preface

Industrialisation of a country is sine-quo-non for economic development. The process of industrialisation has been accelerated since second five year plan. The industrial policy resolution (1948) identified and regulated the areas of operation for the public and private sectors. The industrial policy statement of 1980 was a positive step to ensure participation of private sector in wide sphere. Some of the positive steps of the industrial policy are: (i) delicensing of majority areas; (ii) removal of restrictions on location of industries; and (iii) elimination of provisions relating to expansion and mergers. These policies have helped the growth of industries in India. Further, the liberalisation policy of 1991 has given enormous boost to private investment in the industrial sector. The industrial policy of 2006 further strengthened the growth prospects of industry and its significance in the national economy.

As a policy, Government of India has been very keen to develop the Small and Medium Enterprises (SMEs) since 2006. Through this concept, the Government tries to create the economic development and employment generation in achieving the faster economic growth rate enunciated by the planning commission. In fact, the SMEs, popularly known as Small Scale Industries (SSIs) account for about 95 per cent of industrial units, produce 7500 products and contribute about 40 per cent of the industrial output. The SMEs create largest employment opportunities (18 million persons) and export 36 per cent of the total export from 32 million registered units. It is estimated that the SSIs alone contribute to seven per cent of India's GDP. It provides an opportunity to the nation through harnessing local competitive advantages for achieving global dominance.

In order to enhance the global competitiveness, the definition of SSI is broadened to include medium enterprises in a composite sector of SMEs. As such, the industries, which invest in plant and machineries from Rs.1 crore to 10 crores may be treated as SMEs. The revision and modification assures the SMEs go for all round development and generation of large-scale employment opportunities.

The globalisation policies of the government affected the growth pattern of Indian SSIs to a great extend. There is a shift of policy from "production – led growth to competition – led growth". Nonetheless, there is a continuous increase in the number of SSIs over a period of time. It increased from 19.48 lakhs units in 1990-91 to 35.10 lakhs units in 2002-03. But performance in terms of employment, production, and exports are not satisfactory. The reasons for the dismal performance are:

- under the new policy, the government has de-reserved many goods, which were earlier reserved only for the small scale industries;
- stiff competition between large and small scale industries and also from abroad.
- the use of capital intensive technology in the small scale sector created adverse effect on the employment generation;
- inadequate access to the finance;
- lack of co-ordination in the globalised regime; and
- lack of experiences in managing business in a competitive market economy.

The SMEs are facing great challenges on product standardisation, total quality management, subsidies, and action taken against dumping. They are exposed to direct competition from large scale industries, both from domestic and foreign companies. It is also equally a challenging task for the SMEs to keep world standards like development and implementation of clean development mechanism and reduction of green house gas emission. Besides, the SMEs get proper infrastructure facilities from the government and quality maintenance.

Globalisation has opened the world market through these SMEs- in order to make them competitive and integrate them into world market. There is a lot of opportunities to generate employment for the women and rural unemployed youth for the development of new entrepreneurial activities. Similarly, there is a possibility for developing value added products in agro - and non-agro based industrial products. Thus, there are wide opportunities available for the SMEs to grow faster.

As a result of globalisation, the opportunities and the competitive strength of the Indian SMEs have increased to certain extent. However, it's important to look into the effectiveness of this competition with other global players. The future of Indian economy lies with the growth and diversified competitive activities of SMEs. However, there are some apprehensions about globalisation.

Fundamentally, the globalisation process is a big threat to the rural livelihoods, particularly to the rural industries, cottage and SSIs as the globalisation process exploits the natural resources and produce huge wastages.

Similarly. the capacity level of them are not enough to meet the global competition. Hence, the developing countries are not in a position to derive benefits from globalisation. Instead, the process of development may create artificial dependency on developed countries. Hence, globalisation is not sustainable.

Even the research and development activities are mostly helpful to the large and MNC than SSIs. Hence, the local industries are struggling hard to compete with foreign products.

The Special Economic Zones (SEZs), established in the process of globalisation may lead to both industrial imbalance and regional imbalances. Because, most of the SEZs are being established in prosperous areas than economically backward areas. This type of activity may encourage disparity between agricultural and industrial growth rates. As a manufacturer, the industries located inside SEZs will get preferential treatment, hence, the industries located outside SEZs will face stiff competition in the market. In due course of time even these industries may shift to locate their base in SEZs.

The globalisation process may help the service sector to grow rapidly and the agriculture and allied activities to go backward. While it helped some cities and some states to progress faster, the agriculture and marginalised labourers have been the worst affected people. Incidently, about 35 per cent of Indians are earning less than a dollar a day. Besides, inequalities also widened. It benefited to only 20-30 per cent of the people and 70 per cent of the people were worst affected by the globalisation.

It's said that globalisation opens up opportunities for SSIs. But in all practical sense the so called SSIs are not capable of taking advantages of the growth process. Similarly, globalisation means competition with the best in the world, which means more efficiency, more production, more employment and improvement in welfare of the people. But, it is not operated in developing and poor countries.

Hence, the SMEs have to find out ways to convert challenges into viable opportunities through skill development and effective marketing. Improved productivity and market linkages may bring good return. Encouraging the innovators in various fields of SMEs may help to promote globalisation. The specialised products that come from certain regions of Tamil Nadu and India are to be branded and marketed as branded products at the international level. R&D, access to information, capital, technology, product diversification, supply chain management, and quality management are the other areas that have to be concentrated on for faster development of SMEs.

The book is divided into five parts. First part deals with the SMEs under gobalisation, in which the facets of SMEs and the growth prospects are analysed. Few empirical studies of SMEs under globalisation were discussed in part two. Food processing cases were analysed in part three. The fourth part contains a series of studies conducted on women entrepreneurship in the midst of globalisation. Finally, the fifth part gives an account of challenges and opportunities of SME's under globalisation. In total twenty chapters presents some of the important issues and problems of SMEs under globalisation.

The expected outcome of the book is that it may provide an opportunity for the academicians, researchers, NGO's, industrialists and other ministerial staff to know the research findings on SMEs, policy issues, and as motivating instrument for starting innovative SME enterprises, understanding the reality and may go for adapting suitable strategies to face global competition.

L. Rathakrishnan

Acknowledgements

I wish to express my deep sense of gratitude to all contributors of this edited volume. In fact, the papers were presented in the national seminar, organised and conducted by the author, under the same title on 16-17th October 2006. The papers were thoroughly revised to suit the book format. I am thankful to all paper contributors. I would like to express my gratitude to numerous well wishers who have shared their experience in getting the book published.

The seminar was sponsored by the University Grants Commission, New Delhi and co-sponsored by the Federation of South India Producer Associations, Chennai and Kins Foundation, Gandhigram. My special thanks to them all for their financial support. Without their support this work could not have materialised.

I am under obligation to acknowledge gratefully the kind cooperation received from the Chairman, Registrar and other administrative staff of Gandhigram Rural University, Gandhigram for their support and helpfulness to get the book published in timely.

I also thank all teaching and non-teaching members of the Department of Rural Industries and Management, Gandhigram Rural University, Gandhigram for their kind support and encouragement.

I would like to extend a special acknowledgement to my teachers, namely Dr. M. Ramadoss, Dr. B.S. Nagarajan, Dr. S. Ramachandran, Dr. S. Ramasamy, Dr. S. Ramamoorthy and Dr. P.N. Ramani for their care and unflinching support throughout my career. I am deeply indebted to them all. They inspired me to take up the enterprise of writing this book.

I gratefully acknowledge the assistance and guidance received from friends and my scholars who motivated me to go for this venture. I would like to mention the help I received from my scholars, namely Mr. A. Saravanan Naidu, Ms. P. Uma, Mr.V.P. Sriraman, Mr. G. Pannir Selvam and Mr. B. Prabalolane. They all helped me in proof reading and correction.

My heartfelt gratitude to Prof. S. Lakshmi, Faculty of English and Foreign Languages, Gandhigram Rural University, Gandhigram for her kind cooperation in proof reading.

I thank Mr. Sudhi Kumar, Anandha Computers, Gandhigram for neat typing of the manuscript.

A special thanks to Kalpaz Publications, Delhi for their timely publications. I gratefully acknowledge the kind cooperation extended by the publisher.

I greatly appreciate the silent contributions given by my family members.

There are many others who also helped me indirectly without whose cooperation and support this work could not have been completed in time. I thank them all.

L. Rathakrishnan

List of Contributors

Dhulasi Birundha Varadarajan Professor and Head in Environmental Economics, School of Economics, Madurai Kamaraj University, Madurai-625 021.

Duraisamy, A Reader in Economics, Madras Christian College, Chennai.

Gurumoorthy, V HOD in Sociology, Rani Anna Govt. College, Tirunelveli – 627008.

Haridoss, R Professor and Head in Mathematical Economics, School of Economics, Madurai Kamaraj University, Madurai – 625 021.

James Terance Sekar Superintendent, Pondicherry Engineering College, Pondicherry - 605 014.

Jeyaraj, I Lecturer in Economics, Arul Anandar College, Karumathur – 625 514.

Manivel, S Reader in Cooperation, Gandhigram Rural University, Gandhigram – 624 302.

Murugan, M Senior Lecturer in Economics, Ph.D. Under FDP UGC X Plan, School of Economics, Madurai Kamaraj University, Madurai – 625 021. Email : m_murugan23@rediffmail.com

Murugan, N Assistant Professor of Management Studies, PSNA College of Engineering and Technology, Dindigul – 624 622.

Muthaiyan, P Professor in Economics, Pondicherry University, Pondicherry - 605 014.

Narayanasamy. P Temporary Lecturer in Economics, Gandhigram Rural University , Gandhigram – 624 302.

Nehru, S Selection Grade Lecturer in Economics, Gandhigram Rural University, Gandhigram-624302, Tamil Nadu

Ramachandran, S Professor in Economics, Gandhigram Rural University, Gandhigram – 624 302.

Rathakrishnan, L Reader in Rural Industries and Management, Gandhigram Rural University, Gandhigram-624 302 e-mail: rathakr@rediffmail.com

Sabesh Manikandan Lecturer in Economics, Ayya Nadar Janaki Ammal College (Autonomous), Sivakasi - 626 124.

Sambit Kumar Mishra Sr. Lecturer, Post Graduate Dept. of Management Studies, Siddaganga Institute of Technology, B.H. Road, Tumkur - 572 103.E-mail : sambit_kumar_mishra@rediffmail.com, sambit_mishra_2001@yahoo.co.in

Samwel Kakuko Lopoyetum Senior Post-Doctoral Research Fellow in Cooperation, Gandhigram Rural University, Gandhigram - 624 302.

Sankar, M Research Scholar, Faculty of Agriculture & A.H., Gandhigram Rural University, Gandhigram-624 302.

Sankaran, A Lecturer in Economics, School of Business Studies, Manonmaniam Sundaranar University, Tirunelveli.

Seethalakshmi, M Reader in Dairying, Faculty of Agriculture & A.H, Gandhigram Rural University, Gandhigram-624 302.

Selvanathan, K Registrar, Pondicherry Engineering College, Pondicherry-605 014.

Shahin Sultana. A Lecturer in Social Work, Delhi School of Social Work, Delhi University, Delhi – 7.

Shashi Kumar, R Reader in Economics, Bangalore University, Bangalore-560 056. E-mail: drrshashi@yahoo.com

Sriraman, V.P. S.G. Lecturer, Bharathidasan Institute of Management, BHEL Complex, Tiruchirapalli-620 024.

Thiripurasundari, K Reader in Commerce, Sri Parasakthi College, Courtallam – 627802.

Vaidehi, S Lecturer in Economics, Amman College of Arts and Science, Pilliar Natham, Dindigul

Part – I Small and Medium Enterprises Under Globalisation

1

Economic Analysis of Growth and Resource Use Efficiency of Small Scale Industries in Tamil Nadu

Duraisamy, A

Abstract

This chapter makes an attempt to analyse the growth of employment, production, number of units established, investment and export of SSIs in India and Tamil Nadu since liberalisation. It also aims to analyse the resource use efficiency of the inputs used in the SSIs in Tamil Nadu. Secondary sources of data were used and analysed with growth model and ordinary least squares method. The growth model indicates that the production of SSIs at current prices for 1994-2005 in India has grown at the rate of 10.74 per cent per annum. Hence, the SSIs are coping with challenges and changes needed due to liberalisation. Tamil Nadu has benefited more due to liberalisation. The growth rate of production and employment in Tamil Nadu economy exceeded the national level. The study also found a significant relationship between the inputs used and output produced. The model reveals that an unit added in the total number of SSIs in Tamil Nadu brings about 18.7 lakhs worth of output per annum. However, the marginal productivity of labour in SSIs shows a negative value. Hence, it is inferred that the SSIs have employed more amount of labour, which is not fully utilised efficiently.

Introduction

The small-scale industrial sector plays a pivotal role in Indian economy in terms of employment and growth. In spite of the stiff competition from the large sector and not so encouraging support from the government, this sector has recorded a very high rate of growth. This is evidenced by the number of registered units which went up from 16,000 in 1950 to 36,000 in 1961 and 16.38 lakhs in 2005 in India. This sector progressed from the production of simple consumer goods to many sophisticated and precision products like electronic control systems, micro-wave components, electro – medical equipment, T.V sets etc.

The performance of SSI units in India reveals that the growth rate of the output and employment has increased significantly. The rapid growth of the small-scale industries has great relevance in our national economic policies. The growth of the small sector improves the production of the non-durable consumer goods of mass consumption. This change acts as an anti-inflationary force. If a big push is given to the small scale industrial sector, it can become a stabilising factor in a capital-scarce economy like India by providing a higher output-capital ratio as well as a higher employment-capital ratio.

Industrial policy 1956 projected that SSIs provide immediate large-scale employment, they offer a method of ensuring a more equitable distribution of the national income and effectively mobilise resources of capital and utilise the available skill. The problem of urbanisation may be avoided by starting lot of SSIs all over the country. The concept of self-employment can be extended throughout the economy through this means.

In 1966, the small-scale enterprises were defined as undertakings with a fixed capital investment of less than Rs. 7.5 lakhs and ancillaries with a fixed capital investment of plant and machinery of Rs. 10 lakhs. In 1975 this limit has been raised up to Rs. 10 lakhs and Rs. 20 lakhs respectively. It has been further increased up to Rs. 20 lakhs and Rs. 25 lakhs in 1980. As per the industrial policy statement of 1990 the investment ceiling in plant and machinery for small-scale industries has been raised upto Rs. 60 lakhs and for ancillary units up to Rs. 75 lakhs. In 1997 this has been increased up to Rs. 3 crores which has been reduced to Rs. 1 crore in the year 2000. At the end of March 2002, there were 3.4 million small industry units, accounting for more than 40 per cent of gross value output in the manufacturing sector, about 35 per cent of total exports, and providing employment to over 19.2 million people, which is second only to agriculture (Planning commission, 2002). The present U.P.A Government had set up an national commission on enterprises in the un-organised / informal sector headed by Arjun Sengupta in 2004. This commission recommended to raise the investment from Rs. 1 crore to Rs. 5 crores. This committee also recommended to facilitate technology upgradation and enhancing competitiveness.

This chapter makes an attempt to analyse the growth of employment, production, number of units, investment and export of small-scale industrial sector in India since liberalisation. The objectives are as follows :

(i) To estimate the growth of output, employment investment and exports of SSI units in India with special reference to Tamilnadu, and

(ii) to analyse the resource use efficiency of the inputs in small-scale industrial sector in Tamilnadu.

Sources of Data

For the present study the researcher used various issues of economic survey of India and the reports published by the department of industries and commerce, Tamil Nadu. For India the data covers the period 1994-95 to 2004-05. For the state of Tamil Nadu the researcher used the data from 1991-92 to 2002-03. Thus, the study relied on secondary sources of data.

Statistical Tools used

To fit the trend the researcher used the growth model

$\ln Y = a + b \text{ Time} + U_z$

Production function has also been estimated by using ordinary least squares method to the data related to the inputs and the output of the small-scale units of Tamil Nadu.

Growth Performance of Small Scale Industry

The overall performance and contribution of small-scale enterprises is generally described in terms of its growth in units, employment, production and exports. The growth model gives the rate at which the variables grow per annum.

Dependent Variable – UNIT IND Method.. Growth

R Square 0.99985

Adjusted R Square 0.99983

F = 59793.92558 Signif F = 0.0000

Variables in the Equation

Variable	*B*	*SE B*	*Beta*	*T*	*Sig T*
Time	0.039985	0.000164	0.999925	244.528	0.000(
(Constant)	4.336853	0.001109		3910.443	0.000(

The above results show that for the period 1994-95 to 2004 2005 the number of SSIs in India was growing at the rate o 3.99 per cent per year.

Dependent Variable – PRDN IND Method.. Growth

R Square 0.86171

Adjusted R Square 0.84635

F = 56.08288 Signif F = .0000

Variables in the Equation

Variable	*B*	*SE B*	*Beta*	*T*	*Sig T*
Time	0.107395	0.014341	0.928286	7.489	0.0000
(Constant)	11.656979	0.097263		119.850	0.0000

The growth model indicates that the production of SSIs at current prices in India during the period 1994-2005 has grown at the rate of 10.74 per cent per annum. This reveals that this sector is coping with challenges and changes in the intensifying competitive environment emerging due to liberalisation.

Dependent Variable – PROD IND Method.. Growth

R Square 0.99381

Adjusted R Square 0.99312

F = 14444.14293 Signif F =0.0000

Variables in the Equation

Variable	*B*	*SE B*	*Beta*	*T*	*Sig T*
Time	0.078338	0.002061	0.996898	38.002	0.0000
(Constant)	11.560438	0.013981		827.105	0.0000

When the production values are deflated with the price index based on 1993-94 prices the growth rate has come down from 10.74 to 7.83 per annum during the study period. This shows that on an average during the study period the inflation prevailed at the rate of 3 per cent.

Dependent Variable – EMPT IND Method.. Growth

R Square 0.99810

Adjusted R Square 0.99789

F = 4728.63453 Signif F = 0.0000

Variables in the Equation

Variable	*B*	*SE B*	*Beta*	*T*	*Sig T*
Time	0.039302	0.000572	0.999050	68.765	0.0000
(Constant)	5.206959	0.003876		1343.268	0.0000

The above result shows that the growth of employment by SSI units in India is not on par with the production. During the study period in India the employment has grown at the rate of 3.93 per cent per year.

Dependent Variable – EXPO IND Method.. Growth

R Square 0.98423

Adjusted R Square 0.98197

F = 436.81214 Signif F = 0.0000

Variables in the Equation

Variable	*B*	*SE B*	*Beta*	*T*	*Sig T*
Time	0.128303	0.006139	0.992082	20.900	0.0000
(Constant)	10.1186294	0.034545		294.867	0.0000

The above results indicate the proportionate rate of change in exports with respect to time. It has grown at the rate of 12.83 per cent per annum. This could be because of the impact of liberalisation.

SSIs and its Growth in Tamil Nadu

Though the performance of SSIs in India during the last decade was good it is essential to see whether this trend has been the same for the states also. The researcher has taken Tamilnadu for the state level analysis. This state may not represent all the state of India, but represents most of the developed states in the country. For this purpose the researcher has considered the data for the period from 1991-92 to 2003-04.

Dependent Variable – UNIT TN Method.. Growth

R Square 0.98867

Adjusted R Square 0.98754

F = 872.75695 Signif F =0 .0000

Variables in the Equation

Variable	*B*	*SE B*	*Beta*	*T*	*Sig T*
Time	0.108240	0.003664	0.994320	29.542	0.0000
(Constant)	11.786603	0.026965		437.101	0.0000

The growth of SSI units during the period is comparatively high when compared to the whole nation. It has been growing at the rate of 10.82 per cent per annum while for India it was only 3.99 per cent. This indicates that the state of Tamilnadu has benefited more due to liberalisation and has been able to improve its share in the small-scale industrial sector.

Dependent Variable – INVT TN Method.. Growth

R Square 0.97971

Adjusted R Square 0.97768

F = 482.88710 Signif F =0.0000

Variables in the Equation

Variable	*B*	*SE B*	*Beta*	*T*	*Sig T*
Time	0.131237	0.005972	0.989804	21.975	0.0000
(Constant)	8.010933	0.043954		182.256	0.0000

The increase in the number of units reflected the investment of capital in SSI units in Tamilnadu. During the period 1991 to 2003 the investment was increasing at 13.12 per cent per annum. The higher level of investment growth may be due to modernisation and newer type of products brought under small-scale sector.

Dependent Variable – PRDN TN Method.. Growth

R Square 0.98611
Adjusted R Square 0.98473
F = 710.13270 Signif F =0 .0000

Variables in the Equation

Variable	*B*	*SE B*	*Beta*	*T*	*Sig T*
Time	0.159505	0.005986	0.993033	26.648	0.0000
(Constant)	9.635963	0.044052		218.738	0.0000

The production of SSI units in Tamilnadu has grown at the rate of 15.95 per cent per annum while the rate of growth of production in India was only 10.74. This clearly exhibits the significant role played by the SSI units in the Tamilnadu economy during the last decade.

Dependent Variable – EMPT TN Method.. Growth

R Square 0.98573
Adjusted R Square 0.98430
F = 690.66874 Signif F =0 .0000

Variables in the Equation

Variable	*B*	*SE B*	*Beta*	*T*	*Sig T*
Time	0.094272	0.003587	0.992838	26.281	0.0000
(Constant)	13.921596	0.026401		527.318	0.0000

The employment generating capacity by SSI units in Tamilnadu is higher than those at the national level. Employment has grown at the rate of 9.43 per cent per annum in Tamil Nadu while it was only just 3.93 per cent per annum in India.

The comparison between the state level performance and the national level is unavoidable. This shows that Tamil Nadu has lot of scope in extending the range of products and regional concentration in the coming years.

Comparative Performance of SSI Units in India and Tamil Nadu

Variable	*India* (1994-2005*	*Tamilnadu (1991-2003)*
No.of units	3.99	10.82
Production	10.74	15.95
Employment	3.93	9.43
Investment	--	13.12
Export	3.93	--
Prdn. (1993-94 price)	7.93	--

Resource Use Efficiency

Having proved the performance of SSI units in Tamilnadu was more significant in the growth of Tamilnadu economy it is essential to understand the relationship between inputs and outputs of the small-scale industries in Tamil Nadu. The researcher estimated the production function by using the ordinary least square method. The results are given below:

Prdn_tn = 3313.96 + 0.187 (Unit_tn) + 9.84 (Invt_tn) – 0.0387 (Empt_tn)

(2.59) (4.33) (-2.47)

$R^2 = 0.99$ F = 1005.76

Where Prdn_tn = production in cross of rupees

Unit_tn = number of registered units in Tamil Nadu

Invt_tn = investment in crores of rupees

Empt_tn = employment in numbers

The above results show that there is significant relationship between the inputs used and the output produced. The co-efficient of determination reveals that 99 per cent change in the output is explained by the variations in the input considered in this model. The 't' values are all significant at 5 per cent level. The 'F' value also shows that the model estimated is significant at even 1 per cent level.

One can interpret the results that a unit added in the total number of SSI units in Tamilnadu brings about 18.7 lakhs worth of output per annum. It can also be seen that one crore additional investment in SSI units brings about 9.84 crores per annum in Tamil Nadu. The addition to the total production, which can be also known as marginal productivity of labour in SSI units of Tamilnadu is negative valuing – 0.0387. Every additional labour reduces the production by 3.87 lakhs per annum. This shows that we have employed more amount of labour in SSI units, which is not fully utilised efficiently.

Conclusion

Small-scale industrial sector has been challenged by an increasingly competitive environment due to a) liberalisation of the investment regime in the 1990s, favouring foreign direct investment (FDI) at the international level, particularly in the developing countries like India. Domestic economic reforms bring new scope for investment and also stiff competition for the existing firms. The cumulative impact of these developments forced the small-scale industrial sector to compete or make an exit from the market. The SSIs experienced relatively higher growth rates with high labour absorption and export intensity. The performance of SSI units in Tamil Nadu showed the growth potential with employment generation and more opportunities. It should ensure more equitable distribution of income and flexibility to face the challenges and changes in the policies. This growth of SSI should contribute for decentralisation.

A change of policies from protectionism to liberalisation has helped large Indian industry and multi-nationals to enter in areas reserved for SSIs. This extreme path should be avoided since this will do more harm than good. India should choose those liberalisation policies which should help more of small scale industrial sector rather than inviting more MNCs to occupy more share of Indian market.

Appendix
Table-1
Production, Employment and Exports of SSIs in India

Year	*Units*	*Production*	*Real PRDN*	*EMPT*	*Exports*
1994-95	79.60	122210.0	109116.0	191.40	29068.00
1995-96	82.84	148290.0	121649.0	197.93	36470.00
1996-97	86.21	168413.0	135380.0	205.86	39248.00
1997-98	89.71	189178.0	147824.0	213.16	44442.00
1998-99	93.36	212901.0	159407.0	220.50	48979.00
1999-00	97.15	234225.0	170709.0	229.10	54200.00
2000-01	101.10	161289.0	184428.0	239.09	69797.00
2001-02	105.21	282270.0	195613.0	249.09	71244.00
2002-03	110.10	311993.0	210636.0	261.38	86013.00
2003-04	113.95	357733.0	228730.0	271.36	N.A
2004-05	118.53	399200.0	245747.0	282.82	N.A
Predicted values based on the growth model					
2006-07	133.8399	519443.3	315141.5	316.45	

Table-2

Trend in Growth of SSIs in Tamilnadu

Year	*Units*	*Invest.Cr*	*Prodn.Cr*	*EMPLYT*
1991-92	138404	3210.50	16747.00	1176700
1992-93	157892	3757.50	20219.00	1310500
1993-94	178114	5332.00	24048.00	1425300
1994-95	207357	5184.00	29436.00	1638200
1995-96	234409	5977.00	35161.00	1828600
1996-97	263845	6912.00	41687.00	2033000
1997-98	295004	7966.00	48675.00	2250900
1998-99	324627	9350.00	58432.00	2451000
1999-00	354939	10623.00	70987.00	2667200
2000-01	387597	11567.22	78261.66	2902122
2001-02	419524	12166.19	83904.80	3104477
2002-03	448905	12569.34	89781.00	3142335
Predicted values based on the growth model				
2006-07	742993.7	24605.62	196426.3	5025098

References

1. Bala Subramanya (2004), "Small Industry and Globalisation: Inplications, Performance and Prospects", *Economic and Political Weekly*, 39(18): 1826-34.
2. Subrahmanian, K.K (1995), "Technology Dimensions of Small Scale Industry", *Productivity*, 36(1): 26-30.
3. Verma, S.B. (2005), *WTO and Development Opportunities*, Deep and Deep Publications, New Delhi: 298-304.
4. Bibek Debroy and Laveesh Bhandari (2005), *Small Scale Industry in India: Large Scale Exit Problems*, Academic Foundation, New Delhi.
5. Ruddar Dutt and Sundharam, K.P.M. (2006), *Indian Economy*, S. Chand and Company, New Delhi.
6. Damodar, N. Gujarati (2004), *Basic Econometrics*, McGraw – Hill, New Delhi.
7. www.smallindustryindia.com

2

Globalisation and Growth Prospects of Small and Medium Enterprises in India

Shashi Kumar, R

Abstract

Among the developing countries, India's growth experience during the past five decades has been unique. Unlike many of its East and Southeast Asian neighbors, India did not grow at the "miracle" rates that exceeded 6 per cent and reached as high as 10 per cent. At the same time, unlike Africa and Latin America, it did not suffer periods of prolonged stagnation or decline. For three of the five decades (1950-80), India steadily grew at the so-called "Hindu" rate of three and a half per cent. During the remaining two decades, it grew at rates between 5 and 6 per cent. While the credit for steady growth without prolonged stagnation or decline goes to the macroeconomic stability and policy credibility that the government provided, the blame for the relatively low rate of growth, especially during 1950-80, must be assigned to the myriad microeconomic distortions and heavy state intervention that straitjacketed the entrepreneurs. Through strict investment licensing, the government effectively stamped out domestic competition and through strict import licensing, it eliminated foreign competition. It was only during the second half of the 1980s that the government began to loosen its grip on investment and import licensing followed by more systematic and comprehensive opening up in the 1990s and beyond. The promotion of the small-scale sector in India has been an important thrust of industrial policy since Independence though the focus of concern changed with the priorities of each five year plan. The six industrial Policy Resolutions which have been framed since 1948 have set out the guidelines for the country's industrial development with different degrees of emphasis on the main objectives. This chapter discusses the Small Scale Industries performance of India focusing especially on that since the inception of New Economic Policy; the impact of these policies on SSIs, efficiency and growth; and the future policies.

Introduction

The twentieth century began when the first wave of globalisation was approaching its peak. It has ended on the rising crest of a second wave far more forceful than the first. Globalisation is a source of both hope and of apprehension. One reading of economic change over the past hundred years points to strong benefits from closer integration openness to trade; factor flows, ideas and information have powerfully stimulated progress, economic and political. The most nations are at the forefront of the advance. And when the leading industrial economies turned inwards after the First World War, the retreat from globalisation was a grave setback for the entire community of nations. By some estimates, the spread of tariff and non tariff barriers affected between 50 and 70 per cent of total trade. It was only after the process was resumed slowly and fitfully in the 1950s[1], that the economic tempo quickened and resulted in five golden decades[2].

Small and Medium Enterprises and Economic Development

Small and Medium Enterprises (SMEs) have played a crucial role in economic development in developed as well as developing countries. In recent years they have occupied a pivotal position in the economic development of developing countries. This is primarily due to changing business environment. Concentration on core competencies and business process outsourcing mark the new environment. This has led to sub-contracting of business activities to SMEs. Despite their crucial position in an economy, they are the most vulnerable to rapid technological change. The rapid technological change that had been witnessed in the last decade of twentieth century has created opportunities as well as threat to the existence of SMEs. It is also perceived by many that new WTO regime might also challenge the very existence of SMEs. Globalisation and liberalised economic policies pursued by nations have exposed SMEs to large domestic enterprises and MNCs.

Globalisation and SMEs

Globalisation in a way has not only affected the competitiveness of SMEs but has also threatened the very survival of some of the weaker ones. It has forced them to re-think on their manufacturing and marketing strategies. Small and large sized companies have realised that to compete globally they need to work more closely with each other than ever before. Large enterprises can have the economy of scale, benefits of knowledge, research, marketing, branding and in some cases even financing. Small enterprises can be the low cost engines of production and generate jobs. This could be an ideal combination for Indian industry to remain globally competitive. The paper argues that there are several key and interrelated elements to globalisation and its impact on the performance of India's SMEs.

Small and Medium Enterprises in India

With the advent of planned economy from 1951 and the subsequent industrial policy followed by Government of India, both planners and Government earmarked a special role for small and medium scale industries in the Indian economy. Due protection was accorded to both sectors, and particularly for small-scale industries from 1951 to 1991, till the nation adopted a policy of liberalisation and globalisation.

SMEs always represented the model of socio-economic policies of Government of India, which emphasised the judicious use of foreign exchange for import of capital goods and inputs; labour intensive mode of production; employment generation; non-concentration of diffusion of economic power in the hands of few (as in the case of big houses); discouraging monopolistic practices of production and marketing; and finally effective contribution to foreign exchange earning of the nation with low import-intensive operations. It was also coupled with the policy of de-concentration of industrial activities in a few geographical centers.

Definition of SMEs in India and World

In India the SME is generally referred to as 'small-scale industry' including the tiny sector and the 'Small Scale Services and Business Enterprises' (SSSBE). SMEs have always represented the model of socio-economic policies of the Government of India, which emphasised judicious use of foreign exchange for import of capital goods and inputs; labor intensive mode of production, employment generation; non concentration and diffusion of economic power in the hands of a few (as in the case of the big business houses); discouraging monopolies practices of production and marketing; and finally effective contribution to foreign exchange earnings of the nation with low import-intensive operations.

In India the small and medium enterprises are not well defined. The internal group set up by the Reserve Bank of India has recently recommended that the units with investment in plant and machinery in excess of SSI limit and upto Rs.1 crore may be treated as medium enterprises. The definitions of 'small' and 'medium' sized enterprises differ from one country to another. SMEs have been defined against various criteria such as the number of workers employed, volume of output or sales, value of assets employed, and the use of energy.

As per the Micro, Small and Medium Enterprises Development Act of 2006, (India), a micro enterprise is where the investment in plant and machinery does not exceed twenty five lakh rupees. A medium enterprise is where the investment in plant and machinery is more than five crore rupees but does not exceed ten crore rupees. A small enterprise is where the investment in plant and machinery is more than twenty five lakh rupees but does not exceed five crore rupees. In the case of the enterprises engaged in providing or rendering of services, as (a) a micro enterprise is where the investment in equipment does not exceed ten lakh rupees, (b) a small enterprise is where the investment in equipment is more than ten lakh rupees but does not exceed two crore rupees, (c) a medium enterprise is where the investment in equipment is more than two crore rupees but does not exceed five crore rupees.

Objectives of SMEs in India

It can be observed that by and large, SMEs in India have met the expectations of the Government in this respect. SMEs developed in a manner which made it possible for them to achieve the following objectives, namely high contribution to domestic production, significant export earnings, low investment requirements, operational flexibility, location wise mobility, low intensive imports, capacities to develop appropriate indigenous technology, import substitution, contribution towards defense production, technology – oriented industries, and competitiveness in domestic and export markets. At the same time one has to understand the limitations of SMEs, which are:

low capital base, concentration of functions in one / two persons, inadequate exposure to international environment, inability to face impact of WTO regime, inadequate contribution towards R&D and lack of professionalism.

In spite of these limitations, the SMEs have made significant contribution towards technological development and exports. SMEs have been established in almost all-major sectors in the Indian industry such as; Food Processing, Agricultural Inputs, Chemicals and Pharmaceuticals, Engineering; Electricals; Electronics, Electro-medical equipment, Textiles and Garments, Leather and leather goods, Meat products, Bio-engineering, Sports goods, Plastics products and Computer Software, etc.

As a result of globalisation and liberalisation, coupled with WTO regime, Indian SMEs have been passing through a transitional period. With slowing down of economy in India and abroad, particularly USA and European Union and enhanced competition from China and a few low cost centers of production from abroad many units have been facing a tough time.

Those SMEs that have strong technological base, international business outlook, competitive spirit and willingness to restructure themselves shall withstand the present challenges and come out with flying colours to make their own contribution to the Indian economy.

New Economic Policies and SMEs

In order to help the sector integrate with the industry at large within liberalized economic framework, the government of India has announced new policy measures. In the present context, the following are of particular interest as announced in the year 1991:

- The investment ceiling for the purpose of definition of a small unit has been raised to Rs. 6 million (Rs. 7.5 million if the unit concerned undertakes to export 30 per cent of its output or if it is an ancillary unit i.e. a firm supplying at least 50 per cent of its output to large scale industries).

- Other investors (including large scale enterprises and foreign investors) are now allowed 24 per cent equity participation in a small scale unit
- The Act on Delayed Payments to Small and Ancillary Enterprises has been promulgated. Under this act, buying/ mother units will be required to pay interest on delayed payments for supplies bought from SSI units if the payments are delayed beyond the negotiated and agreed upon time period.
- The Reserve Bank of India has announced a package of measures to ensure a better flow of credit to the SSI through measures such as expansion of 'single window' loan scheme. Banks are encouraged to open specialised SSIs branches and to give greater priority to the sector in their annual credit budgets.
- Access to inputs has been improved by giving SSIs priority to allocation of iron and steel from public sector undertakings and by removing obstacles to imports of a range of raw materials and intermediate products.
- The number of products, which are reserved for SSIs stands at 836 in 1994. This represents a decrease of only 7 items since the economic reform process has been initiated in 1991.

The Government's Promotional Framework

The Small Industries Development Bank of India (SIDBI) was established as the principal financial institution in April 1990 under an Act of the Indian Parliament. SIDBI has been assisting the entire spectrum of Small Scale Industries (SSIs), including the small village and cottage industries, through suitable schemes tailored to meet the requirements of setting up of new projects, expansion, diversification, modernisation and the rehabilitation of existing units. The SSIs sector, including the small units, comprises the domain of SIDBI's business. The bank also finances industrial infrastructure projects for the development of the SSIs sector.

Non-government Promotion Structure

There are three national associations representing all type of industries, small and large. These are 'Federation of Indian Chambers of Commerce and Industries' (FICCI), Confederation of Indian Industries (CII) and 'Association of Chambers of Commerce and Industries' (ASSOCHAM). These associations represent mainly the interests of large scale industries. However, these associations have membership of small sector as well and represent mainly the policy related interests of SSI sector.

The exclusively small industry related associations are diversified geographically and sectorally and are supposed to have been linked with 'Federation of All India Small Scale Industries' (FASSI), 'Federation of Small and Medium Industries' (FOSMI) and also Indian Council of Small Industries (ICSI). However, these institutions are weak in character due to their working for cross purposes and lack of dynamic perspective for small scale sector growth. They have virtually no linkages with the small industry in general and their local associations in specific. Another institution that is concerned with the small and medium enterprises is 'World Assembly of Small and Medium Enterprises' (WASME). There are only a few of the local associations that are involved in providing specific individual level services to the small industry. However, all the associations are involved in lobbying with the government to provide one or the other facilities or benefits to the sector.

Policy of 2007

The Government of India has announced a Promotional Package for Micro, Medium and Small Enterprises on 27 February, 2007. Shri. Mahabir Prasad, Union Minister for Small Scale Industries and Agro and Rural Industries announced a policy package for stepping up credit to Micro, Small and Medium Enterprises in Lok Sabha on 27 February 2007, keeping in mind the goals of the National Common Minimum Programme

(NCMP). SMEs will be promoted since they are labour-intensive in nature and generate employment, which is one of the objectives of the NCMP. By enacting the Micro, Small and Medium Enterprises Development Act, 2006, the Government seeks to facilitate promotion and development and enhancing competitiveness of these enterprises.

The Government will also soon enact a law on Limited Liability Partnerships covering, among others, micro, small and medium enterprises, with a view, inter alia, to facilitating infusion of equity and venture capital funding in these enterprises. To strengthen the data base for the MSME sector, statistics and information will be collected in respect of number of units, employment, rate of growth, share of GDP, value of production, extent of sickness/closure and all other relevant parameters of micro, small and medium enterprises, including khadi and village industry units set up under Rural Employment Generation Programme and Prime Minister's Rozgar Yojana as well as coir units, through annual sample surveys and quinquennial census.

Globalisation and SMEs

The small enterprises sector is a vibrant segment of the Indian economy, which has contributed over 39 per cent of the industrial sector output and 34 per cent of the nation's exports and provided employment to over 19.965 million persons through 3.572 million units spread both in the urban and the rural areas of India. It has been estimated that 100,000 rupees of investment is fixed assets in the small-scale sector generates employment for four persons.

Along with agriculture, the small enterprise sector including SMEs provides the largest employment generation potentials in the country. During 2006-07 the small sector registered a growth rate of 8.6 per cent as against 7.0 per cent for overall industrial growth.

Growth of Units and Employment in SMEs

Although SMEs have been in focus in the literature, there is no unified definition of what constitutes these enterprises. The scale of enterprise can be measured in terms of total workforce, turnover, investment, and number of business units. In labour intensive industry the turnover of a firm might be large despite little investment. On the other hand in case of capital and skill intensive industry, an enterprise might have large turnover with few skilled workers. Hence, it is very difficult to have a unified definition of SMEs. SSIs has emerged a very dynamic sector of the Indian economy, which contributes nearly 40 per cent of the total industrial production and over 34 per cent of the national exports. The growth of units and employment in SSIs is presented in Fig. 1.

Figure 1

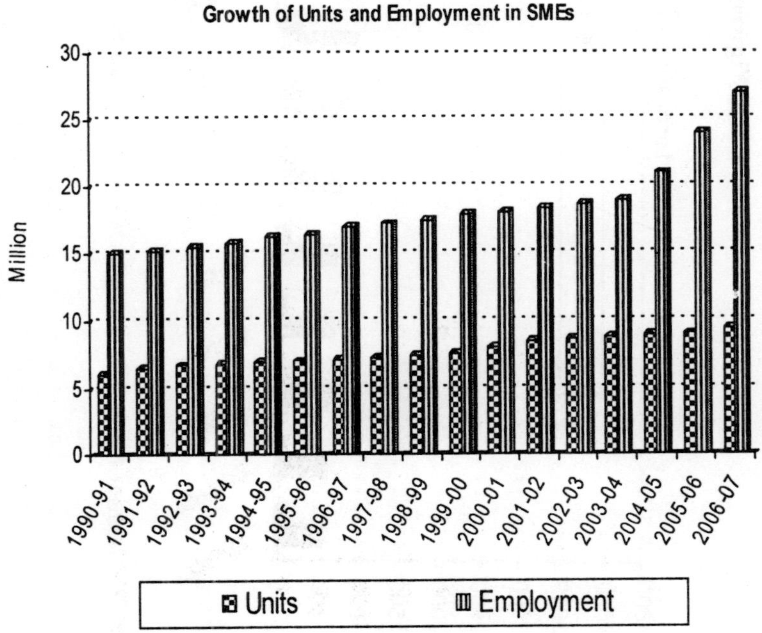

Source: CMIE Reports.

Figure 2

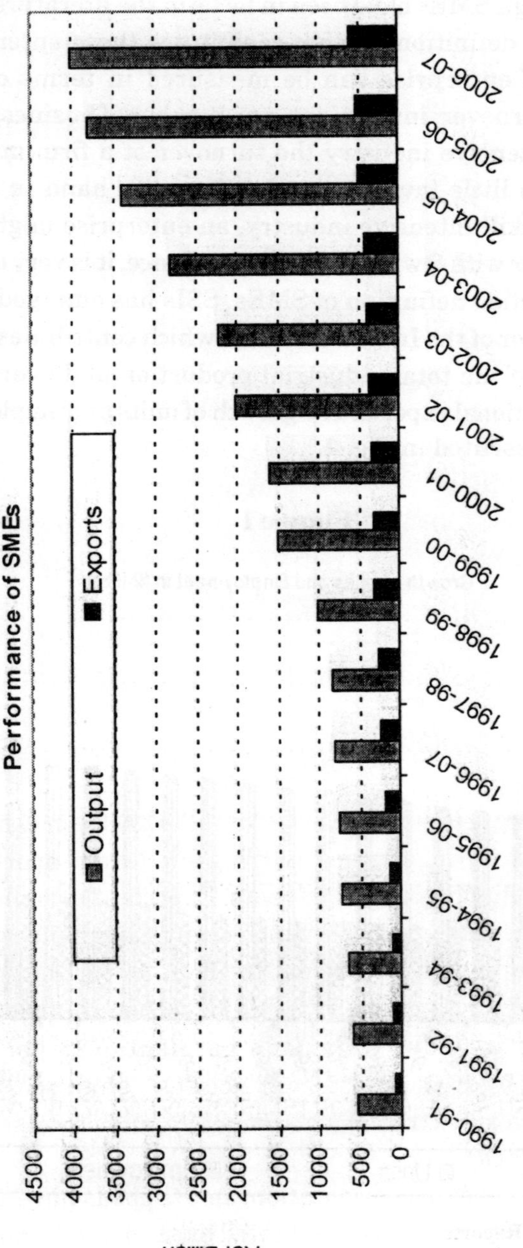

Source: Development Commissioner (SSI), Ministry of Small Scale Industries, Government of India

The SSIs sector in India employs around 26 million people and is involved with the production of over 7500 industrial items with the product range varying from very simple items produced with traditional technology to high tech products. At present, the SSIs sector accounts for over 90 per cent of industrial units in the country, 40 per cent of value addition in the manufacturing output and approximately 35 per cent of India's exports.

The Compound Annual Growth Rate (CAGR) of units has been 3.94 per cent since 1990-91 while employment has grown at 4.10 per cent during the same period. According to an estimate of annual survey of industries, average contribution of SSIs in total employment has been roughly 70 per cent since 1990-91.

Output and Exports Performance

As far as the performance of SSIs is concerned, the output has experienced CAGR of 14.15 per cent while exports have grown at 18.11 per cent annually since 1990-91. The performance of SSIs is presented in Fig. 2. It can be also seen from Fig. 3 that the percentage of exports to total output has been fluctuating during this period. It attained 25.61 per cent in 1993-94 and declined until 1998-99. It has been increasing since then and reached 27.57 per cent in 2002-03.

Small Scale Industries sector in India has been exhibiting a striking export performance. Barring few years, exports have grown double digit in the last 10 years. Exports at current prices in 2002-03, the latest year for which data is available, stood at Rs. 86,000 crores. This works out to about 34 per cent of total exports in India in the same year. Major sectors contributing to SSIs exports include readymade garments (27 per cent), engineering goods (14.5 per cent), chemicals and pharmaceuticals, electronics and computers, and processed foods (11 per cent each).

In terms of export orientation, sports goods have 100 per cent exports from SSIs sector, followed by readymade garments (90 per cent), leather (70 percent), marine products (47 per cent)

Figure 3

Export Performance Percentage

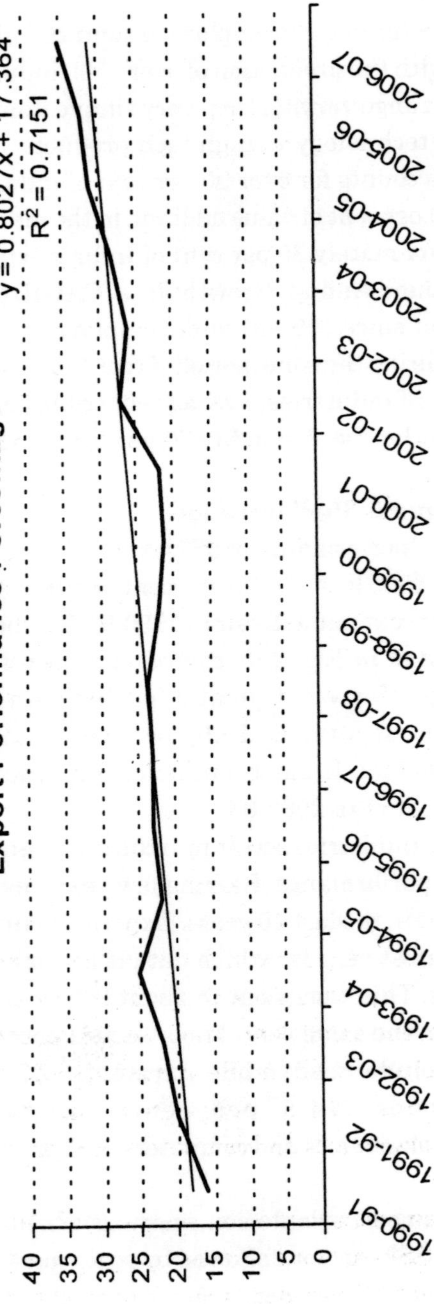

Source: National Accounts Statistics (Base 1993-94)

and chemicals and pharmaceuticals (44 per cent). Over the last 10 years, the share of SSIs exports has increased in most of the sectors. At the same time, in some sectors, the share of SSIs in total exports has come down. The SSIs intensive sectors that have witnessed increase in export share include engineering goods, chemicals and allied products, plastic products, processed foods, marine products, woolen garments and knitwear, processed tobacco. Sectors like basic chemicals & pharmaceuticals, finished leather and leather products, synthetic and rayon products have witnessed declining share in total exports. Sectors like readymade garments and sports goods were observing neutral trend, with the share remaining the same.

These 12 SSIs intensive sectors accounted for about 95 per cent of total SSI exports from India, in the year 1991-92. However, the share has come down to 85 per cent in 2002-03. While these sectors have improved their cumulative share in India's total exports from 51.6 per cent in 1991-92 to 55.5 per cent in 2002-03, the export share by SSI units in these sectors have come down from 58.4 per cent in 1991-92 to 52.4 per cent in 2002-03. Thus, it may be inferred that, since liberalisation, more and more exporting units from SSIs sector have been increasing their capital investment to come out of the SSIs net and emerge as global players.

Such a trend is happening especially in sectors like basic chemicals, pharmaceuticals, engineering goods, leather and textile sectors. There are no official data for compilation of export performance by the medium scale units. However, analysis has been made using the CMIE's India Corporate Database, which represents more than two thirds of Indian manufacturing sector. Analysis has been made to measure the export performance of medium scale units in select sectors, using two definitions, viz., based on capital investment, as defined by RBI, and based on sales turnover of units up to Rs. 75 crores. The analysis revealed that sectors like food and beverages, chemicals, auto components, machinery, electronics, metals, castings and forgings have witnessed increasing export orientation trend over the last decade.

However, the export orientation of sectors like leather, textiles and readymade garments has more or less remained static over the period. It may be inferred that these sectors, since they require plenty of capital investment to meet the global challenges, need to be kept out of any limit on capital investment, to emerge as global players.

Findings

In India, small and medium industries play a vital role in the growth of the economy. Small industries have a 40 per cent share in industrial output, producing over 8000 value-added products. They contribute nearly 35 per cent in direct export and 45 per cent in the overall export from the country. They are one of the biggest employment-providing sectors after agriculture, providing employment to 28.28 million people. The following are the important findings of this paper.

- SMEs in India, which constitute more than 80 per cent of total number of industrial enterprises and form the backbone of industrial development, suffer from the problems of sub-optimal scale of operation and technological obsolescence.
- Innovation has always been the hallmark of small and medium enterprises. SMEs that integrate innovation can reap significant benefits.
- Although Indian SMEs realise the importance of technological innovation, most of the Indian SMEs still believe in importing technology, rather than developing them in-house or through/in association with, national Research and Development (R&D) centers.
- It is estimated that 400 modern SSEs and 2000 rural and artisan based clusters exist in India. These contribute to 60 per cent of India's manufacturing exports. Some of the clusters are so big that they produce 70 to 80 per cent of the total volume of that particular product produced in India. For example Panipat produces 75 per cent of the

total woolen blankets produced in the country; Tirupur produces 80 per cent of the country's cotton hosiery

- The problems faced by the SMEs, particularly in accessing technology and maintaining competitiveness have been formidable. It has been found that sharing of information at local and national clusters are mostly informal. Information regarding the latest development and competency understanding is much less. Work sharing is not seen in the local and national clusters, as it is a fight for the same customer, in the same market. Eventhough the product and technology used by the entrepreneurs are similar, the tendency to share is less among the cluster participants

Constraints

The constraints faced by the SSIs sector include product reservations, regulatory hassles–both at the entry and exit stages, insufficient finance at affordable terms, inflexible labour markets and infrastructure related problems-like high power tariff, and insufficient export infrastructure. These are briefly elaborated below:

- The policy of product reservations has restricted operation of economies of scale and greater efficiency in the small scale sector.
- Starting a business in India requires number of permits, even after the initiation of liberalisation programme, as compared to many other developing Asian nations.
- Insufficient finance at affordable terms is another challenge daunting the performance of Indian SME sector.
- Infrastructural bottlenecks such as transportation / communication facility and insufficient export infrastructure increase the transaction cost of SME units in India.
- Problems in assessing adequate and reliable power at affordable price are another key constraint of Indian SMEs.

Opportunities

The opportunities that globalisation has unfolded include:

- *Increased flow of foreign investment and technology*. The globalisation process has attracted more and more foreign companies to bring investments and technology into the country and establish joint ventures. This has provided an opportunity to the local SMEs to build up their capabilities and capacities.
- *Outsourcing or re-location of pieces of supply chain*. The globalisation process has opened up many opportunities for design outsourcing and contract manufacturing for the local SMEs.
- *Access to foreign markets*. The globalisation process has enabled the local SMEs to look beyond the national boundaries and access foreign markets for their products and services.
- *Mergers and acquisitions*. The globalisation process has promoted mergers and acquisitions among companies resulting in enhancement of economies of scale, quality, delivery schedules, etc. of the local SMEs.
- *New areas of business*. The process of globalisation has resulted in opening up new areas of business for local SMEs such as business process outsourcing, medical transcriptions, clinical research trials, etc. It has also encouraged some of the SMEs to look at emerging technologies such as biotechnology, nanotechnology, etc.

Some of the forward looking and dynamic SMEs have seen these opportunities and integrated themselves with the global supply chains. Globalisation has also given rise to a number of Preferential Trade Agreements (PTAs) or Free Trade Agreements (FTAs) between nations, which also present opportunities as well as threats.

Recommendations

- SMEs will have to integrate with global supply chains. They will have to identify their core areas of strength and concentrate solely on them.

- SMEs will have to adopt a technology strategy, which is well integrated with the business strategy to stay competitive in the globalised economy.
- In order to increase the percentage of beneficiaries, there should be a widespread publicity of the available technology transfer schemes and the norms for availing the benefits of technology transfer schemes should be further simplified.
- Participation of SMEs in international exhibitions, business delegations and buyer-seller meets must be facilitated to assist them in accessing foreign technology for their production requirements
- FDI limit of 24 per cent equity participation in SMEs need to be liberalised to enable them to attract foreign technology.
- There is a need to set up specialised agencies that acquire technologies from labs and foreign suppliers, add value to them and then offer a complete technology package to the SMEs.
- Innovative mechanisms need to be put in place to promote technology transfer from institutions and R&D establishments.
- The SMEs will have to establish intense linkages with R&D institutions to bring about adaptations in acquired technology and carry out technology upgradation in the long term to keep pace with the rapid technological obsolescence in the globalised economy
- SMEs must not lose sight of patenting the value additions that they bring about in acquired technology and build a patent portfolio in the long run. This would enhance their long term competitiveness and also build their brand image.

Conclusion

It is well known that survival of SMEs is very crucial for Indian economy. Any adverse impact on the growth of firms will have serious implications on employment and foreign trade. The findings of the study suggest that government needs to provide basic and technological infrastructure to SMEs without which firms cannot use ICTs effectively. And without adoption of appropriate ICTs firms may not remain competitive in the era of liberalisation and globalisation. A large number of garment manufacturing firms reported that they had to have their own alternative arrangement for regulated and sufficient electricity which ultimately results in higher cost of production. Many firms were surviving in export markets due to MFA quota and not because of lower cost of production. In view of the fact that MFA provisions are no more available to garments sector firms since January 1, 2005, export-oriented firms need to be cost effective. Hence, there is a necessity to embark on providing technological, physical, and communication infrastructure at a globally competitive rate so that SMEs can withstand the onslaught posed by large firms and MNCs.

Until 1991, the high protectionist walls surrounding India's SMEs helped them to cope with competition, big businesses, globalisation etc., Such protection under the different policy frameworks have become vulnerable due to the shift in economic planning reforms adopted since 1990-91 with emphasis on globalisation, liberalisation and privatisation. In this context and for facilitating growth with wider employment generation, there is a growing realisation that India should adopt SME concept for its own survival, existence and growth.

Notes and References

1. The first GATT round was completed in 1947.
2. However, five decades of growth did not help to close the gap between the rich and the poor, except for a "convergence club" comprised of East Asian countries. A study using household survey data drawn from 91 countries for 1988 and 1993 found that inequality measured by the Gini index rose from 63 to 66.

This was mainly the result of changes in mean incomes and not rising inequality within countries.

3. Brynjolfsson, E., (1992), 'Productivity Paradox of Information Technology: Review and Assessment', *Working paper*, MIT Sloan School of Management: USA, 25.
4. Card, D., Kramarz, F. and T. Lemieux, (1997), 'Changes in Relative Structure of Wages and Employment: A Comparison of United States, Canada, and France, *NBER Working Paper* 5487.
5. Anon (2006), CMIE Reports, Mumbai.
6. DiNardo, J. E. and Jorn-Steffen Pischke, (1997), 'The Returns to Computer use Revisited: Have Pencils Changed the Wage Structure too?', *The Quarterly Journal of Economics,* CXII : 291-303.
7. Dosi, G., (1988), 'The Nature of the Innovative Process' in G. Dosi, C. Freeman, R. Nelson, G. Silverberg and L. Soete (eds), *Technological Change and Economic Theory*, London Pinter Publishers Limited: 221-38.
8. Anon (2007), *Economic Survey*, GOI, New Delhi: 56.
9. Lefebvre, E. and L. A. Lefebvre, (1996), *Information and Telecommunication Technologies: The impact of Their Adoption on Small and Medium-sized Enterprises*, International Development Research Centre, Ottawa, USA: 185.
10. Lucking, R. and T. Franks, (1989), 'Microcomputers in Public Investment Planning: Harnessing the Potential', *Information Technology and Development*, 5(1): 23-44.
11. Anon (2006), *MSSI Annual Report* 2005-06, Ministry of Small Scale Industries, New Delhi, Government of India.
12. Rahim, S. A. and A. J. Pennings, (1987), *Computerisation and Development in South East Asia,* Asian Mass Communications Research and Information Centre, Singapore.

3

Facets of Small Scale Industries in the Liberalised Regime

Sankaran, A

Abstract

Industrialisation is sine quo non of economic development. Within the industrial sector small-scale industry plays a pivotal role. In India, SSI is currently defined in terms of units for which investment in fixed assets such as plant and machinery, whether held on ownership terms or on lease or hire purchase, does not exceed Rs.10 million. Approximately, in the national economy the small-scale industries contribute 18 per cent on national income, 20 per cent of export and 25 per cent of employment. The small scale industries account for 40 per cent of the gross turnover of the manufacturing sector and about 35 per cent of the total exports of India. The small-scale sector has grown rapidly over the years. The growth rates during the various plan periods have been very impressive. With the globalisation of the Indian economy and the implementation of liberal industrial policy, the overall industrial climate at the global and national level have become vibrant. Technological import boosted foreign direct investment and free mobilisation of labour. From the point of the growth of SSIs, the present study has concentrated on the performance of small-scale industries during the liberalised regime. This study has yielded various results related to contribution of the small-scale industries, its growth performance, employment generation, production and export. Finally, a brief note has been given on the problems faced by these small-scale industries in India, during the liberalisation regime.

Introduction

Industrial development is a precursor of economic development. It has been widely accepted over a long period that within the industrial sector the small-scale industries are playing a vital role. The global level definition of small-scale industries, it differs from country to country. In USA the small-scale industry is defined as the production units, which employed less then 100 workers, and in UK it is considered as those manufacturing units employing less than 200 employees and similarly, in the retail trade outlet as having a turnover less than 50,000 pounds, and in wholesale trade turnover below 200,000 pounds is considered as SSI. In case of construction units those who employed less than 25 employees and in transport units having less than 5 vehicles are taken as small units. But in Malaysia, a small-scale unit is defined as a unit employing investment of less than R.M 250,000 and there is no ceiling on the number of persons employed (Hussain, 2003).

In the case of India, the small scale industries have been defined based on the investment i.e., up to Rs. 10 million (Ministry of SSI, 2005). Development of small scale industries is essential to an economy. While explaining the importance of small scale industries, Bhandari (1998) rightly underlined that the small-scale industries are vital not only in producing different varities of goods but also for the generation of sizeable amount of employment particularly in rural areas. In addition, Mehla

(1989), explained that for a long period of time the small scale industries have occupied a prominent place in the Indian economy. The significance of developing small scale industries in India lies in the fact that they are instrumental in removing the imbalance in the distribution of wealth among the people and the various regions of the country.

Small-scale industries have been given an important place in the framework of Indian economy. The small-scale industries have been imbued with a multiplicity of objectives, important among these being (a) the generation of immediate employment opportunities with relatively low investment, (b) the promotion of more equitable distribution of national income, (c) effective mobilisation of untapped capital and human skill and dispersal of manufacturing activities all over the country, leading to growth of villages, small towns and economically lagging regions (Suri 1988).

The above context rightly suggests that the small-scale industries are playing a pivotal role in almost all walks of economic development. Hence, the development of small-scale industries is essential particularly in recent periods. In addition, there is no scientific study on the current scenario relating to the growth and development of small scale industries in India. Therefore, the present study is an attempt to give a note on the growth and development of small scale industries in the liberalised regime.

Liberalisation Scenario

Prior to 1991, Indian government had imposed several types of controls on Indian economy, e.g., Industrial licensing system, price control of financial control on goods, import licence, foreign exchange control, restrictions on investment by big business houses etc. As a result of the above mentioned control mechanism the economy experienced an unprecedented economic crisis. Reserves of foreign exchange were just sufficient to pay for two weeks imports. New loans were not available, large amounts were being withdrawn from the accounts of NRI's due to which, the faith of international community in Indian economy was shaken. Industrial progress was on reverse gear and prices were sky-rocketing. The causative factors for these above mentioned problems underlined the widespread political instability, gulf crisis, inflation, excessive rise in fiscal deficits, rise in balance of payment deficits and tremendous fall in foreign exchange reserves. In order to pull the economy out of economic crisis and to put it on the path to rapid and steady economic growth the economic reform was introduced on 24th of July 1991 (Guptha and Kaur, 2004).

New Policy on Small Enterprise

The prime motto of this policy is to improve more vitality and growth impetus of this sector. The essences of this policy are (a) increase on ceiling of investment from Rs. 2 lakhs to Rs 5 lakhs. (b) removal of locational destructions on setting up of these industries (c) equity participation by other industrial units in small scale industry not exceeding 24 per cent of the total share holding (d) introduction of new legal form of organisation of business, namely destructed or limited partnership, (e) Other related factors were setting up of a monitoring agency to ensure that the genuine credit needs of this sector are fully met, review of all regulations, procedures and modification to ensure their operations, encouraging industry associations, expansion of entrepreneurship development programmes and further liberalization of schemes of national equity fund and single window loans (Shyamala, 2002). Due to the liberalisation measures the shape of the small-scale industries has had a tremendous change. Several studies have been concentrated on the development of small-scale industries in India for the past few decades. But in the recent past there is no scientific study in this regard. Hence, the present study tries to find out the growth performance of the small scale industries during the period of liberalised régime. *The prime objective of the present chapter is to ascertain the progress of small-scale industry in terms of number of factories, capital, production, employment and export.*

Methods and Materials

The present study is an intensive investigation based on the secondary time series data from Annual Report of Ministry of Small Scale Industries, Economic Survey, and RBI Report on Currency and Finance. The data on small-scale industries have been collected for the period of 14 years, after the introduction of the new economic policy and this period has been deliberately classified into two folds. The first fold covers the period from 1991-92 to 1997-98 and the second fold encompasses the period of 1998-99 to 2004-05. The variables for this study comprise the number of units, production, employment and export. To obtain fruitful results, simple statistical tools such as percentage shares and annual average growth rates have been used.

Analysis and Discussion

The statistics on small-scale industries shows that the number of units have increased steadily over the period, which is shown in Table 1. A similar trend has been detected in the capital production and employment also. The small-scale industry plays a predominant role in the growth of the country as it contributes approximately around 40 per cent of the gross manufacture of the Indian economy. It has been estimated that if one lakh rupee of investment is done on fixed assets in SSIs sector it produces 4.62 lakh worth of goods or services. Mention should be made that the small-scale industrial sector generates a sizable employment next to agriculture in the developing countries like India. It has been estimated that one lakh rupee investment in fixed assets in the small scale sector generates employment for four persons. The remarkable progress among the small-scale industries in India is due to emergence of new products and expansion of markets for these commodities.

Table: 1. Performance of SSIs in India

Year	*No of Units (in million)*	*Fixed Capital (in billion-current prices)*	*Production (in billion-at current prices)*	*Employment (in million)*
1973-74	0.416	22.96	72	3.97
1980-81	0.874	58.50	280.6	16.43
1990-91	1.948	64.32	1553.4	96.64
2001-02	3.312	79.70	6390.24	697.97
2002-03	3.572	90.45	7420.21	860.12

Source: Ministry of SSIs, India.

Right from the neo-classical economy, export has been one of the important indicators of the growth performance of an economy. From this point of view, the analysis on export of

Table 2. Contribution of SSIs to Total Export

Year	*Total Export (in Crores)*	*Export from SSI Sector (in Crores)*	*Percentage Shares*
1951-52	761	Negligible	-
1961-62	660	Negligible	-
1971-72	1608	155	9.6
1981-82	7809	2071	26.5
1991-92	44040	13883	31.5
2002-03	252790	86013	34.03

Source: Ministry of SSIs, India.

small-scale sector has been undertaken. Export from the small-scale sector over a period of time has acquired great significance in Indian's foreign trade. It is observed from Table 2 that the export of small-scale industrial sector had accounted very negligible percentage upto 1961-62 and it registered nearly 10 per cent in the total export in 1971-72. The amount of export of small-scale industries has risen from 155 crore to 86,013 crores. In percentage terms it has increased from 9.6 per cent in the year 1971-72 to 34 per cent in 2002-03. The favorable liberalisation policy on export may have been the causative factor for the sharp increase in the export of small-scale industrial products in India during this period.

Growth Performance of Small Scale Industries in India

The growth rate is a suitable indicator to asses the performance of the industrial economy. Very often, our economists are using this technique to identify the growth performance of different sectors. In the industrial economy of India the growth of small scale industries is very impressive year after year, which is clearly evident from Table 3. The annual average growth rate has been computed for different periods with respect to number of units, capital, production, employment and export.

Here it is transparent that the number of small-scale industries has recorded 4 per cent growth for the study period. In the absolute term, the number of industries has steadily increased from 67.87 lakh units in 1990-91 to 118.59 lakh units in 2004-2005. The growth rate of capital, production and employment has been accounted 4.7, 8.10 and 4.25 per cent respectively for the analysed period. Mention should be made here that the growth rate of export has reached around 19 per cent during the study period. This appreciable growth in the small-scale industries for the overall study period could be due to the expansion of internal market and favorable government policy for small-scale industries

Table 3 Growth Performance of SSIs in India

Year	*No. of Units (in lakhs)*	*Fixed Capital (in crore)*	*Production (in crore-at 93-94 prices)*	*Employment (in lakh)*	*Export (in crore)*
First Phase 1991-92 to 1997-98	4.06	5.21	8.15	4.39	25.03
Second Phase 1998-99 to 2004-05	4.07	4.28	8.06	4.19	9.44
Entire Period 1991-92 to 2004-05	4.06	4.75	8.10	4.25	18.53

Source: Computed form Ministry of SSIs data.

In comparison to the first phase and second phase, it is evident that the overal rate of growth has slightly decreased (except number of units). In particular, the growth of export and capital has slipped down considerably. This saturation is experienced by the Indian small-scale industries, particularly during the second phase. This gloomy performance may be due to the liberalisation process. With the liberalisation of imports, a number of countries in the world have dumped their commodities in the Indian market, which has led to the decrease in the demand for domestic commodities. In addition, the outdated technologies in the manufacturing processes of Indian companies, are not competent enough to compete with the multi national companies.

Problems of Small Scale Industries

A number of studies conducted in this field by several authors in India, have identified the following problems. The major problems are credit constraints, low level of technology, limited opportunities for marketing, low accessibility to business services, low entry barriers and shortage of raw materials. It is also to be highlighted that the chronic problem for the last couple of years has been the increase in sick industries in the Indian small scale industries. The All India Census of Small Scale Industries (1992) rightly underlined that the closure of 35 per cent of the units is mainly due to financial crisis. In addition, problems in marketing and non-availability of raw materials are other basic reasons for the sick units. Now-a-days due to the open door system followed by the government, there is a stiff competition faced by the small scale enterprises. Non-availability of skilled and specially trained labourers is also one of the major problems for small-scale industries.

Suggestion to Improve the SSIs

As our Indian companies have been using outmoded techniques they face tough task to compete in the global market, hence the SSIs must pave avenues for upgradation of technology in production. Infrastructural bottlenecks is another important problem in the third world countries like India. It is cumbersome to bring raw materials and to take the finished products to market. Hence, the infrastructural facilities like roads, power, water, and telecommunication need to be given more importance that would result in effective networking. Awareness on global market conditions should be imparted more among the Indian entrepreneurs to suit the global requirements. Entrepreneurs involved in the production process in India are not well educated and hence simplification of process with regard to registration of companies and export may lead to the boost up of the Indian Small-scale industries. The government may establish district level raw material bank to fill the gap between demand and supply of raw materials. The government should commence some special schemes to upgrade the outmoded techniques presently used by many SSI units. Special attention may be given to research and development related to small scale industries. In addition, the confederation of Indian Industry has rightly given several suggestions that include establishment of a small industry technology development fund with SIBDI, establishment of single small business establishment act and reduction of the special excise on selected items.

Conclusion

From the analysis it is observed that the small scale industries have occupied a prominent place in the socio-economic development of the country. Particularly, it has been assigned an important place commensurate with its potential for employment generation, dispersal of industry in rural areas and export promotion. With the sprit of liberalisation, the number of industries in the small-scale sector of India has increased during the analysed period. The same trend has appeared in the case of capital, employment, output and export also. Mention should be made here that among the above said factors the growth of export has undergone a perceptible increase. However, in the recent phase the performance of export growth has saturated. It could be due to erosion of markets for commodities of the Indian SSIs at international level. It is a striking feature of this study that the effect of the liberalisation policy is not evenly distributed in the analysed period. While discussing the performance of the small scale sector in the liberalised regime Latha (2005) has underlined that "in view of the weaknesses and threats to the small-scale sector, not only the government but also the entrepreneurs have to provide additional facilities, schemes, incentives and encourage innovative activities for the development of this sector in the present era of globalisation and competition".

References

1. Bhandari, R.C.S. (1998), *"State and Industrial Development – Institutions Incentives in the Backward Regions in India"*, Commenwealth Publication, New Delhi: 151.

2. Bibek Debry and Leveesh Bhandari (2005), *"Small Scale Industries in India – Large scale Exit Problems"*, Accademic Foundation, New Delhi: 19-38.
3. Chandawarkar and Kulkarni (2006), *"Small Scale Industries: A Glance"*, *Southern Economics*, 45 (1): 35.
4. Hussain, S.V(2003), *"Small Scale Industries in the New Millennium"*, Sarup Publications, New Delhi: 4-5.
5. Latha, K.L (2005), "Small Scale Sector: A Nursery of Economic Development", in SEDME, 32(2): 23.
6. Mehla, H.S (1989), *"Industrial Growth and Regional Development in India"*, Printwell Publications, Jaipur: 125.
7. Suri, K.B (1988), *"Small Scale Enterprises in Industrial Development"*, Sage Publications, New Delhi: 175
8. Shyamala, B (2002), *"An Evaluation of New Economic Policy on SSI"*, in M. Soundarapandian (ed.), Small Scale Industries, Vol: 2, Concept Publication, New Delhi: 146-152.

4

Growth of Khadi and Village Industry Sector in India

Murugan, N and S. Manivel

Abstract

This chapter on "Growth of Khadi & Village Industrial Sector in India" traces the performance of KVIC sector during the Indian five year plan periods. It also makes year wise analysis of performance in the last fifteen years. It presents a comprehensive picture on the performance of the sector.

Introduction

Small-scale and cottage industries play an important role in integrating the rural economy with the urban economy in an agro-based country like India. These industries contribute significantly to achieve the social and economic development in a number of ways particularly through labour absorption, income distribution, rural development, poverty eradication, regional balance and through promotion of rural entrepreneurship. Infact, they play a vital role in the process of country's industrial development. Particularly, developing countries like India, small labour – intensive industries have been favoured basically to create employment opportunities in an economy with abundant unskilled labour even though such industries may not always be supported on the grounds of economic efficiency.

In addition, low capital requirements and appropriate market environment are believed to have stimulated the growth of numerous indigenous industries with wide dispersal. This helps to promote balanced growth, more equitable income distribution, as well as diversification of the industrial structure, which often lead to increased productive and profitable utilisation of the available resources. This would help the rural class and boost capital formation as well as growth of industries in the small scale sector in urban and rural areas. It creates the basis for transformation of technology and management and also paves the way for creative development while sustaining national heritage and skills.

Rural Industry

Rural industry embraces different kinds of village and small industries. The cottage industries also form an important component of rural industries. The rural industry serves the requirements of rural people as well as other markets. By and large, the financial needs of rural industry are small. More importantly, they function even in the absence of sophisticated infrastructure facilities and as such they are environment friendly. These industries are labour intensive and provide additional employment opportunities, raise production and improve economic conditions of the people in rural areas.

Need for Rural Industries

Agriculture is the primary sector and the main stay of the rural economy. The rural industry though accounts for a second place in the rural economy plays complementary role to industrial sector in the country. The pressure of population on land is high and ever increasing. In the process, it results in a large surplus of labour, both educated as well as uneducated. Agriculture alone cannot absorb the entire surplus force and hence the need for rural industries. If one considers rural industry as a main stay, agriculture is an important part of this process. So the concept of rural industrialization emerged. Rural industrialization aims at the maximum productive employment of local resources, revival and development of traditional industries and skills, establishment of new units, integration of agriculture and industrial development for local prosperity, progressive reduction of disparities between urban and rural income and prevention of migration of rural population. Hence rural industrialisation has been assigned a crucial role in the development of industrially backward areas in rural India.

Importance of Rural Industrialisation

Rural industrialisation is an important means for generating employment opportunities to raise the real income of the people in the rural areas with limited capital cost. It also contributes to the development of agriculture and urban industries. Without rural industrialisation, it would be considerably more difficult to solve the problems of agriculture unemployment and widespread under employment. Rural industrialisation promotes rural industry. The development of rural industries increases the level of income in rural areas, and tends to embolden the self sufficiency of the rural families and its cohesiveness, by creating opportunities for youth, women and the able bodied by changing the pattern of leisure and work. Rural industrialisation should be looked upon not merely as the way of containing the rural workers and stopping them from migrating to urban areas by providing them some kind of remunerative employment in the villages, but as a dynamic element in the process of raising the productivity and income levels of the workers in rural areas. During the process of rural industrialisation many industries were given due importance for the planned economic development. One such industry in this line is Khadi & Village Industries.

Khadi and Village Industries

Khadi and village industries play an important role in the Indian economy in creating income and employment opportunities in the rural, semi-urban and urban areas. These industries generate production at low capital cost, promote use of local material, utilise local skills, widen entrepreneurial base, facilitate balanced regional growth and prevent the migration of labour force to urban centers (Yaswanth and Pandit, 1994). The Khadi and Village Industries Commission (KVIC) was established in April 1957, under the Khadi and Village Industries Commission Act, 1956.

Under the guidance of Mahatma Gandhi, the Father of the Indian Nation the provisional activities of Khadi was strated in 1922, when Khadi was the symbol of "Fight for Freedom". The Khadi programme was thus closely linked with the struggle for freedom. The All-India congress Committee, then known as the All-India Spinner's Association (AISA), was established in 1925 to organise hand spinning and hand weaving. This was followed by the establishment of another organisation called the All-India Village Industries Association (AIVA) in 1935, to look after other village industries such as hand-pounding of paddy, power ghani, palm gur, bee-keeping, hand made paper, etc. The establishment of the Khadi commission was the culmination of the efforts to organise the cottage/village industries during the freedom movement. In 1951, the sarva seva sangh took over the work of AISA and AIVA, as a part of an integrated plan for rural industrialisation.

KVI Sector during Five-Year Plans in India

The important role which KVI industries can play in ameliorating the socio-economic conditions of the rural people, has received emphasis in most of the major policy pronouncements on development in India. The industrial policy resolution of 1948 emphasized the "utilisation of local resources and the achievement of local self-sufficiency in respect of certain

Table 1

Annual Rate of Growth of Production and Employment in KVI Sector (per cent)

Plan	Production			Employment		
	Khadi	Village Industries	Total	Khadi	Village Industries	Total
Second 1956-61	20.8	24.8	23.5	21.1	17.3	19.9
Third 1961-66	13.5	11.0	11.8	2.0	6.3	3.3
Anaul 1966-69	-4.5	10.4	6.0	-11.0	-5.9	-9.2
Fourth 1969-74	7.0	10.3	9.5	-7.9	3.7	-2.9
Fifth 1974-79	14.7	9.5	10.6	0.8	9.9	5.9
Sixth 1980-85	11.4	18.3	17.0	3.1	9.0	6.8
Seventh 1985-90	13.7	16.0	15.7	3.9	3.8	5.7
Eighth 1992-97	10.3	17.4	13.7	4.2	8.0	7.0
Ninth 1998-2001	8.2	19.6	17.5	3.1	13.1	11.2

Source: Annual Reports, KVIC

essential consumer goods" as the most suitable characteristic of cottage and small industries. This approach was followed in the first five year plan. But the development of rural industries was conceived largely in isolation of the rest of the economy. The Industrial Policy Resolution of 1956 pointed out that rural industrialisation as favourable for creation of employment opportunities, equitable distribution of income and mobilisation of capital and skills. The industrial policy of 1980 emphasised the industrialisation of industrially backward areas / rural areas in India. The second plan (1956-57 - 1960-61) looked upon the rural industries as an integral component of the national economy. In the 26 pilot industrial projects, a spatial dimension was added to the programme of development of rural and small industry. The approach was followed up in the third plan (1961-62 - 1965-66) with the formulation of rural industries projects in 49 selected areas to promote village and small industries including ancillary industries.

The programme was continued during 1966-69 and then during the fourth five year plan (1969-70 - 1971-74) when a backward area development programme was adopted. The fifth plan broadened the rural industries programme spatially to cover the entire districts, except the towns in each project; and 100 new districts were included in the programme. The Sixth Five Year Plan (1980-85) emphasised the need for revitalisation of traditional industries and raising their productivity by upgradation of skills and techniques. A positive effort was made to disperse these industries over a wider area, particularly in the rural and semi-urban areas. The VII plan (1985-86 to 1989-90) emphasised the planned economic development at faster rate in rural industrial units in order to promote socio-economic justice to all who live in the rural India. During the VIII and IX plan period greater emphasis was given to create more infrastructure facilities to this sector and also to adopt modern management techniques, development and dissemination of appropriate technology to reduce drudgery, improvement in productivity and quality and lessening the dependence on subsidies. In this way, the government was committed and has been encouraging the production of textiles and non-textile products in the Khadi sector. Considering its large employment potentials it would be the endeavor of the Government to make the products of cottage and small scale sector more competitive and of better quality.

Importance of KVI Sector

The KVI sector has been attaining a steady growth plan after plan and has been considered as an important component in plans because of its inherent qualities such as generation of large scale employment in the areas where nothing else can be done. Khadi provides employment not only to the poorest of the poor, but 80 per cent of the beneficiaries are women. It needs relatively very little investment. Khadi has become either a part-time or a whole time occupation in deprived regions like hill areas as well as arid and drought prone districts. Khadi has 'great quality'– uniqueness as a material, none of the machine made fabrics can achieve. Fine khadi of 100 and 120 counts has a growing market and colored khadi is becoming a popular fabric, which has a clear and unassailable niche in the fashion market.

Khadi

Khadi is a handspun and woven material made from cotton, silk and woolen yarn. It is a mixture of any two or all such yarns. Started with the spinning on Takli, 2-Spindle new model Charkha, 4-Spindle, 6-Spindle, 8-Spindle, 10-Spindle and 12-Spindle new model charkas have been introduced in spinning of Khadi yarn. Similarly, a number handloom including Wardha loom, Gram Laxmi loom and Pit loom are also available for weaving Khadi cloth. Khadi is considered very comfortable to wear especially in temperate countries. It prevents skin rash etc., and is more comfortable to wear when compared to the fabrics made of artificial synthetic yarns like Nylons, Rayons and Terelyne etc. As a matter of fact, Khadi symbolised the spirit of self-reliance in the pre-independence India. There are four varieties of Khadi produced throughout the country viz., cotton Khadi, silk khadi, woolen khadi and muslin khadi. In India many institutions produce very fine varieties of khadi in cotton, silk and mixture of both i.e., cotton and silk, cotton and polyester, woolen and polyester, etc.

Village Industries

Village industries otherwise called cottage industries provide immediate large-scale employment and offer a method of ensuring a more equitable distribution of national income and facilitate an effective mobilisation of capital resources and skill (Venkatasamy, 1999). According to KVIC, any industry located in a rural area (Dahiya, 2004) village or town with a population of 20,000 and below and per capita investment of Rs. 50,000 in plants and machinery is classified as a village industry. At present the KVIC has approved about 115 industrial units as village industries. These industries have been grouped into seven major categories, viz. mineral based industry, forest based industry, agro and rural industry, polymer and chemical based industry, and rural engineering and bio-technology, hand made paper and fiber industry and service industry.

KVI - Programmes - Implementing Agencies

At present, the various development programmes of KVIC are implemented through 5549 registered institutions (registered under the societies act, 1860), cooperative societies, 33 states/ UTs, khadi and village industries boards which are statutory organisations, 30,080 cooperative societies, 27 public sector banks, RRBs and few selected cooperative banks. Khadi programmes are implemented only through registered institutions which are to be registered either with KVIC or SKVIBs, the village industries programmes. In addition to registered institutions / cooperatives, the village industries programmes are implemented through individual entrepreneurs by availing credit from banks. KVIC also assists individual artisans / entrepreneurs through state / union territory and KVI boards. About 17.5 lakh individuals have been benefited up to 2003-04.

Financial Support to KVI Sector

The budget support being provided by Government of India every year is the main source of finance for KVIC to implement the promotional and development programmes. In order to facilitate the formulation of the plan every year, KVIC conducts discussion with its implementing agencies and fixes the financial and physical targets for each of them, taking into account factors like availability of infrastructure, past performance and potentiality of various KVI programmes. As per the KVIC Act, the funds provided by Government of India under its budgetary sources are credited under broad heads such as (1) Khadi, (2) Village Industries, and (3) General and Miscellaneous. Besides the budgetary support, KVIC also generates resources every year in the form of credit from the consortium banks (since 1995-96), refunds of non utilised grants and loans from its subsidiary state units and institutions (Planning commission evaluation study report, 2001).

Table 2
Indicating Budgetary Support to KVI Sector

(Rs. in Crores)

Year	*1997-98*	*1998-99*	*1999-00*	*2000-01*	*2001-02*	*2002-03*	*2003-04*
Budgeted	441.54	364.58	300.75	320.00	354.00	394.65	444.75
Released	440.78	346.23	201.93	261.48	182.18	340.55	423.60

Source: Annual Report, OKVIC, Mumbai (2003-04).

The funds are provided by way of grants and loans and the KVIBs in turn allocates them to implanting agencies. Further the commission, administration expenditure including pension payments are also being met out of Governments budgetary support. The details of funds provided to the KVIC from budgetary sources (Both under plan non-plan during the period from 1997-98 to 2003-04) are shown in Table 2.

The commission also extends support by means of financial assistance to the development of Khadi and Village Industries and organisation of infrastructure facilities. It provides support in different forms. It includes sanctioning of capital expenditure loans, share capital loans and capital formation loans. In addition, the commission provides financial assistance as managerial grants for newly started institutions.

The loans provided by the commission for the promotion of Khadi activities are interest free and the loans for village industries carry an annual interest of 4 per cent. At present nationalised banks are extending working capital loans to Khadi and Village Industries Institutions on the basis of the recommendations of the commission. For such loans banks charge higher rate of interest (more than 4%). But still the borrowing institutions need to pay only the annual interest of 4 per cent and the interest rate over and above this four per cent is paid by the commission under interest subsidy scheme. Even in the case of working capital loans for Khadi activities the borrowing institutions need to pay 4 per cent, whereas such loans from the commission is interest free. Khadi and Village Industries products enjoy exemption from sales tax and central excise Industrial institutions are exempted from income tax. KVIC also conducts research programmes and imparts training to artisans and supervisors in the field of KVIs.

Rebate on Sale of Khadi and Silk

One of the major financial supports extended by the State Government and Khadi and Village Industries Commission,

Mumbai is the rebate on sale of khadi and silk as a promotional measure. The Government announced every year 30 per cent rebate on sale of khadi and 20 per cent rebate on sale of silk throughout the year including the rebate on sale offered by the Khadi and Village Industries Commission. The rebate is extended to the state KVIBs and also all the Certified Institutions of the Khadi and Village Industries Commission.

Performance of KVI Sector in India during 1995-2004

The overall performance of KVI sector in India has been encouraging in terms of production, sales and employment during the last ten years from 1994-95 to 2003-04 and attained the overall growth rate of 12-14 per cent. The volume of production of KVIs in India during the period between 1994-95 and 2003-04 has increased substantially. The total volume of production rose by 10.32 per cent between 1994-95 and 2003-04. However, the increase in the volume of production of Khadi sector is lower than the rate of increase shown by village industries.

The contribution of Khadi sector to the total K & VI production has declined from 10.75 per cent in 1994-95 to 4.68 per cent in 2003-04. Thus, the village industries have emerged as major contributor to the total production in the KVI sector.

Table 3

Trends in Volume in Production of KVI Sector in India

(Rs. in Crores)

Year	*Production*		
	Khadi	*Village Industries*	*Total*
1994-95	389.71	3234.35	3624.6
	(10.75)	(89.25)	(100)
1995-96	522.23	3504.22	4026.45
	(12.97)	(87.03)	(100)

(Contd.)

(Contd. Table 3)

Year	*Production*		
	Khadi	*Village Industries*	*Total*
1996-97	626.40 (13.87)	3889.86 (86.13)	4516.26 (100)
1997-98	624.10 (13.91)	3895.21 (86.19)	4519.31 (100)
1998-99	635.89 (12.43)	4476.48 (87.57)	5112.37 (100)
1999-00	551.94 (8.9)	5613.41 (91.05)	6165.35 (100)
2000-01	431.57 (6.23)	6491.69 (93.77)	6923.26 (100)
2001-02	416.69 (5.51)	7140.52 (94.49)	7557.21 (100)
2002-03	443.07 (5.17)	8126.30 (94.83)	8569.37 (100)
2003-04	453.50 (4.68)	9228.27 (95.32)	9681.77 (100)
Average	509.51 (8.39)	5560.03 (91.61)	6069.54 (100)
Growth rate	1.53	11.05	10.32

Source: Gramodaya Kshitij, April – 2005

* Figure in parenthesis indicates percentages

The total turnover of KVIs in India during the period between 1994-95 and 2003-04 has also increased substantially. The total sales of KVIs products rose by 11.02 per cent between 1994-95 and 2003-04. However, the increase in the sale of Khadi products is lower than the increase in the sale of village industries products. The contribution of Khadi sector to the total sales has declined from 12.06 per cent in 1994-95 to 5.07 per cent in 2003-04. Whereas, the contribution of VI sector has increased from 87.94 per cent in 1994-95 to 94.93 percent in 2003-04. The rate of growth of sales of Khadi sector for the entire period is lower than the growth rate of sales of village industries items.

The employment generation by the KVI sector is significant. Major proportion of the labour force of the country is employed in this sector. The employment in KVIs rose from 54.46 lakh persons in 1994-95 to 71.19 lakh persons in 2003-04.

Table 4

Trends in Volume of Sales of KVI Sector in India

(Rs. in Crores)

Year	*Production*		
	Khadi	*Village Industries*	*Total*
1994-95	490.86	3578.33	4069.19
	(12.06)	(87.94)	(100)
1995-96	567.35	3861.77	4429.12
	(12.81)	(87.19)	(100)
1996-97	581.11	4232.90	4814.01
	(12.07)	(87.93)	(100)
1997-98	745.9	4319.38	5065.28
	(14.73)	(85.27)	(100)
1998-99	647.83	4953.18	5601.01
	(11.57)	(88.43)	(100)
1999-00	631.79	6137.41	6769.20
	(9.33)	(90.67)	(100)
2000-01	570.55	7384.55	7955.10
	(7.17)	(92.83)	(100)
2001-02	527.86	8383.49	8911.35
	(5.92)	(94.08)	(100)
2002-03	577.63	9615.71	10193.34
	(5.67)	(94.33)	(100)
2003-04	587.04	10988.17	11575.21
	(5.07)	(94.93)	(100)
Average	592.79	6345.49	6938.28
	(8.54)	(91.46)	(100)
Growth rate	1.81	11.87	11.02

Source: Gramodaya Kshitij, April – 2005

* Figure in parenthesis indicates percentages

The rate of increase in employment by 2003-04 over 1994-95 is 30.72 per cent. The employment increment in village industries sector is 51.64 per cent over the 1994-95 level.

Thus, the employment composition of KVIs changed significantly in favour of village industries. The village industries have emerged as a major source of employment for the rural masses. The share of Khadi sector in the total KVIs employment has declined from 24.32 per cent in 1994-95 to 12.09 per cent in 2003-04.

Table 5

Trends in Employment in KVI Sector in India

Year	*Production*		
	Khadi	*Village Industries*	*Total*
1994-95	13.19	41.27	54.46
	(24.22)	(75.78)	(100)
1995-96	13.97	42.75	56.72
	(24.23)	(75.37)	(100)
1996-97	14.97	42.38	57.35
	(26.10)	(73.90)	(100)
1997-98	14.01	42.49	56.50
	(24.80)	(75.20)	(100)
1998-99	13.85	44.44	58.29
	(23.76)	(76.24)	(100)
1999-00	12.35	46.88	59.23
	(20.85)	(79.15)	(100)
2000-01	9.56	50.51	60.07
	(15.91)	(84.09)	(100)
2001-02	8.40	54.16	65.56
	(13.43)	(86.57)	(100)
2002-03	5.58	57.87	66.45
	(12.91)	(87.09)	(100)
2003-04	8.61	62.58	71.19
	(12.09)	(87.91)	(100)
Average	11.75	48.53	60.28
	(19.49)	(80.51)	(100)
Growth rate	-4.18	4.25	2.72

Source: Gramodaya Kshitij, April – 2005

* Figure in parenthesis indicates percentages

Conclusion

The growth rates of KVI sector in terms of production, employment and productivity is significant. The entire KVI sector recorded the highest growth rate over the years. Within the KVI sector the improvement of Khadi sector is diminishing gradually sending warning signals to everyone interested in the promotion of Khadi.

The development of KVI sector has acquired even more relevance today on account of: (i) growing population pressure in rural areas; (ii) rapid expansion of the labour force especially among the marginal farmers and landless agriculture laborers; (iii) inadequate opportunities for non-agricultural work; (iv) limitation of the organised sector in absorbing the labour force; (v) prevalence of substantial under employment in the economy; and (vi) need and the capacity for creating employment opportunities at or near the place of residence so as to avoid migration from rural to urban areas. It is for these reasons the governments support is considered essential for the continuous progress of the KVI sector.

References

1. Vasant Desai. (2000), *Small-scale Industries and Entrepreneurship* (5th edition), Himalaya Publishing House, Mumbai, 2000: 123.
2. Yashwant, A., and Pandit Rao, (1996) "Experiences of the Khadi & Village Industries Commission in Technology Transfer", *The Technology Transfer of Rural India,* Edited: Balla, A.S., and Amulya, K.N. Reddy, Oxford University Press, New Delhi: 113-132.
3. Dhanasekaran, K. (1999), "Role of KVIC in rural industrialisation", *Rural industries in India*, Vol.1, Mohit publications, New Delhi: 180-184.
4. Natwar Thakkar, (2004), "The Meaning and Role of Khadi", *Santhakul*, 34 (9):3-6.

5. Pushpalatha, A., (1999), "Role of KVIC in Rural Industrialisation", *Rural Industries in India*, Vol. II, Mohit Publications, New Delhi: 180-184.
6. Arjun Ray Chandhuri (2004) "Khadi Industry to the Rescue as Rural Land Productivity Dips", *Economic times* : 5.
7. Dahiya, K.S., (2004), "Artisans the focus of KVIC schemes", *Gramodaya Kshitjit*:40.

5

Kyoto Protocol's Clean Development Mechanism and It's Feasibility to Indian Small Scale Industries Under Globalisation

Dhulasi Birundha Varadarajan

Abstract

Over tl last few years the Clean Development Mechanism (CDM) has generated a lot of hype, hope and skepticism. The ratification of the Kyoto protocol hinges mainly on the resolution of issues related to the operationalisation of the CDM. In the meantime efforts have been made to identify possible opportunities for the implementation of CDM projects in developing countries. The Government of India is a signatory to the UNFCCC (United Nations Convention on Climate Change) and ratified the convention in November 1993. In India, industrial pollution is regarded as the worst among the many environmental impacts that are causing damage through excessive exploitation of resources and degradation of environment. India has a strong industrial base. However, a considerable number of industries use outdated equipments, resulting in significant pollution and environmental degradation, such as over-exploitation of ground water, increasing air pollution and highly contaminated water bodies. Illegal discharges from small-scale industry are difficult to regulate and control in India. The collective environmental damage done by small-scale industries can obviously be much higher than envisaged. World over business environment has been changing fast. Three features of this change are of critical importance to industrial units: first, there has been a shift for the past two decades, in the economic policies of the nations, especially developing nations, from policy regulation to market orientation exposing their industrial units to market competition to a greater extent. Second, globalisation in the sense of increasing integration of world economics is taking place resulting in intensifying market competition. Thirdly, past few decades have experienced rapid technological development in numerous areas. In this context this paper analyses the following aspects: (i) Challenges of Globalisation,(ii) Small-scale industries in India and its environmental problems, (iii) Policy initiatives to overcome environmental problems of small-scale industries and, (iv) Feasibility of cleaner technology promotion to small-scale industries under Kyoto Protocol's Clean Development Mechanism.

Introduction

Over the last few years the CDM (Clean Development Mechanism) has generated a lot of hype, hope and skepticism. The ratification of the Kyoto protocol hinges mainly on the resolution of issues related to the operationalisation of the CDM. In the meantime efforts have been made to identify possible opportunities for the implementation of CDM projects in developing countries. The Government of India is a signatory to the UNFCCC (United Nations convention on Climate Change) and ratified the convention in November 1993. The Ministry of Environment and Forests, which is the nodal ministry for all environment related activities in the country is the nodal ministry for co-ordinating the climate change policy as well.

Clean Development Mechanism is one of three international flexibility mechanisms included in the Kyoto Protocol to facilitate cost –effective fulfilment national emissions reduction commitments for industrialised countries. The mechanisms provide incentives for these countries to meet their Green House Gas emissions reduction targets. The other two flexibility mechanisms are: International Emission Trading (IET) and Joint Implementation (JI). The CDM has two goals to promote sustainable development in developing countries and to allow industrialised countries to earn emission credits for their investments in emission-reducing projects in developing countries. According to the article of the Kyoto Protocol, to earn credits under CDM the project proponent must prove and have verified that the greenhouse gas emissions reductions are real, measurable and additional to what would have occurred in the absence of the project.

In India, industrial pollution is regarded as the worst among the many environmental impacts that are causing damage through excessive exploitation of resources and degradation of environment. India has a strong industrial base, however a considerable number of industries use outdated equipment, resulting in significant pollution and environmental degradation, such as overexploitation of ground water, increasing air pollution and highly contaminated water bodies.

Pressure from Government is coming through the pollution control board as well as through the judiciary system which increasingly is ordering companies to shut down for environmental offences. Illegal discharges from small-scale industry are difficult to regulate and control in India. Although small-scale Industries are promoted in a large way by the Indian Government and play an important role within the economy with their prime role and vast scope in employment, the unsafe practices of these industries for a long time have gone unnoticed. The collective environmental damage done by small-scale industries can obviously be much higher than envisaged.

World over the business environment has been changing fast. Three features of this change are of critical importance to industrial units: first, there has been a shift for the past two decades, in the economic policies of the nations especially the developing nations from policy regulation to market orientation exposing their indusial units to market competition to a greater extent. Second, globalisation in the sense of increasing integration of world economies is taking place resulting in intensifying the market competition. Thirdly, past few decades have experienced rapid technological developments in numerous areas. All these developments have changed the methods of production marketing and doing business. In this context this paper analyses the following aspects:

- Challenges of globalisation
- Small-scale industries in India and their environmental problems
- Policy initiatives to overcome environmental problems of small-scale industries
- Feasibility of cleaner technology promotion to small-scale industries under Kyoto Protocol's Clean Development Mechanism.

Challenges of Globalisation

Globalisation is seen to be the world's mega trend over the next 15 years causing the global economy to grow by about 80 per cent compared with 2000, and raising average income per head world wide by about 50 per cent over the same period. The benefits will be a much richer world. Economists world over believe that most of this growth will be in Asia, especially in China and India, driving Asia to displace the West over the next 15 years as the focus of global economic dynamism. In brief, India has moved from managing external sector to implementing an optimal integration of domestic and external sectors and the global economy.

Global economic integration is technology induced and policy managed. The BRIC report reflects considerable confidence in the future of the Indian economy, though it is necessary to see it in fine print to realise that India would be a super power in 2050. What is important to recognise is that the report leans on the relevant skills that need to be sustained, reoriented and upgraded in a globally competitive era and need to provide link between supply and demand for labour through increase in productivity (Economy Watch 2005).

Globalisation whether in a limited way in terms of multilateral trade liberalisation (Bhalla 1996) or in the broader sense of increasing internationalisation of production, distribution and marketing of goods and services (Harris 1993), has resulted in the opening of the markets and thus leading to intense competition. For example, the WTO regulates multilateral trade enforcing its member countries to remove import quotas and other import restrictions and to reduce import tariffs. In addition, countries especially the developing countries are asked to stop subsidies to exports as well as to domestic goods. Time limits are prescribed and strictly enforced by WTO in all these respects. India has been asked to remove quantitative restrictions on imports by 2001 and all export subsidies by 2003 (Kumar 2000).

Equally important are the non trade issues of WTO such as TRIMS, TRIPS and the stringent sanitary environment and labour standards. The Sanitary and Photo Sanitary Measures (SPMS) empower countries to deny imports from certain regions for reasons like spread of diseases. Under this, U.S.A has already banned the import of Indian beedies (Kumar 2000). Whatever be the status of agreements on environment and labour standards, these have already been imposed on export units by the importing agencies. The environment standards enhance the importance of new technologies, labour standards, if agreed and implemented also remove totally the comparative advantage of having cheap labour for the Indian industry especially the small-scale industries. (Bhavani 2000).

India is a highly populous country and to sustain its population growth economic development and industrialisation are the compounding factors, that are environmental burden. An approach first used by Ehrlich and Ehrlich (1990) was to consider per capita environmental impacts on citizens. Stikker (1992) further expanded Ehrlich and Ehrlich's approach and defined the Environmental Burden as:

Environmental Burden* = *Global population* X *GNP per capita* X *Environmental impact per unit of GNP

On an individualistic approach, if one considers individual country populations' India and China would be the countries with the highest burden. What Stikker and Ehrlich and Ehrlich suggested was that if an industry is to operate within a level of Global Environmental Quality, it must reduce its Global Environmental impact. Resources are required to sustain population growth, as well as the outputs of industrialisation and economic growth. Said (1997) provides two logical solutions to the Ehrlich's theory, one is that humanity should breed less and the other is that we should consume less and produce lower environmental impacts in the process. Changing life style and consumption habits in the long run will be effective but will not directly address environmental impact unless industries themselves take the stance and priority of protecting the environment and measures are enforced to curb population growth (Souza 2001).

Small-Scale Industries in India

The small-scale industry has emerged as India's engine of growth in the New Millennium. The ongoing programme of economic reforms based upon the principle of liberalisation,

Table 1: Performance of Small Scale Industries

year	*No. of units (lakh).*			*Production (Rs. crore)*		*Employment*	*Emport*
	Regd.	*Unregd.*	*Total*	*(at current)*	*(at constant*	*in lakh*	*(Rs. crore)*
2000-01	13.10	88.00	101.10 (4.1)	2,61, 289 (11.6)	1,84,428 (8.0)	239.09 (4.4)	69, 797 (28.8)
2001-02	13.75	91.46	105.21 (4.1)	2,82,270 (8.0)	1,95,613 (6.1)	249.09 (4.2)	71,244 (2.1)
2002-03	14.68	94.81	109.49 (4.1)	3,11,993 (10.5)	2,10,636 (7.7)	260.13 (4.9)	86,013 (20.7)
2003-04	15.54	98.41	1113.95 (4.1)	3,57,733 (11.6)	2,28,730 (8.6)	271,36 (4.3)	N.A.
2004-05	16.38	102.15	118.53 (4.0)	3,99,020 (11.5)	2,45,747 ** (7.4)	282.82 (4.2)	N.A.

* 1993-94 prices

** Based on growth rate of 7.44 per cent which is the average growth rate of the last years

Note : Figures in parenthesis indicate percentage growth over previous years

Source : Development Commissioner SSI.

Source : Economic Survey : 2004-2005.

globalisation and privatisation and the changes at the international economy scene including the emergence of WTO have brought certain challenges and several new opportunities before the small-scale industrial sector. The most important challenge faced by the sector is that of growing competition both globally and domestically.

Contributions of small-scale sector to India's industrial production, exports and employment are significant. About 3 million units employing nearly 16.7 million persons account for 35 per cent of India's total exports and about 40 per cent of industrial manufacture (SIDBI report on small scale industrial sector 1999). By the end of March 2000, the small-scale industrial sector accounted for nearly 40 per cent of gross value of output in the manufacturing sector and 35 per cent of total exports from the country. The SSIs (32 lakh units) provided employment to about 18 million people (SIDBI NEWS 2000). In real terms, the small-scale sector recorded a growth rate of 10.1 per cent in 1994-95 as against 7.1 per cent in 1993-94 and 5.6 per cent in 1992-93 (Parthasarathy 1996). During 2001-05, this sector registered continuous growth in the number of units, production, employment and even in exports (till 2002-2003). During this period the average annual growth in the number of units was around 4.1 per cent, while employment grew by 4.4 per cent annually. Further, the average annual growth in production, at current and constant prices, was 10.6 per cent and 7.6 per cent respectively (Table1 Economic Survey 2004-2005).

Policy Initiatives

Since independence, India has had strong policies to promote the small-scale industrial sector. Small-scale units were protected from the competition of large scale units through numerous protective measures. Despite numerous policy measures for the past four decades, Indian small-scale units have remained mostly tiny, technologically backward and lacking in competitive strength. (Tendulkar and Bhavani 1997). Not withstanding their lack of competitive strength, small-scale industrial units of India could survive so far due to product and geographical market segmentation and policy protection, which gave them only isolated sheltered markets.

For example, product differentiation in terms of quality coupled with the existing income inequalities segmented the product market into two parts: price sensitive and quality insensitive segment and price insensitive and quality sensitive segment. Small-scale industrial units mainly being producers of lower quality but cheaper products cater mainly to the price sensitive and quality insensitive market segment. Under development of infrastructure like transport created sheltered local markets for small-scale units. The only competition these units have so far faced is the competition with each other due to the overcrowding (Sandesara 1982)

The small enterprises sector, however, faces several problems, which prevent it from achieving its full growth potential. Some of the major problems faced by the sector are access to timely and adequate credit, technological obsolescence, infrastructural bottlenecks, marketing constraints and a plethora of rules and regulations. Some policy initiatives taken during 2004-2005 are as follows:

The national commission on enterprises for the unorganised sector was established in September 2004 to recommend measures considered necessary for improvement in the productivity of enterprises, generation of large scale employment opportunities on a sustainable basis, linkage of the sector to institutional framework in areas like credit, raw material supply, infrastructure, technology upgradation, marketing facilities and skill development.

- 85 items reserved for exclusive manufacture in the small-scale sector were dereserved in October 2004. The total number of reserved items now stands at 605.

- To facilitate technology upgradation and enhancing competitiveness, the investment limit (in plant and machinery) has been raised in October 2004, from Rs.1 crore to Rs.5 crore reserved for manufacture in the small scale sector.
- The small and medium enterprises (SME) fund of Rs.10,000 crore was operationalised by the SIDBI since April 2004. Eighty per cent of the lending from this fund will be for SSI units at interest rate of 2 per cent below the prevailing PLR of the SIDBI
- The Reserve Bank of India enhanced the corporate loan limit for the SSIs sector to the Rs.1 crore.
- With a view to integrate small and medium enterprises, facilitating their growth and enhancing their competitiveness (including measure for freeing the sector from "Inspector Raj") a suitable legislation is being finalised.
- Under technological support, the scheme of capital subsidy of 12 per cent for investment in technology upgradation was given preference which will be given to tiny sector and ISO 9000 certification units will be getting Rs.75000.
- The cluster development programme was initiated to strengthen rural development by creating common facilities for innovation, technology upgradation, packaging, processing and e-commerce.

Environmental Problems of Small-Scale Industries

Industrialisation enables India to utilise its resources optimally, diversify the economic base, raise the living standards of people and attain balanced regional development through fiscal incentives and concessional finance for backward regions. At the same time industry can contribute significantly to pollution. Small industries have contributed more and they have acute environmental problems. Industrial effluents largely come from 3 million small and medium sized units that are scattered throughout the country. Industrial disposal of polluted effluent taken via open drains into streams and reservoirs or through lakes or waste water treatment systems (US-AEP 1996).

In these units western technological systems are getting adopted far and wide, which produce enormous gaseous, liquid and solid wastes. The pollution control technologicies developed in the west are not economically suitable for these small enterprises. The number of such enterprises is huge and so is the pollution for them. They contribute some 40 per cent of the total industrial waste water in India. These enterprises tend to form strong clusters with serious water pollution problems. The total waste water generated amount to some 3900 million litres per day. Of this the contribution of engineering industry is 54 per cent, paper and board mills 28 per cent, textile industries 12 per cent, organic chemicals two per cent, tanneries one per cent and others 3 per cent. To specify, clusters of textile dyeing industries have led to serious problems in towns situated on small rivers like Pali, Batotra and Jodhpur in Rajasthan, Jetpur in Gujarat and Tiruppur inTamilnadu (Anil Agarwal 2000).

Small industries by comparison with large industries lack environmental commitment, technical expertise in environmental management and the financial capabilities to address environmental problems. Nor do they have standards or effective treatment opportunities and services (Nyati 1988). Small industries also lack additional space for pollution control facilities. There are difficulties in obtaining the technical assistance of knowledgeable consultants. Since most of the units are dispersed, they find it difficult to come together for a joint or common treatment plant. Environmental legislation in India, although seemingly as tough as that in major developed nations, is not well enforced. Though multinational and the large domestic companies are monitored poorly funded regulatory bodies find it nearly impossible to police the millions of small and medium small units (Roberts 1995). These small industries lack incentive to set up treatment equipment or to operate equipment, if it already is installed, operating that equipment has been more expensive than non-compliance (Dasgupta *et al.* 1998).

The government's prime role has been to encourage growth of theses industries, often neglecting environmental considerations. To minimise the environmental impact of these small-scale industries several policy initiatives have been taken recently by the government. India, being in the process of globalisation, is making initiatives towards Clean Development Mechanism of Kyoto protocol through emphasis on cleaner technology promotion especially in small-scale industries.

Initiatives of Clean Development Mechanism in India

The detrimental effect of industrial processes on the environment can be reduced either during, or at the end of the process, or by a combination of both. The United Nations Industrial Development Organisation's (UNIDO) clear technology promotion projects in India and China would promote the transfer of cleaner technologies not yet commonly in use in India from Switzerland or other OCED countries. The entrepreneur would adopt if it is competitive with another technology assuming the same product output and quality. Factors determining the competitiveness are the investment cost, operation cost, technology risk, environmental pressure and the complexity of the technology. The entrepreneur must also be aware of the existence of such technologies (information and seek cost) and must have the necessary know how to use them efficiently (know-how cost).

Cleaner production focuses on the process, by reducing pollution at the source. It covers actions that conserve raw materials and energy, eliminate the use of toxic or hazardous toxicity or hazard of all emissions and wastes. End-of-pipe actions process the pollutants after they are emitted. The kinds of cleaner production actions that an enterprise can take can be classified into one of the eight categories.

(1) House keeping
(2) Better process control
(3) Substitution of input materials
(4) Reuse or Recycling of waste material on site.
(5) Modifications or replacement of equipment or hardware.
(6) Substitution of existing process technology by cleaner technology.
(7) Sale of waste as a useful by-product
(8) Product modification

UNIDO's holistic cleaner production approach is a preventive integrated strategy that is applied to the entire production cycle to:

- increase productivity by ensuring more efficient use of raw materials, energy and water;
- promote better environmental performance through reduction at source of wastes and emissions; and
- reduce the environmental impact of products throughout their lifecycles by the design of environmentally friendly but cost-effective production.

The net effect is to give enterprises in developing and transition countries a more competitive edge, thereby facilitating their access to international markets. Union's holistic approach to cleaner production includes its sectional activates as well as implementation of multilateral environmental protocols through development of CP technology and investment promotion.

Cleaner Technology Promotion in India

The confederation of Indian industry (CII) has been quite involved in the cleaner production field. Its major function is on the policy level but it also has major activities in the energy field, ISO 14000 and an active environmental department. The environmental department mainly performs training services, awareness raising and assessments, with Canadian assistance. The basic focus is capacity building. The energy division of the

CII basically undertakes energy audits and energy auditors. It has developed some CDM projects. Together with American support the CII is currently establishing a green business center in Hyderabad.

The Tata Energy Research Institute is strong in the field of energy services and environment studies. It has made various studies on the cleaner development mechanism, CDM of the Kyoto protocol, in India as well as in other Asian countries.

The Asian and Pacific Center for Transfer of Technology (**APCTT**) located in Delhi involves the transfer of technology, including environmental technology. But this centre could not reach small and medium sized enterprises due to different operating structure of companies in these countries. The APCTT jointly with **UNIDO,** the government of India and **Small Industries Development Bank of India** (**SIDBI**) has created the **Technology Bureau for International Industrial Partnership (TBIIP).** Its goal is investment and technology acquisition from India towards African Countries and from International corporations to India. Currently some 10 projects have focused on the assessments and medium term exchange programmes. The relationship to cleaner technology promotion is fairly weak, the focus is on technology in general.

Quite similar to this is the **International Center for Advancement of Manufacturing Technology** (ICMAT) initiated in1999 in Bangalore which piggy back of the Central Manufacturing Technology Institute (CMIT). The focus of the institute is not on the cleaner technology but on technology in general assuming that new technology will be cleaner.

The Ministry of Environment and Forests has introduced the scene of adoption of clean technology in small scale industries. This scheme aims at promotion, development and adoption of clean technologies including waste reuse or recycling in small scale industries. Under this scheme, the ministry sponsors training and awareness programmes for entrepreneurs and studies on waste minimisation and demonstration in potential small-scale industrial sectors. Besides, a project on waste minimisation in small scale industries has been launched by the ministry with the National Productivity Council (NPC) as nodal agency under the World Bank assisted industrial pollution prevention project. The objective of the cleaner technology is to increase the awareness, interests and confidence of Indian small and medium scale industries to take up waste minimisation activities on a sustained basis. It also aims at generating enough indigenous capacity to create an environment of self help in waste minimisation in the industries. The project has two components to achieve these two objectives.

- Development of **communication strategy** for launching an awareness campaign on waste minimisation and
- Establishment and running **waste minimisation circles (WMCS)** in small-scale industries in the country.

Under the capacity building activity of this project, National Productivity Council has trained about 118 participants from 84 organisations. If these 84 organisations are selected they could act as facilitators for promoting the concept of waste minimisation circles (WMCS). If these 84 facilitators succeed the 43 WMCS in different sectors will be established.

Environmental Control

The method of granting consent under water and air pollution to SSI has been simplified except for 17 pollution indsutries, Viz: fertilizers (Nitrogen Phosphate), Cement, Aluminum Thermal Power, Sulphuric Acid, Copper Smelter, Iron and Steel Sugar, Fermentation and Distillery, Petrochemicals, Oil refinery, Tanneries, Zinc Smelter, Pulp and Paper, Dyes and Dye intermediaries, Basic Drugs and Pharmaceuticals, Pesticide manufacturing and formation.

Energy Conservation Programme

Office of District Industrial Centre has been pursuing programmes on energy conservation in small-scale Industries.

There are many energy intensive areas in small scale as foundry, forging, rolling mills, glass and ceramics industry, etc., where thermal efficiency is very poor. In order to make aware the SSIs on the advantages of taking up energy conservation measures, awareness programmes by different SISIs/RTCs are conducted every year. In addition, energy audit studies, survey on energy consumptions pattern and any other issue related to energy conservation are also being taken up by SISIs/RTCs.

Regarding the adoption of pollution control measures, it is the policy of the government that the industrial undertakings desiring to use the wastes and effluents for manufacture of new products should be encouraged to do so. Many of the chemicals recovered from pollution control processes and recycling of waste products are reserved for exclusive manufacture in the small scale and they should be permitted without the mandatory export obligation.

Thus, in accordance with Kyoto protocol's Clean Development Mechanism efforts is taken to tune the small scale industries towards minimum environmental damage.

Conclusion

The major environmental concerns in India today are poverty coupled with growing population and side effects of enhanced industrial activities. As long as poverty remains the main stumbling block, industrialisation provides hope of significantly improving the standard of living. Removal of poverty and environmental protection are two sides of the same coin that is sustainable development (Dwivedi and Khator 1995). The SSIs must realise the importance of environmental management and quality that it could be highly effective if it is administered by the small units themselves. Changing life style and consumption habits in the long run will be effective but will not directly address environmental impact unless industries themselves take the stance and priority of protecting the environment and measures are enforced to curb population growth.

Porter and Linde (1995) suggest that environmental regulations can spur innovation that increase product value and decrease total costs, seem appropriate. The trade off between economy and environment for production processes, customer needs and technology is dynamic and complex. Porter and Linde suggest that innovation-friendly regulations can improve resource productivity and competitiveness, but the problem is getting small industries to cooperate to view it as along term solution rather than a short term goal. So far, Indian Industrial units especially small units are operating in isolation, which can not continue any more. However, to get into the international production and trade net works, individual units have to satisfy the buyers' standards in terms of price, quality and delivery schedules (Geneffii 1995).

In sum, the process of globalisation is intensifying the market competition by allowing imports and multilateral corporations relatively easily into India. This in turn is creating pressure on industrial units to pay more attention to quality, price and delivery considerations rather than profitability. All these requires substantial improvement in various dimensions of technology i.e., transformation, organisation and information (Chandra and Sastry). Non trade issues of WTO such as environmental standards are further adding to the importance of new technology adoption. Cleaner project to be successful, it is necessary to be aware of the potential barriers that might exist to the transfer of cleaner technology (or any other environmental sound technology). Cleaner production requires changing attitudes, exercising responsibility of environmental management and promoting technological change.

Thus, the initiatives taken in India towards cleaner production as per Kyoto Protocol's rules on clean development mechanism should benefit sustainable development, help alleviate poverty, create clean technology in a environment damage-free economy and produce local benefits among others. To achieve this, millions of small-scale industries should adopt clean technology, which are environmental benign technology by availing the incentives offered by the national government as well as international organisations like UNIDO. For this a concerted effort is necessary on the part of government and other small-scale Industries promotion agencies to disseminate the message of Cleaner Production coupled with cost minimisation and quality orientation to the consumers and small-scale producers. Then only the objective of globalisation towards clean world can be achieved.

References

Anil Agarwal, (2005), "Small Scale Industries Drive, India's Economy, But Pollute Heavily ,What can be done," *Dilemma in the Developing World*, Web Page.

Anil Kumar (2000), "World Trade Organization Agreement; its Impact on Small Scale Sector," in Laghu Udyog Sam char 24 (6-8), January – March: 28-39.

Bhalla, A.S (1996), *Facing the Technological Change*, Macmillan Press Ltd., London.

Bhavani, T.A.(2000), "Small-Scale Units in the Era of Globalisation, Problems and Prospects," Web Page.

Chandra, P. and Sastry.T.(1998)" Competitiveness of Indian Manufacturing, Futures Survey" in *Viklpa Journal for Decision Makers*, 23(3): 25-36.

Das Gupta et al (1998), "Capital Market Responses to Environmental Performance in Developing Countries," *World Bank Policy Research Paper*, No: 1909.

Dwivedi and Khator (1995) "India's Environmental Policy Programs and Policies in O.P.Dwivedi and D.K.Vajpayi (Eds.), *Environmental Policies in the Third World: A Comparative Analysis,* Greenword Press: 47-70.

Economy Watch, (2006), "India and Global Economy", Web Page.

Ehrlich, P. and Ehrlich, A (1990), "The Population Explosion" Arrow Ltd., London.

Gerreffi, G. (1995), "Global Production Systems and Third world" in Stallings. (Ed). *Global Change and Regional Response: The New International Context of Development*, Cambridge University Press: 100-142.

Nyati, (1998), "Problems of Pollution and its Control in Small-Scale Industries," New Delhi, India.

Parthasarathy, S. (1996), "Whither Small Scale Industry?", *Hindu Survey of Indian Industry*, National Press: 4-26.

Porter, M and Linde, C (1995), "Green and Competitive Ending of Stalemente", *Harward Business Review:* 120-134.

Roberts Michael, (1995), "Indian Public Demands Industry Responsibility" *Chemical week*, 1(157): 89.

Said, David, (1997), Green Australia, Mapping the Market, St.Leonards, N.S.W, Australia, Prospect Publishing.

Sandesara, J.C. (1982), "Efficiency of Incentives for Small Industries" IDBI, Bombay.

SIDBI (1999), *Report On Small Industries Sector*, Small Industries Bank of India, Lucknow.

SIDBI NEWS (2000). *Comprehensive Policy Package for SSI and Tiny Sector*, Small Industries Bank of India, New Delhi.

Souza, C.M.D, (2001), "Integrating Environmental Management in Small Industries of India.", *Electronic Green Journal Issue*, 14, Spring.

Stikker, A.(1992), "Sustainability and Business Management," *Business Strategy and the Environment*, I: 1-8.

Part – II Empirical Studies of Small and Medium Enterprises Under Globalisation

6

Benefits of Globalisation: Small and Micro Enterprises – A Case Study

Ramachandran S. P. Narayanasamy

Abstract

Micro level studies on impact of Globalisation are warranted since they could reveal the realities of situation at the grass root level. Therefore, the present study is carved out with a main focus on identifying the accrued benefit flow to spinning mills operating in Dindigul District and the perculated benefits to a micro-enterprise which is a supporting unit to the spinning mills. This is a case study based on both secondary and primary data. A detailed and an in-depth analysis of benefits of globalisation on the selected two cases has been attempted. Further, the scope for small and micro enterprises of this region is also explored during the era of globalisation. Major findings of the study were: (i) As a result of the adaptation and implementation of policies and programmes by the government since 1991, the number of spinning mills functioning in Dindigul district has increased which in turn resulted in an increase in the use of imported machines for production of fine yarn for exports. (ii) Additional employment opportunities are created, causing income generation to labour force particularly to women workers and foreign exchange earnings of these mills. These direct flows of benefits of globalisation to the spinning mills perculate in terms of creation of additional demand for varities of brushes for cleaning the imported machines and packing materials for export of yarn to a micro enterprise at the grassroot level and (iii) Indirect flow of benefit includes the creation of business opportunities to the selected micro enterprises which has been already engaged in manufacturing these items. The dynamic entrepreneurs have utilised business opportunities for further expansion and business diversification.

The growth and development of this enterprise over the past one and half decades is steady and it is noted that it is the pioneering and the only unit manufacturing varieties of brushes for industrial use, artisans use and quality packing materials for the spinning mills. The entrepreneur has become the owner of a factory building worth of Rs.6 lakhs and created employment opportunities to 20 rural educated, unemployed men and women. The advantages and gains listed out by them include (i) Creation of infrastructure-building, machines, tools and equipments, (ii) Creation of employment opportunities, (iii) Increase in procurement of raw materials, (iv) Increase in production of products, (v) Product diversification, (vi) Increase in family saving and investment in gold, (vii) Educating the children and diversification in business. A close examination on the scope for small and micro enterprises during the era of globalisation also reveals that of some of the specific/ resources based industries have lot of export potential in this region.

Introduction

India's textile industry is one of the economy's largest industry. India is the world's third-largest producer of cotton and second-largest producer of cotton yarns and textiles. India's textile industry is also significant in the global context, ranking second to China in the production of both cotton yarns and fabrics and fifth in the production of synthetic filers and yarns. Policy reforms, which began in the 1980s and continued in to the 1990s, have led to significant gains in technical efficiency and international competitiveness particularly in the spinning sector. The modern spinning mills first appeared in response to the Textile Policy of 1985, which removed entry and exit barriers, encouraged the importation of modern machinery and lowered duties on synthetic raw materials. Since 1985, additional reforms, including the 1991 industrial Policy, the 1992 Textile Order and the 1996 Tax Policy, aided the sector by removing restrictions on domestic and foreign investment, easing industry entry and reducing tax differentials between cotton and man made fiber and yarn. As a result of these measures, the spinning sector in India now includes a number of technologically advanced spinning mills of recent vintage, which are able to compete on international markets. At present, India is particularly competitive in the production of yarns and fabrics based on both the "Ring" and "Open-ended" (O.E) spinning methods and India enjoys cost advantages which stem from its comparatively low cost of labour and raw materials as well as low wastages.

The cost competitiveness of the Indian spinning and weaving industries, even with the cunnent scale and state of technology enables and ensures that India will continue to be a highly competitive global player. In this context, the present study has made an attempt to find out the peculated flow of benefits of policy measures on spinning mills that too at the grass root level confining to globalisation era.

The Present Study

Impact studies (both positive and negative) of globalisation on small, medium and micro enterprises that too at the grass root level are warranted which could reveal the realities of the situation regarding globalisation to spinning mills and its perculative advantages to a micro enterprise functioning at Dindigul district, Tamil Nadu.

The specific objectives of the present study are:

(1) To identify and record the direct benefits of globalisation to the selected spinning mills (export units);
(2) To find out the indirect benefits of globalisation perculated to a micro enterprise (supporting unit of sample spinning mills) and
(3) To assess the scope of small, medium and micro enterprises of this region during the globalisation era.

Methodology

This is a case study. Based on both secondary and primary data, a detailed and an in-depth analysis of positive effects of globalisation on selected two cases has been attempted.

Sampling and Selection of Cases

Spinning mills (export of yarn) operating in Dindigul District are purposively selected and grouped under Case I and a micro enterprise which is a supporting unit to the sample case I is also purposively selected as Case II in accordance with the objectives of the present exercise.

Sources of Data Collection

Secondary sources include the annual reports and records of the sample spinning mills and the annual reports of the Textile Association functioning in Dindigul district. Primary data and information regarding case II are collected and gathered from the entrepreneur of the same case by administering a structured and pre-tested interview schedule. Data and information pertaining to both cases (I&II) are confined to a period of one and a half decade i.e., from 1991-to 2006. However, the present exercise is confined to only spinning units-an important segment of the textile industry and has covered only an important micro enterprise which has enabled spinning mills export performance over the year.

Analysis and Discussion

Part –A

Case I

Direct benefits of globalisation to spinning mills in Dindigul district

Part A of this section deals with the profile of spinning mills (Case I) including export units. A detailed analysis of the export performance of these mills is presented here over the past years as a result of adoption of policies and programmes of the government for textile industry during the era of Globalisation.

Profile of Spinning Mills

Dindigul district is the venue of the present study. The existing industrial clusters of this district include leather and leather tanneries, lock industry, iron scrapes, coir and coir products, brass metal products, rice mills, etc... Availability of suitable climatic condition, cheap labour, infrastructural facilities, the emergence of existing and migrated enterprising entrepreneurs and availability and accessibility of transport for procuring raw material and marketing the products enabled the starting of textile units (Cotton yarn spinning, mixed fibre spinning, processing and other related works) in this district. There were only seven spinning units functioning in 1981. The favorable industrial climate induces the entrepreneurs of different locations to start their spinning unit in Dindigul. As a result of this, the number of spinning mills has escalated to 50 in 1991 and further increased to 79 in 1997 and as on today there are 134 mills operating in different locations of this District. This recent increase in the number of industrial units (1997-2006) is mainly due to the shift in the ban on the quota system and the policy measures of the government of India towards textile industry. These industrial units provide employment to 24,000 labourers of which 15,000 workers are permanent and 80 per cent of them belong to women. As a result of the recent measures implemented, these industrial units have export opportunities and 30 out of 134 units are producing fine quality cotton yarn for exports. The number of export units has increased from one in 1991 to 30 in 2006 and the increase in export of cotton yarn works out 26 per cent during the period 2005-2006. This is mainly attributed to incentive measures like easy to start the spinning mills (no license required), power subsidy, easy procedures of importation of textile machineries, and exportation of cotton yarns. These are the contribution of globalisation to spinning mills functioning in Dindigul District.

Part –B

Case II

Perculated Benefits of Globalisation to Micro Enterprise

Part B of this section presents the profile of the sample micro enterprise which is followed by an in-depth analysis and discussion on the perculated benefits of globalisation.

Profile of the Micro Enterprise

Amuthalakshmi Traders – a micro enterprise engaged in production and service is functioning at Settynayakkan patti village, Dindigul district. This enterprise represents the selected case II for an in-depth analysis. This micro unit has been engaged in the production of (a) 60 varieties of brushes for cleaning the machineries of spinning mills (b) Quality wooden frames used for packing the bales of quality yarn for exports (c) Wooden hammers for the use of goldsmiths (d) Wooden handle frames for files for rural artisan use and (d) providing technical service-cleaning and preparing spares for the brushing parts of the imported machineries of the spinning mills operating at Dindigul, Rajapalayam, Coimbatore, etc. This unit is the only enterprise in Dindigul district manufacturing brushes for industrial purposes, packing materials throughout the year by utilising the locally available wood and, packing materials throughout the year by utilising the locally available wood and employing rural uneducated, unemployed youth (both men and women) and providing on job training with the application of simple technology by using simple machines and tools. The enterprise has its continued operation for the past one and half decades and it is housed in its own building, fully equipped with the required machines, tools and equipments worth Rs. 6 lakhs.

Starting production with 2 labourers, as on to –day, the unit has 16 women and 4 men employees. The entrepreneur of this enterprise belongs to the Hindu religion and hails from Coimbatore, the textile city of South India. He has completed his higher secondary schooling and is well trained in wooden technology (2 years). He is married and supported by wife and two children. His wife is a well trained technician in brush knitting. He entered into business supplying rods to welding units at his middle age (31 years). Though he earned profit and generated surplus at the early stages of his business, he lost everything due to mismanagement of funds by his relatives. The entrepreneur of this unit has moved from Coimbatore to Dindigul, where a number of spinning mills are functioning and there exists lot of scope for doing business. The entrepreneur's educational background along with technical knowledge in manufacturing wooden items coupled with failure of his earlier business and the experience of his wife in brush knitting induced the entrepreneur to start his own unit at Dindigul district.

Perculated Benefits of Globalisation to Micro Enterprise

The direct flow of benefits of globalisation to the spinning mills are causing the flow of indirect benefits (perculated) to the sample micro enterprise. An in-depth analysis of the accrued advantages (indirect benefits to micro enterprise) arising out of the positive impact of globalisation on spinning mills has been attempted and presented.

At the time of start up stage (1991), production in the sample micro enterprise was in limited scale with limited amount of investment, employing two workers. The unit could produce one or two varieties of brushes and marketed the same to a limited number of spinning mills. Efforts were taken by the entrepreneur to push his product in the market by direct contact. The growth strategy of the enterprise was "buy my product and try my product". Some time brushes are given free to spinning mills with a view to get the satisfaction on the use of quality products. Quality products with lowest quoted price and timely supply at the door enabled the enterprise to have its share in the market and the spinning mills gave orders to the sample enterprise by stopping their earlier purchase of these items at a higher rate from other places. The entrepreneur of the enterprise utilised this available business opportunities. He contacted the production and general managers of the spinning mills for getting orders of his products. Gradually, he created confidence over the timely supply of his quality products among the managers of the mills and they have recommended his products to other mills. His business transitions are done by cash only and he has adopted "Fixed Price Policy" for his product during the past 15 years ensuring the quality of products. He has taken efforts and action towards minimising the cost of production – item-wise. He is looking after procuring the required quantity and quality raw materials from different parts of Tamil Nadu and is getting orders for his products from spinning mills during his business tour.

His wife is in-charge of the production department, manges the entire production process including management of workers. She is also making transport arrangements for the timely supply of products to the spinning mills. He expanded his business slowly but steadily through market penetration by increasing the production and sale of products to the existing and new customers by effectively utilising the resources of his enterprise and gradually increasing the number of workers from 2 in 1991 to 7 in 1997 and the unit could produce 10 varieties of brushes for the mills which in number has also escalated to 75 in 1997 from 50 in 1991 and further increased to 134 in 2006.

This has opened business opportunities not only in terms of increased demand for brushes for cleaning the machineries but also opened the service opportunities of cleaning the spare i.e., brush part of the mill's machines for the production of quality yarn for exports. Again, the sample unit utilised this chance and the entrepreneur of the sample unit started providing this technical service to the mills. By providing this technical service, the entrepreneur was able to earn a sizeable amount, which ranges between Rs.4000/- and Rs.10000/- depending on the techniques and by preparing various sizes of spares for the brushing part of machineries, which could remove the dust and enable the spinning mills to produce fine quality of cotton yarn for exports.

The service charges for preparing these "Spares" are relatively cheaper compared to the import of these spares; that too very costly from the supplier of machines. The entrepreneur of the sample micro enterprise utilised this service opportunities by learning and acquiring skills in techniques of preparing different varieties of 'spare brushing' part of the machineries that too at lower cost through experience over the past years and as on to-day, he has become an expert in providing this service to the spinning mills. As a result, the micro enterprise has become a production cum service unit and extended its service gradually to the existing and new spinning mills, which made their entries during the period 1997-2006. This necessitated the entrepreneur of the sample unit to link after the service, procurement of raw materials and marketing aspects of his enterprise and his wife had to become the full time in-charge of the production department of enterprise.

Meanwhile, yet another progress happened during the later part of the study period (between 2002 and 2006). As a result of abolition of quota system in textile sector, entry of unit into the industry is made simple and there exists lot of scope for exporting fine cotton yarn to Japan, Korea, Taiwan, Italy and USA. Enterprising community (both local and migrated) started their spinning unit in Dindigul district where the climate is more conducive coupled with availability and accessibility of infrastructure facilities and cheap labour. The number of mills has gone upto 134 of which 34 have started their entry in foreign market by enhancing the production and export of quality cotton yarn. Their entry into international trade compelled them not only to produce fine quality of cotton yarn with specification but also quality wooden packing materials to the bale of cotton yarn for exports.

The main reasons for the requirements of quality wooden packing to the bales of cotton yarn are: (1) To avoid the damage caused to the bundles while transporting them to ports through containers and (2) to maintain the quality of exported cotton yarn in stock till the use of the same by the importers after one or two years of imports. As a result, the spinning mills, entered in external trade demand quality, wooden packing materials in the form of wooden frames, which could be used for neat and damage free packing of cotton yarn for exports. This in turn opened yet another business opportunity to the sample micro enterprise, which was already engaged in the same product line. The entrepreneur of the sample unit, a technician in wood technology, approached the exporting units and received orders for producing wooden packing frames by supplying the samples in accordance with quality and specifications. The exporting units are fully satisfied with quality products and started giving orders to the enterprises as per their requirements. This has necessitated the entrepreneur to construct his own factory shed with more space in 2005 and this has fulfilled the dream of the entrepreneur to become "the owner of fully equipped factory".

During the initial stage of manufacturing the wooden frames, the enterprise was able to produce 60 to 80 frames per day and as on to day it produces 100 to 120 frames by fully utilizing the capacity of the enterprise and engaging more number of rural women workers (15). The reason behind the employment of women workers are (i) Creation of permanent job in this factory to the under employed and unemployed women work force in agriculture. (ii) Women can learn the techniques of manufacturing wooden frames very easily and quickly by using simple machines. (iii) They concentrate on work with sincerity and punctuality and (iv) They have the pride over the production of these products, which are earlier confined to men.

Apart from payment of wages (daily wage ranges between Rs.60/- and Rs.75/-) the enterprise covers the other frinch benefits to the workers including medical, educational and expenses on family function of its employees. The sample enterprises turnover per year (for all the items produced and services rendered put together) is to the tune of Rs. 5/- lakhs and it generates net profit which amounts to Rs. 75,000/- which accounts for 15 per cent of its investment. The surplus generated by the enterprise enabled the entrepreneur in diversifying his business that too in trading and he has become the dealer of the branded ice cream 'ARUN ICE CREAM' opening the retail outlet accessible to the spinning mill and extension area of the Dindigul Township mainly catering to the demand for this item by the people in the neighbourghood.

During the past one and half decades the enterprise has grown successfully by completing its various stages of growth i.e., from start up to growth, further business expansion to diversification in business. Entrepreneur of his enterprise pointed out that the emergence, survival and continued operations of this unit during the past 15 years (from 191 to 2006) had been mainly due to the growth and development of spinning mills not only in Dindigul district but also in other districts of Tamilnadu. It is clearly understood that the emergence, growth and future development of this micro enterprise depend on the performance, progress, growth and development of spinning mills during the era of globalisation. Though the entrepreneur of the sample unit is still living in a rented house, the time is too short to have his own house. At present he has availed Rs. 6/- lakhs as loan from the State Bank of India, Dindigul, timely and easily after the pre-loan supervision done by the bank official for further expansion of business activities so as to meet the increasing demand for the products and services. Once the enterprise took serious efforts to push its products in the market, to-day, the situation is entirely different and there exists lot of scope for this micro enterprise since Dindigul is becoming another textile city in Tamil Nadu.

Conclusion

A closer examination on the scope of small, medium and micro enterprises of this region reveals that there exists business opportunities in exporting fruits, vegetables, flowers, processed food/fruit items including industrial finished products like leather goods, quality locks, herbals, herbal based medicinal and cosmetic products and natural dye products. The potential present and future generation of entrepreneurs of this region can start, run, successfully operate these potential enterprises as micro, small and medium levels with the main objectives of creating employment and generating income through internal and external trade.

7

Profitability Analysis of Select Cottage Industry – A Case Study

Manivel, S and N. Murugan

Abstract

This study on production units of the selected Sarvodaya Sangham is an outcome of empirical research. The study applied case study method. It makes and indepth analysis of profitability applying ratio analysis. The profitability of the sangham is studied in terms of various ratios such as (i) Gross Profit margin (ii) Operating margin (iii) Operating expenses ratio (iv) Operating profit ratio and (v) Net profit ratio. The results of these ratios were also subjected to further statistical analysis and correlation and regression analysis to understand the degree of influence these variables exert on the profitability. The study found that the high cost of production, inadequate demand for KVI products and managerial incompetence are the major reasons for the low net profit ratios of the sangham.

Introduction

Khadi and Village Industries have been recognised as the instruments of social transformation, enlarging employment opportunities, broadcasting entrepreneurship and securing dispersal of industries. Village industries occupy an important place in the economy as they provide employment for a major chunk of work force. They have a strategic role to play in the economic development. The Khadi & Village Industries Commission is the apex body which promotes Khadi & Village Industrial activities in the country. KVIC is having 30 State Khadi and Village Industries Boards which guide and provide all kinds of services to over 3500 institutions and over 29000 cooperative societies. There are about 14200 sales outlets in the country in the KVI Sector.

The Khadi Board is looking after the production and supply of khadi yarn for making khadi cloth. It has training, production and sales centers through out the country. A large proportion of women labour is engaged in the KVI units. Women account for 46 per cent of the total workforce in the sector. KVI Boards assist over 5 lakh artisans. It has reached 2.35 lakh villages in the country in the last few decades.

Role of NGOs in Promoting K&VI Industries

Non-Government Organisations provide services in fields such as health, agriculture, welfare of children, women education and capacity building. NGOs and Trusts with Gandhian ideology have been taking up economic programmes even in the pre-independence era with a view to provide employment to the ever increasing population. The economic programmes are implemented with the fundamental objective of alleviating poverty. Their motive is to generate gainful employment to those who are semi-skilled and traditionally involved in the village industrial activities.

The available studies on financial management practices are mostly confined to private and public sector industrial units.

The scholars have shown scant-attention to study the financial aspects of K&VI units. One reason might be their smallness. These units are tiny and cottage in nature. They involve less capital and are not sufficiently supported financially by the KVIC. The units are managed by people with, of course, rich experience but poor professional background. Therefore, they by and large failed to capture the attention of the researchers. But, in a more and more globalised economy, even the smallest and the micro enterprises need to adopt appropriately the modern management tools, techniques and approaches to remain competent and to withstand market competition.

The K&VI units have adopted labour intensive production technologies and therefore they have more proportion of investment in current assets such as raw materials. Their primary motive being generation of employment to millions of people living in our villages, they continue to produce goods without heeding to market demand and conditions. This again results in piling up of inventory. But still, we need to keep their wheels moving in the interest of the millions of people. Here comes profitability, which is the driving force behind the furtherance of business. That is, the circumstances force these K&VI units to be sufficiently liquid and at the same time profitable in their operations.

Objective of the Study

The major objective of the study is to analyse the profitability of a cottage industrial unit run by a sarvodaya sangham in Tamil Nadu.

Nature and Sources of Data

The data required for the study have been collected from the records and account books of the K&VI unit. Financial Statements for a period of ten years have been obtained. These were the main sources for preparing this analysis. In addition, formal and informal interviews and individual discussions were held with the employees for getting adequate clarification with regard to the working of the selected K&VI unit. The study covers a ten-year period from 1994 to 2003.

Methodology

The study adopts case study method. The Kangeyam Sarvodaya Sangham was selected purposively for the study. The study predominantly relied on ratio analysis for studying the profitability performance. Multiple correlation and regression techniques have been used to study the joint influence of corresponding independent variables on the dependent variable. A linear regression model has been constructed and tested with the help of 'F' test whereas 't' test has been applied to judge the significance of the computed multiple regression co-efficient.

Profitability Analysis

Profitability means the profit making capacity of an organisation. The term profitability may be defined as the ability of a given investment to earn a return. Profit cannot be ignored since it is both a measure of success of the business and a means for its survival and growth. In other words, profit is the engine that drives the business enterprise to achieve its objectives, and is the reward for entrepreneurship. It is the most common yard stick to measure the operating efficiency of the enterprise, the greater the profitability more the efficiency. Profitability also indicates public acceptance of the products produced by the organisation. It also reflects the ultimate impact of various policies and decisions adopted by the enterprise on its business operations.

The term profit is viewed by different people in different perspectives. From the view point of financial management, profit is the test of efficiency and measure of worth of their investment; to the creditors, the margin of safety; to the employees, source of fringe benefits; to the Government, the measure of taxable capacity and basis for legislative action; to the customers, demand for price cut; and finally, to the country an index of economic development, national income generated and rise in the standard of living. It is, therefore, imperative that profit should be the basic thing for which the business firm should strive in the interest of all the stake holders.

Profitability Ratios

Profitability ratios measure how effectively a firm's management is generating profits on sales, total assets and most importantly on the investment. There are two types of profitability ratios. They are profit margin ratios and rate of return ratios. Profit margin ratio shows the relationship between profit and sales. Rate of return ratios reflect the relationship between profit and investment. Following are some of the profitability ratios in relation to sales which are used for the purpose of analysing the profitability of Sangham. These ratios help studying the relationship between sales and various kinds of expenses viz., cost of goods sold, operating expenses, non-operating expenses, interest and tax.

- Gross Profit Ratio
- Operating Ratio
- Operating Expenses Ratio
- Operating Profit Ratio
- Net Profit Ratio

Gross Profit Ratio

The gross profit ratio reflects the efficiency with which the organisation operates its business. The difference between the net income from sales and direct costs involved in goods sold is known as the gross profit. A high ratio is a sign of good management as it means that the cost of production / cost of goods sold is relatively lower as compared to the income. It is also an indication of a higher sales price fixed for selling goods. The standard gross profit ratio is usually taken as 30 per cent for a business unit. The gross profit ratio not only varies widely

Table – 1
Profitability Position in Relation to Sales

Particulars / Year	GP	COGS + OE	Op. Exp.	OP	NP	Sales	GPR	OR	OER	OPR	NPR
			(Rs. in Lakhs)				(in percentage)				
1993-94	43.71	409.69	35.75	7.96	3.97	417.65	10.47	98.99	8.56	1.91	0.95
1994-95	45.51	415.05	38.33	7.18	1.79	422.23	10.8	98.30	9.08	1.70	0.42
1995-96	67.79	545.30	49.41	18.58	3.19	563.88	12.06	96.70	8.76	3.30	0.57
1996-97	84.25	650.36	55.63	28.62	4.57	678.98	12.41	95.78	8.19	4.22	0.67
1997-98	6828	645.51	62.31	5.97	2.57	651.48	10.48	99.08	9.56	0.92	0.39
1998-99	83.65	579.08	65.57	18.08	3.21	597.16	14.00	96.97	10.98	3.03	0.54
1999-2000	69.44	500.72	61.89	7.55	1.29	508.27	13.66	98.51	12.18	1.49	0.25
2000-01	48.27	426.99	46.46	1.81	2.43	428.80	11.26	99.58	10.83	0.42	0.57
2001-02	40.97	319.07	39.66	1.31	1.33	320.38	12.79	99.59	12.38	0.41	0.42
2002-03	41.21	323.22	39.31	1.90	0.80	325.12	12.68	99.42	12.09	0.58	0.24
Growth Rate (%)	-0.59	-2.34	0.95	-13.35	-14.80	-2.47	-	-	-	-	-
Mean	59.33	481.50	10.26	9.90	2.52	41.44	12.06	98.20	10.26	1.80	0.5
Standard Deviation (%)	16.40	23.98	10.67	5.83	1.16	121.71	1.20	1.41	1.54	1.26	0.20
Co-efficient of Variation (%)	27.64	23.98	21.58	86.16	46.03	24.76	9.95	1.43	15.01	70.00	40.00

Source: Computed from financial Statement of the Sangham

from one unit to another, but also varies from one year to another in the same unit.

The gross profit position of the sangham has gradually increased from Rs. 43.71 lakhs in 1993-94 to Rs. 84.25 lakhs in 1996-97. Thereafter, a sudden decline was noticed in the gross-profit in 1997-98 followed by steep increase in 1998-99 (Rs. 8.65 lakhs). But, again from 1999-2000 there was a gradual decline in gross-profit except 2002-03. In general, it fluctuated between Rs. 10.97 lakhs in 2001-02 an Rs. 84.25 lakhs in 1996-97 declining annually on an average at the rate of 0.59 per cent. The average amount of gross-profit was Rs. 59.33 lakhs. The standard deviation being 16.40, the co-efficient of variation was 27.64 per cent.

The quantum of sales had increased gradually from Rs. 417.65 lakhs in 1993-94 to Rs. 678.98 lakhs in 1996-97. The increase in the volume of sales was notably high during the years 1995-96, 1996-97 from the previous years. Thereafter, a gradual decline was noticed from Rs. 651.48 lakhs in 1997-98 to Rs. 320.38 lakhs in 2001-02. The position started improving during the last year of study (2002-03) with a sales turnover of Rs. 325.12 lakhs. However, there has been a decline in the sales performance. It recorded an annual average of 2.47 per cent. It is observed from the table that the sales position during the last two to three years was not that much encouraging when compared to mid 90's. During this period the average sales turnover was Rs. 91.44 lakhs. The standard deviation being 121.71, the fluctuations in this ratio would be more due to larger variations in sales than gross-profit which has shown more consistency.

The GPR has increased from 10.47 per cent in 1993-94 to 14.00 per cent in 1998-99 with little fluctuation in 1997-98. From the year 1999-2000, it has decreased from 13.66 per cent to 11.26 per cent in 2000-01 with notable fluctuations in the last two years under study. In general, this ratio has increased year after year with minor fluctuations in some of the years under study. The average ratio being 12.06 per cent, is far below the standard norm. The lower GPR could be attributed to the non-adoption of modern technology, for it is a labour intensive industry. This has adverse impact on the profitability. The standard deviation and co-efficient of variation were 1.20 and 9.95 per cent respectively. This is an indication of lack of variability in this ratio during entire period of study.

Net Profit Ratio

Net profit margin establishes the relationship between net profit and sales. It indicates the efficiency of the management in managing the business. It is the overall measure of company's ability. If the net profit margin is inadequate, the company will fail to achieve a satisfactory return on owners equity. A high net profit ratio would reveal an advantageous position in the face of falling sales price, rising cost of production or declining demands for the product. A lower profit margin has the opposite implications. Net profit ratio is measured by dividing net profit by sales. The standard net profit ratio usually adopted is 3.2 per cent.

The NPR registered a fluctuating trend during the period under study. It ranged between 0.24 per cent in 2002-03 and 0.95 per cent in 1993-94. The nature of this ratio was so erratic during the entire period of study. Another important point noticed from the table is that the ratio was, in general, found to be lower in the last three to four years compared to the initial period. The average ratio was 0.50 per cent. The standard deviation and co-efficient of variation were 0.20 and 40.00 per cent respectively.

NPR being the relationship between net profit and sales the fluctuation in the NPR might be due to changes in the net profit or in the sales. The net profit of the sangham has also shown a fluctuating trend during the study period. It ranged between Rs. 0.80 lakhs in 2002-03 and Rs. 4.57 lakhs in 1996-97.

The net profit pattern of the sangham has shown comparatively better position in the initial and middle of the study period than in the later years, except a few variations in some of the years. During the period, it declined at an average rate of 14.80 per cent per annum. The average net profit, standard deviation and co-efficient of variation were Rs. 2.52 lakhs, Rs. 1.16 lakhs and 46.03 per cent respectively.

The fluctuations noticed in the net profit and sales have reflected in the net profit ratio. The co-efficient of variation was the highest with 46.03 per cent in case of net profit when compared to sales (24.76).

Operating Profit Ratio

Operating profit divided by net sales is an important indicator of the efficiency of an enterprise. This ratio is particularly helpful in predicting the sickness of a corporate enterprise. Net operating margin for an industrial unit should be about 6.5 per cent.

The OPR has shown a fluctuating trend during the study period. It fluctuated between 0.41 per cent in 2001-02 and 4.22 per cent in 1996-97. It is observed from the table that this ratio was found to be very poor during the last four years from 1999-2000 to 2002-03. But it was comparatively better in the mid 90's except 1997-98. On an average a ratio of 1.80 per cent was recorded. The standard deviation being 1.26 co-efficient of variation was 70 per cent.

The operating profit of the sangham has recorded a fluctuating trend. It fluctuated between Rs. 1.31 lakhs in 2001-02 and Rs. 28.62 lakhs in 1996-97. The operating profit registered an upward trend in the first half of the study period (from Rs. 7.18 lakhs in 1994-95 to Rs. 28.62 laksh in 1996-97), with little fluctuations, whereas in the second half it recorded a declining trend from Rs. 7.55 lakhs in 1999-2000 to Rs. 1.31 lakhs in 2001-02, followed by an upward movement in 2002-03. The average operating profit recorded was Rs. 9.90 lakhs. There has been a declining trend in the rate of growth (13.35 per cent per annum). The standard deviation and coefficient of variation were 8.53 and 86.16 per cent respectively.

Further, the co-efficient of variation was highest with 86.16 per cent in the case of operating profit compared to sales (24.76 per cent). This indicates that the fluctuation in this ratio was more due to variations in the operating profit than in the sales.

Operating Ratio

The operational efficiency of the Sangham could also be understood from the operating ratio. Lower operating ratio shows availability of higher operating profit to the organization.

The operating ratio has shown a fluctuating trend during the period between 1993-94 and 2002-03. It fluctuated between 97.58 per cent in 1996-97 and 99.59 per cent in 2001-02. It is observed from the table that, this ratio was more or less consistent during the entire period of study. This would be further supported by standard deviation (being 1.41 per cent) and co-efficient of variation (1.43 per cent). The average ratio was 98.20 per cent.

The cost of goods sold and operating expenses of the sangham had increased from Rs. 409.69 lakhs in 1993-94 to Rs. 650.36 lakhs in 1996-97. It is also observed from the table that this increase was gradual during the first two years, but thereafter a steep increase was noticed (1994-95 to 1996-97). Thereafter, from 1997-98 onwards a gradual decline was noticed; it decreased from Rs. 645.51 lakhs in 1997-98 to Rs. 319.07 lakhs in 2001-02 with minor fluctuation in 2002-2003 (Rs. 323.22 lakhs). The rate of decline recorded was 2.34 per cent. the average, standard deviation and co-efficient of variation were Rs. 481.50 lakhs, Rs. 115.47 lakhs and 23.98 per cent respectively.

Since the co-efficient of variation of cost of goods sold, operating expenses and sales recorded more or less a similar trend; there has been less variability in the operating ratio.

Operating Expenses Ratio

The operating expenses ratio has shown a fluctuating trend during the last ten years from 1993-94 to 2002-03. This could be understood from the data pertaining to the range. The range indicates a ratio of 8.19 per cent in 1996-97 and 12.38 per cent in 2001-02. It is also observed from the table that this ratio was found to be higher in the second half of the study period (from 1998-99 to 2002-03) as compared to initial years (from 1993-94 to 1997-98). This indicates that the sangham has incurred more operating expenses during the last five years compared to first half of the study period. The average ratio was 10.26 per cent. While standard deviation was 1.54, the co-efficient of variation was 15.01 per cent.

The fluctuations in OER may be due to the variations in the operating expenses or in the sales. The operating expenses of the sangham have shown an increasing trend during the first five to six years of study. It had increased from Rs. 35.75 lakhs in 1993-94 to Rs. 65.57 lakhs in 1998-99. Thereafter, a sudden decline was noticed. It decreased from Rs. 61.89 lakhs in 1999-2000 to Rs. 39.31 lakhs in 2002-03 and recorded an annual average growth of 0.95 per cent. The average operating expenses during this period was Rs. 49.43 lakhs. The standard deviation and co-efficient of variation were Rs. 10.67 lakhs and 21.58 per cent respectively.

The fluctuation in this ratio is explained more by the changes in sales than by changes in the operating expenses.

Multiple Regression and Correlation Analysis

The general Linear Regression Model (LRM) of Y on X_1 and X_2 has the form of

$$\mathbf{Y = A + B_1X_1 + B_2X_2}$$

Linear Regression equation constructed for the dependent variable Gross-Profit Ratio (Y) and independent variables Gross Profit (X_1) and sales (X_2) for the industrial unit is as follows.

Results of Multiple Regression & Correlation Analysis

Variables	*Regression Co-efficient (Beta)*	*t - value*	*Sig.*	*F – value*	*Sig.*	*Correlation Co-efficient (r)*	R^2
GPR	12.06	33.024	0.000				
GP	0.186	13.456*	0.000	90.756	0.000	0.981	0.963
Sales	-0.02261	-12.136*	0.000				
OR	98.20	244.161	0.000				
COGS+OE	0.160	11.054*	0.000	122.867	0.000	0.986	0.972
Sales	-0.158	-11.569*	0.000				
OER	10.26	16.073	0.000		0.000		
Op. Exp	0.198	9.031*	0.000	58.169		0.971	0.943
Sales	-0.02061	-10.768*	0.000				
OPR	1.80	2.175	0.066				
OP	0.16	11.054*	0.000	122.867	0.000	0.986	0.972
Sales	-0.001355	-1.340#	0.222				
NPR	0.50	7.289	0.000				
NP	0.217	12.266*	0.000	77.928	0.000	0.978	0.957
Sales	-0.001063	6.268*	0.000				

Source: Computed from financial statements of the KASS

* Significant at 0.01 level # Significant at 0.10 level

The table value of t at 0.01, 0.05 and 0.10 levels of significance for 7 degrees of freedom are 3.499, 2.265 and 1.90 respectively. The table value of 'F' at 0.05 and 0.01 levels of significance (2, 7) are 4.74 and 9.55 respectively.

Gross Profit Ratio

GPR = 12.06 + 0.186 Gross-Profit – 0.02261 Sales

The regression co-efficient for exogenous variable gross-profit indicates positive relationship while sales indicates negative relationship with the dependent variable GPR.

$\mathbf{B_1}$ **= 0.186** represents the partial effect of gross-profit, holding sales constant. The estimated positive sign implies that such effect is positive while the absolute value implies that the gross-profit ratio would increase by 0.186 units for every one-unit increase in gross-profit.

For alpha = 0.05 and V = n-k-1 = 10-2-1 = 7, this implies that a critical't' value of

$t_{cv} = \pm 2.365$.

For gross profit, t_{cv} = 13,456. Thus, H_0 must be rejected in favour of Ha; in which case, gross-profit can be said to have a significant influence on GPR at 5 per cent level.

$\mathbf{B_2}$ **= 0.02261** represents the partial effect of sales on GPR, holding gross-profit constant. The estimated negative sign implies that such effect is negative while the absolute value implies that GPR would decrease by 0.02261 times for every additional one unit of sales.

For sales, t_{cv} = -12.136, H_0 must be rejected in favour of Ha; in which case, sales is said to have a significant influence on GPR.

F – test

From the ANOVA table, under the degree of freedom column V_1 = 2, V_2 = 7, V = 9 and F_{ov} = 90.756. Using the significance level of 0.05 implies the critical F value or $F_{cv} = F_{.05}$ (2,7) = 4.74 from the F distribution table.

From the above it is concluded that the null hypothesis (H_0) is rejected in favour of H_a. This means that the estimated LRM proves that the relationship between GPR and gross-profit and sales is not a mere theoretical construct; indeed it does exist and is statistically significant.

The correlation co-efficient (R) being 0.981 indicates that the relationship between the dependent variable GPR and the independent variables gross-profit and sales is quite strong and positive. Further, it confirms the existence of a high degree of positive correlation among the variables.

The co-efficient of determination (R^2) of value 0.963 simply means that about 96.30 per cent variations in the dependent variable GPR is explained or accounted for by the estimated regression equation that uses the corresponding independent variables.

Operation Ratio

The Estimated Linear Regression equation constructed for the dependent variable Operation Ratio (Y) and independent variables cost of goods sold & operating expenses (X_1) and sales (X_2) is as follows.

Operating Ratio = 98.20 + 0.160 cost of goods sold and operating expenses – 0.158 sales

The regression co-efficient for exogenous variable cost of goods sold and operating expenses indicates positive relationship while the variable sales indicates negative relationship with the dependent variable.

B_1 = 0.160 represents the partial effect of cost of goods sold and operating expenses, holding sales constant. The estimated positive sign implies that such effect is positive while the absolute value implies that the operating ratio would increase by 0.160 units for every one-unit increase in cost of goods sold & operating expenses.

For alpha = 0.05 and V = n-k-1 = 10-2-1 = 7, this implies that a critical 't' value of

$t_{cv} = \pm 2.365$.

For cost of goods sold and operating expenses, $t_{ov} = 11.054$ Thus, H_0 must be rejected in favour of H_a; in which case, cost of goods sold and operating expenses can be said to have a significant influence on operating ratio at 5 per cent level.

B_2 = 0.158 represents the partial effect of sales on operating ratio, holding cost of goods sold and operating expenses constant. The negative sign implies that such effect is negative while the absolute value implies that the operating ratio would decrease by 0.158 times for every additional one unit of sales.

For sales, t_{ov} = -11.569, thus H_0 must be rejected in favour of H_a; in which case, sales can be said to have a significant influence on operating ratio.

F – test

From the ANOVA table, under the degree of freedom V_1 = 2, V_2 = 7, V = 9 and F_{ov} = 122.867. Using the significance level of 0.05 implies the critical F value or $F_{cv} = F_{.05}$ (2,7) = 4.74 from the F distribution table.

From the above it is concluded that the null hypothesis (H_0) is rejected in favour of H_a. This means that the estimated LRM proves that the relationship is not a mere theoretical construct; indeed it does exist and is statistically significant.

The correlation co-efficient (R) being 0.986 indicates quite strong and positive relationship between the dependent variable operating ratio and the independent variables cost of goods sold and operating expenses and sales. Further, it confirms the existence of a high degree of positive correlation among the variables.

The co-efficient of determination (R^2) of value 0.972 simply means that about 97.20 per cent variations in the dependent variable operating ratio is explained or accounted for by the corresponding independent variables.

Operating Expenses Ratio

Linear Regression equation constructed for the dependent variable operating expenses Ratio (Y) with independent variables operating expenses (X_1) and sales (X_2) is as follows.

OER = 10.26 + 0.198 operating expenses – 0.02061 sales

The regression co-efficient for exogenous variable operating expenses indicates positive relationship while the variable sales indicates negative relationship with the dependent variable viz., OER.

B_1 = 0.198 represents the partial effect of operating expenses, holding sales constant. The positive sign implies positive effect while the absolute value implies that the OER would increase by 0.198 units for every one-unit increase in operating expenses.

For alpha = 0.05 and V = n-k-1 = 10-2-1 = 7, this means the critical 't' value

$t_{cv} = \pm 2.365$.

For operating expenses, t_{ov} being 9.031, H_0 must be rejected in favour of H_a; in which case, operating expenses can be said to have a significant influence on OER at 5 per cent level.

B_2 = -0.02061 represents the partial effect of sales on OER, holding operating expenses constant. The estimated negative sign implies that such effect is negative while the absolute value implies that OER would decrease by 0.02061 times for every additional one unit of sales.

For sales, t_{ov} = -10.768, H_0 must be rejected in favour of H_a; in which case, sales is said to have a significant influence on OER.

F – test

From the ANOVA table, under the degree of freedom column V_1 = 2, V_2 = 7, V = 9 and F_{ov} = 58.169. Using the significance level of 0.05 implies the critical F value or $F_{cv} = F_{.05}$ (2,7) = 4.74 from the F distribution table.

From the above, it is concluded that the null hypothesis (H_0) is rejected in favour of H_a. This means that the LRM proves that the relationship is statistically significant.

The correlation co-efficient (R) being 0.971 the relationship between the dependent variable OER and the independent variables operating expenses and sales is quite strong and positive. Further, it confirms the existence of a high degree of positive correlation among these variables.

The co-efficient of determination (R^2) being 0.943 simply means that about 94.30 per cent variations in the dependent variable OER is explained by the independent variables.

Operating Profit Ratio

Linear Regression equation constructed for the dependent variable Operating Profit Ratio (Y) and independent variables operating profit (X_1) and sales (X_2) is as follows.

OPR = 1.80 + 0.160 Operating Profit – 0.001355 sales

The regression co-efficient for exogenous variable operating profit indicates positive relationship while the variable sales indicates negative relationship with the dependent variable viz., OPR.

B_1 = 0.160 represents the partial effect of operating profit, holding sales constant. The positive sign implies positive effect while the absolute value implies that the operating profit ratio would increase by 0.160 units for every one-unit increase in operating profit.

For alpha = 0.10 and V = n-k-1 = 10-2-1 = 7, implies a critical 't' value of

$t_{cv} = \pm 1.190$.

For operating profit, t_{ov} = 11.054, H_0 must be rejected in favour of H_a; in which case, operating profit has a significant influence on OPR at 5 per cent level.

B_2 = -0.001355 represents the partial effect of sales on OPR, holding operating profit constant. The estimated negative sign implies negative effect while the absolute value implies that OPR would decrease by 0.001355 times for every additional one unit of sales.

For sales, t_{ov} = -1.340, thus, H_0 must be rejected in favour of H_a; in which case, sales has a significant influence on OPR even at 10 per cent level.

F – test

From the ANOVA table, under the degree of freedom column V_1 = 2, V_2 = 7, V = 9 and F_{ov} = 122.867. Using the significance level of 0.05 implies the critical F value or $F_{cv} = F_{.05}$ (2,7) = 4.74 from the F distribution table.

From the above, it is concluded that the null hypothesis (H_0) is rejected in favour of H_a. This means that the relationship is statistically significant.

The correlation co-efficient (R) being 0.986 indicates that the relationship between the dependent variable OPR and the independent variables operating profit and sales is quite strong and positive. Further, it confirms the existence of high degree of positive correlation among these variables.

The co-efficient of determination (R^2) with the value 0.972 simply means that about 97.20 per cent variations in the dependent variable OPR is explained by the independent variables viz., operating profit and sales.

Net Profit Ratio

Linear Regression equation constructed for the dependent variable Net-Profit Ratio (Y) and independent variables Net Profit (X_1) and sales (X_2) is as follows.

NPR = 0.50 + 0.217 Net Profit – 0.001063 sales

The regression co-efficient for exogenous variable gross profit indicates positive relationship while variable sale indicates negative relationship with the dependent variable NPR.

B_1 = 0.217 represents the partial effect of net-profit, holding sales constant. The positive sign implies that such effect is positive while the absolute value implies that the net-profit ratio would increase by 0.217 units for every one-unit increase in net-profit.

For alpha = 0.05 and V = n-k-1 = 10-2-1 = 7, the critical 't' value i.e.

$t_{cv} = \pm 2.365$.

For net profit, t_{ov} = 12.266, H_0 must be rejected in favour of H_a; in which case, net-profit is said to have a significant influence on NPR at 5 per cent level.

B_2 = -0.01063 represents the partial effect of sales on NPR, holding net-profit constant. The estimated negative sign implies that such effect is negative while the absolute value implies that NPR would decrease by 0.001063 times for every additional one unit of sales.

For sales, t_{ov} being -6.268, the H_0 must be rejected in favour of H_a; in which case, sales is said to have a significant influence on NPR.

F – test

From the ANOVA table, under the degree of freedom column $V_1 = 2$, $V_2 = 7$, $V = 9$ and $F_{ov} = 77.928$. Using the significance level of 0.05 implies the critical F value or $F_{cv} = F_{.05}$ (2,7) = 4.74 from the F distribution table.

From the above, it is concluded that the null hypothesis (H_0) is rejected in favour of H_a. This means that the LRM has shown that the relationship is not a mere theoretical construct; it does exist and is statistically significant.

The correlation co-efficient (R) being 0.978 the relationship between the dependent variable NPR and the independent variables net-profit and sales is quite strong and positive. Further, it confirms the existence of a high degree of positive correlation among these variables.

The co-efficient of determination (R^2) of value 0.957 means that about 90.70 per cent variations in the dependent variable NPR is accounted for by the estimated regression equation that uses the corresponding independent variables.

Conclusion

From the foregoing analysis, it can be concluded that the gross profit ratio of the sangham increased from 5.04 per cent to 14.00 per cent with notable fluctuations in one or two years. This is mainly due to the variations in selling price of the goods and cost of goods sold. The operating profit ratio of the sangham has also increased during the study period (from 95.78 per cent to 99.59 per cent). This indicates that the operational efficiency of the sangham has declined year after year with downward trend in the operating profit from 4.22 per cent to 0.46 per cent. Similarly, the operating expenses ratio of the sangham revealing an increasing trend from 2.51 per cent to 12.38 per cent with notable fluctuations in one or two years indicate that factory and administrative expenses are not effectively managed. The study also revealed that the gross profit ratios remained almost constant in these years and the net profit ratio show a fluctuating trend from 1.07 per cent to 0.17 per cent, especially in the later period under study. This indicates that the operational expenses like administrative expenses have not been effectively controlled during the period of study. It is concluded that the high cost of production, inadequate demand for KVI products and managerial incompetence are the major reasons for the poor profitability of the sample K & VI units of the sangham.

References

1. Mahammad Rafiqul Islam (2000) "Profitability of Fertilizer Industry in Bangladesh", *The Management Accountant:* 338-345.
2. Debasish Sur (1999), "Inter-Company Profitability Analysis of Indian General Insurance Industry", *The Management Accountant*, July: 495-501.
3. Agarwal, R.S. (2002), "Physical, Financial and Operational Efficiency Analysis of State Transport Units: a Case Study", *The Management Accountant*: 452-459.
4. Moyer. Mc Guigan. Kretlow (2003), *Contemporary Financial Management* 9th edition, Thomson South-Western Publishing House, New Delhi: 77.
5. Thirupurasundari, K (2002). "Financial Analysis of Fishnet Works-A Case Study", *The Management Accountant*: 674-676.
6. Paul, S.Kr (1997), *Advanced Financial Management* 1st Edition, New Central Book Agency (P) Ltd., Calcutta: 557.
7. Vijaya Kumar, A. (1998), "Determinants of Corporate Size, Growth and Profitability – the Indian Experience", *The Management Accountant*: 327-329.
8. Khan, M.Y., and Jain (1993), *Management Accounting*, 2nd edition, Tata Mc Graw Hill (P) Ltd., New Delhi: 81.

9. Benmont Smith, M (2001) "Modeling Associations between Working Capital and Operating Profit: Survey findings", *The Journal of Financial Management and Analysis:* 56-60.

8

Micro-Enterprise in Bamboo Based Activity

Rathakrishnan, L

Abstract

Bamboo based activities have tremendous potential in non-farm sector. It gives employment and livelihood to millions of people in the rural and urban areas. In order to analyse the significance and scope of this enterprise, 50 basket weavers were interviewed and data analysed with simple statistical tool. The younger generations are not interested to take up this job due to meager return on investment and un-attractiveness. Although three-fourth of the entrepreneurs are educated they do not know how to improve the craft work. On an average a basket weaving enterprise provides employment to the tune of 2.44 persons. By and large the bamboo based enterprise produce tomato baskets big and small size, mats and flower baskets. The entrepreneurs face a lot of problems. However, majority viewed that they would like to continue this occupation in near future also. It is found from the SWOT analysis that the enterprise has lot of scope in future, if it is properly directed. It is concluded that bamboo

Table 1: Growth of Village Handicrafts and Cottage Industry

Year	*No.of units (in lakhs)*	*Output at current prices (Rs. in crores)*	*Employment (in lakhs)*	*Exports (Rs. in crores)*
1997-98	20.8	178699	129.8	13883
1998-99	22.5	209300	134.1	17785
1999-2000	23.8	241648	139.4	25307
2000-01	25.7	293990	146.6	29068
2001-02	77.2	356213	152.6	36470
2002-03	28.57	412636	160.0	39429
2003-04	30.14	465171	167.2	44437
Growth rate	8.03	44	5.2	6.6

based enterprises are to be promoted through improved technology and other government assistance.

Introduction

The cottage and traditional industries play a significant role in shaping the life of rural people. On the one hand the industries encourage rural entrepreneurs and on the other hand this sector keeps alive the technical skills of the less affluent people. Being a traditional industry the bamboo sector contributes significantly to the social and economic life of the poor people. Poverty reduction through employment, maintaining regional balance, promoting rural entrepreneurship, helping industrial development of the country and also raising the standard of living of the people are other contribution to the Indian economy.

In addition, the cottage and village handicraft industries have vast scope for development. These industries have earned foreign exchange. The growth of the industry, output, and employment is shown in Table 1. The industry is growing at 8 per cent per year; the output (at current price) grows at the rate of 44 per cent per year; employment by five per cent; and the export of the products is about seven per cent. By all yardstick the village handicrafts and cottage industry is growing on par with other manufacturing large scale industries.

Characteristics of Bamboo Industry

Bamboo substitutes timber in many respect. It finds a large number of fascinating uses in the rural areas. They are used for fuel, basket making, packing, furniture, ladders, mats, walling, huts, thatching and roofing. The consumption pattern of bamboo is shown in Table 2. The table shows that more than one-third of bamboo is used by the pulp industry for manufacturing paper. It is followed by house uses and other uses in the rural areas. Only five per cent of the bamboo is used by the bamboo basket weavers including packaging. Another two per cent is used by the furniture and other wood based industries.

Table 2: Consumption Pattern of Bamboos in India

S.No	*Uses*	*Consumption Percentage*
1.	Pulp	35.00
2.	Housing	20.00
3.	Non-residential	5.00
4.	Rural uses	20.00
5.	Fuel	8.50
6.	Packing including basket	5.00
7.	Transport	1.50
8.	Furniture	1.00
9.	Other wood working industries	1.00
10.	Others including ladders and mats etc.	3.00

The industry has tremendous potentiality for generating employment throughout the year because of good market demand for the products. The industry falls under the broad category of forest based industries. More than 1,17,989 family units, 400 registered institutions and 450 cooperative societies are functioning in the country (KVIC 1995-96). The industry provides employment to the tune of 2.72 lakhs to rural artisans and craftsman, besides providing many indirect employment opportunities. Bamboo craft provides year-long employment and income. The annual production of the unit is Rs. 129 crores and sales is about 161 crores. However, the technology used in this sector is either traditional or poor technology, which causes large waste of raw materials, loss of time, low output and poor quality of final products.

Micro-Enterprises in Bamboo Sector

Materials and Methods

The major objective of the present study is to appraise the employment and income potentiality of the bamboo basket weaving industry and its present status in the selected area. Fifty bamboo basket weaving cottage industrialists were randomly selected. Interview schedule was adopted to collect the data from the respondents. Through this interview schedule data related to entrepreneurs' background, investment, output, sales, marketing, profit, employment, income and their problems have been listed. Thus, both primary and secondary data were used for analysing the status and problems of bamboo basket weavers in Dindigul district, Tamilnadu.

Agriculture is the primary occupation of the people in the district followed by industries and service sector. The district has extensively hilly and rocky areas with undulating plains. The Palani Hills forms northern side of the western ghats, ranging the height from 1000-2700 meters. Forests cover 19 per cent of the total area of the district. About 700 species accounting for 50 to 80 per cent of the flora of the whole Indian peninsula have been identified in the district. Of which a large number of species are peculiar. Bamboo is one main species in the district. Hence, a forest based traditional industry was selected for the study.

Analysis and Interpretation

Bamboo basket weaving is an important occupation of the respondents in the study area. Males dominate (80 per cent) in this occupation is due to tradition and also their devotion in this occupation. As females have to do all the household activities, it is natural that they get very limited time to do basket weaving occupation. However, the females support males. Moreover, it is a cottage industry. Therefore, all the family members, one way or the other contribute to the family income.

It is found from the study that 82 per cent of the respondents are in the age group of 31 years to 50 years. Only six per cent of the respondents are above 60 years. Table 3 shows that as age increases the bamboo basket weaving entrepreneurs health condition does not allow them to continue this occupation. Hence, less number of respondents are found in the age group of 60 and above.

Table 3: Distribution of Sample Respondents According to Age

S.No	*Age*	*No. of Respondents*	*Per cent*
1.	Below 30	6	12
2.	31-45 years	20	40
3.	46-50 years	21	42
4.	Above 60	3	6
	Total	50	100

The table further shows that the involvement of younger generation is found to be less (12 per cent). It is due to poor monetary return from this enterprise. The younger generation is not interested to take up this occupation as their fathers and forefathers did. More-over the younger generation also has a feeling that basket weaving occupation is neither remunerative nor attractive. Their attitude is further supported by the fact that 78 per cent of the respondents live in nuclear family than joint family.

Almost all types of religious people are involved in this occupation. However, 70 per cent of the respondents are Hindu and 20 per cent of are Christians and the rest (10 per cent) falls under the category of Muslims. Nevertheless, 56 per cent of them are coming under the category of MBC community and 16 per cent are SC respondents.

Family size is another indicator of the standard of living of the respondents. It is depicted in Table 4. It is surprising to

Table 4: Distribution of Sample Respondents According to Family Size

S. No	*Education*	*No. of Respondents*	*Per cent*
1.	Primary	9	18
2.	Middle school	14	28
3.	High school	12	24
4.	Illiteracy	15	30
	Total	50	100

note that more than half of the respondents (54 per cent) are having a family size of 3-4 members. The entrepreneurs prefer to have a small family size. Only a few have (12 respondents) large family size. This is owing to joint family system followed in these households. This shows the respondents' positive attitude to have a smaller family than larger family. They follow the Governments policy of "We two, ours two" or "We two, ours one".

Table 5: Education of the Respondents

S. No	*Family Size*	*No. of Respondents*	*Per cent*
1.	1-2 members	11	22
2.	3-4 members	27	54
3.	5-6 members	11	22
4.	6 and above members	1	2
	Total	50	100

Educational qualification of the respondents is shown in Table 5. It is found from the study that 70 per cent of the respondents are literate and remaining 30 per cent are illiterate. Among the literates some have studied upto high school, namely

10th standard only. Among the respondents its only the old people who are found in illiteracy category. As this occupation does not require any formal literacy the respondents have not shown interest in studies especially in higher education.

As this industry is a traditional one almost all members of the family are involved in this occupation. However, the number of respondents in this occupation is only to a maximum of four in a family. The study found that two to three people are working in the same family. As such, 90 per cent of the respondents' family involved 2-3 workers. On an average the bamboo based basket weaving occupation provides employment to the tune of 2.44 persons. In total all these 50 micro-enterprises provided employment to 122 persons in a year.

Table 6: Distribution of Sample Respondents According to the Types of Goods Produced

S. No	*Types of Good Produced*	*No. of Respondents*	*Per cent*
1.	Tomato basket	42	84
2.	Mats	1	2
3.	Big basket	5	10
4.	Flower basket	1	2
	Total	50	100

Bamboo based products find a large number of fascinating uses in the rural and urban sector. They are used for walling, huts, thatching and roofing. They are also used for medicinal purpose. The other items that can be made from bamboo are baskets, brooms, brushes, chairs, combs, dustbins, fences, flutes, furniture, handicrafts, toys, umbrella handles, room divider, hotel decoration item and incense stick, etc.

The type of goods produced by our sample respondent is shown in Table 6. Five types of goods are produced in the study area, namely tomato basket, mats, big size basket, flower basket and small basket. Nevertheless, 84 per cent of the respondents are producing tomato basket only. Another 12 per cent of the respondents produce big and small basket. As Dindigul district is the major centre of tomato production, the demand for tomato basket is also high. Hence, there was a heavy demand for the tomato basket. The bamboo basket is also relatively cheaper than other similar products available in the market.

Table 7: Marketing Channels

S. No	*Marketing Channel*	*No. of Respondents*	*Per cent*
1.	Direct	48	96
2.	Society	2	4
	Total	50	100

Table 7 reveals the channels of marketing of the products produced by the respondents in the study area. Only two types of marketing is followed, namely direct marketing and marketing through society. More than 95 per cent of the respondents are selling their goods directly without the help of the society and only 4 per cent of the respondents sell their goods through society. The table clearly shows that the marketing of the products is carried out directly without any assistance from other sources, namely middlemen.

Table 8: Respondents Problems

S. No	*Problems*	*No. of Respondents*	*Per cent*
1.	Marketing	10	20
2.	Finance	5	10
3.	Competition	4	8
4.	Raw material scarcity	3	6
5.	Decrease in demand	3	6
6.	No problem	25	50
	Total	50	100

In general, the entrepreneurs have to undergo many hardships in marketing the bamboo products. This cottage industry is also facing some issues like problem of marketing, problem due to other alternative packing materials available in the market, financial problems, problem due to scarcity of raw materials and lack of demand. Table 8 further reveals that 50 per cent of the respondents have undergone lots of hardships due to the above mentioned problems and the remaining 50 per cent had not experienced any such problems. This shows that due to experience in this field, about 50 per cent of the respondents have managed to overcome all the problems mentioned here and the remaining 50 per cent of the respondents are new comers to this occupation. Hence they face all the above stated problems.

Future options: S.W.O.T Analysis for the Industry

Strength: The bamboo industry is nature based. Hence, it is eco-friendly. Mostly the industry supports economically weaker sections. It provides self employment to the downtrodden community. Besides employment is generated in non-farm sector. It requires low capital to invest and also traditional technology. This again will not spoil the eco-system. The industry uses local skill and produces aesthetic products with beauty and tradition.

Weakness: The micro-enterprises are unorganised, hence difficult to bring under any networking system. As the products are manually produced, defects and deficiency are common. Hence, they face marketing problems. Application of modern management concept such as total quality management is difficult. As networking is difficult, marketing of the bamboo products, especially the basket sales is difficult.

Opportunities: As the industry is natural resource based, the opportunities for the bamboo based products are brighter. Another advantage is that the raw material namely bamboo can be grown naturally in the forest or in the farm. We can involve women and tribals for supply of raw materials to the manufacturers or so called bamboo based micro-enterprises. The bamboo craft can provide year long employment and income as against less than 150 days employment in the farm sector. The average earning capacity will also go up depending upon the skill they acquire in this craft work. A small training on eco-pen making can change the life-style of the micro-enterprises. Better opportunities are available targeting low-end domestic market to premium export market. A London based Green stationery company has evinced interest in the bamboo pen as an eco-friendly alternative and business groups in the country have promoted the pens as a corporate gift items (Raghaviah 2006:8).

Threats: Threats for this enterprises are many. All products manufactured with bamboo can be substituted by synthetic industry. Hence, marketing is a big threat. As the bamboo has to grow, it takes long time to supply raw materials to the bamboo micro-enterprises. Again, the artisans are moving to other occupations because bamboo based craft work is not attractive and yields less profit. Organising the village artisans under a networking system is once again a great challenge to this industry.

Conclusion

In general, the cottage industry plays an important role in the development of rural areas and in particular the importance of basket weaving industry can not be under-estimated. So, a study was under taken to analyse the working conditions and problems of basket weavers in Dindigul District. The study reveals that due to the advancement of scientific technology in the field of backing, the demand for baskets is drastically reduced. Besides the basket weavers are also facing lots of problems and one of the important problem is finance. However, the basket weaving community can see some alternative modes of bamboo products making such as refill pens, business cards, cell phone stands, incense stick containers, bangles and flower vases. Cooperative thrift and credit societies or other commercial or scheduled bank linkages may be identified for their future survival. Rural market training to the artisans may help them to lead a better life. Exhibitions and government mela will again help this industry to grow. Though they are not economically well they are willing to continue the same occupation in future also. In this scenario, the government should come forward to help the basket weavers by providing them with some incentives and subsidies so as to bring them up both economically and socially through which the problem of unemployment in rural areas can be reduced. At any cost this industry, being a traditional one and also natural resource based needs to be protected and promoted by vigil and care.

References

1. Anon (2006), *A Study on Basket Weavers in Dindigul District,* Gandhigram Rural University, Gandhigram.
2. Arora (1978), *Industry and Rural Development,* S. Chand & Co. New Delhi.
3. Arora (1995), *Project Profiles of Cane and Bamboo Industry*, Directorate of Cane and Bamboo Industry, KVIC, Bombay – 54.
4. Basu, S.K. (1998), *Place and Problems of Small-Scale Industries,* A Mukherji & Co. Calcutta.
5. Ragaviah Maleetha, (2006), "Micro-Enterprises in Bamboo Sector Generate Income, Employment: Set Up Under Rashtriya Sam Vikas Yojana programme in Wayanad district", *The Hindu*, April 4, 2006:8.
6. Satish Tiwari (2000), *Environment and Forest,* Anmol Publications Private Limited, New Delhi.
7. Sharma, V.M.L (1959), *Lessons in Forestry* Indian Council of Agricultural Research, New Delhi: 215.

8. Whiltakaj, R.H. (1961), "Estimation of Net Primary Production of Forest and Shrub communities", *Ecology*, (42): 177-180.

9

Non–Timber Forest Products Based Small and Medium Enterprises: Vehicles for Lessening Rural Poverty

S. Vaidehi

Abstract

There is a new and increasing emphasis on poverty alleviation and livelihoods improvement through forestry, representing both a challenge and an opportunity. Small and Medium Enterprises (SMEs) give large number of employment throughout the developing countries. SMEs can also provide many opportunities for poverty reduction. The role and the potential of a forest product is determined more by the socio-economic and environmental context of the production, processing and marketing system than by the physical characteristics of the product itself. There are an estimated 100 million people in India who live in and around forests and another 275 million for whom forests constitute an important source of livelihood. Non-timber forest products (NTFPs) are a vital source of livelihood for a large proportion of the poor living in or close to the forest in most tropical countries. Managing forests for production of NTFPs also implies maintaining biological diversity of both plant and animal species. Moreover, local processing of NTFPs can increase off-farm rural employment opportunities. Small-scale forest-based enterprises, many of them based on NTFPs, provide up to 50 percent of income for 20 to 30 percent of the rural labour force in India. NTFPs provide about 40 percent of total official forest revenues and 55 percent of forest-based employment in India. Under these circumstances, the present paper flushes out the new opportunities arising through increased control of resources by local people and new markets for forest products and helping to achieve poverty alleviation through forestry, enhancing income and employment options, taking advantage of opportunities to build and strengthen SMEs in rural areas.

Introduction

Small and Medium Enterprises (SMEs) have played an important role in industrial production in particular and economic growth in general in less developed, developing and transitional economies world wide. They have generally provided the bulk of entrepreneurs and employment and contribute to poverty reduction and wider distribution of wealth in developing economies. Ironically, however, SMEs in these economies have usually been neglected and even discriminated against in terms of government attention, access to finance, management and marketing enterprises. This has been particularly true in developing economies where large enterprises have usually been given the primary role in economic and industrial development.

In India, forests are an important natural resources, which provide raw materials to a number of important industries, namely furniture, matches, paper, rayon construction, tanning etc., The role and the potential of a forest product (Non-timber forest products – bamboo, canes, grasses, essential oils, resins, medicinal plants, lac, gums, tanning materials, dyes, etc.,) are determined more by the socio-economic and environmental context of the production, processing and marketing system than by the physical characteristics of the product itself. It is a fact, that the state government receive about Rs. 450 crores annually by way of these non-timber forest products. Non-timber forest products are a vital source of livelihood for a large proportion of the poor living in or close to the forest in most tropical countries. According to one estimation 100 million people in India live in and around forests and another 275 million are those for whom forests constitute an important source of livelihood. Moreover, local processing of NTFPs can increase off-farm rural employment opportunities. Small-scale forest-based enterprises, many of them based on NTFPs, provide up to 50 per cent of income for 20 to 30 per cent of the rural labour force in India. NTFPs provide about 40 per cent of total official forest revenues and 55 per cent of forest-based employment in India. Under these circumstances, the present paper flashes out the new opportunities arising through increased control of resources by local people and new markets for forest products and helping to achieve poverty alleviation through forestry, enhancing income and employment options, and taking advantage of opportunities to build and strengthen SMEs in rural areas.

Definition of SMEs

Countries do not use the same definition for classifying their SME sector. Nor does a universal definition appear to be necessary. The definitions in use depend on the purposes these definitions are required to serve and the policies which govern the SME sector thus defined. The three parameters generally applied by most countries, singly or in combination, are:

- Capital investment on plant and machinery;
- Number of workers employed; and
- Volume of production or turnover of business.

• Despite the lack of universal quantitative norms, the SMEs as a class are clearly distinguishable in any country, developed or developing. The factors that set them apart are essentially qualitative and comparative. On the qualitative side are their internal management structures, decision-making process, financial practices, trading styles, attendant risk factors, etc. Most SMEs are one-person shows or are run by two or three individuals, usually relatives, friends or business partners, who take most of the decisions. There is usually no distinction between private and business assets, and subjective and personal factors play a large role in decision-making. The personal stakes SME entrepreneurs have in their business are much higher than those of corporate executives in their companies. This enhances the attendant risks and commits entrepreneurs even more strongly to the success of their ventures.

The comparative factors have to do with the way SME's are situated vis-à-vis large enterprises. In the corporate sector, they are small and medium sized in comparison with the large corporate entities with which they share a given economic space. SMEs therefore come in varying sizes and SME's in on country may well be larger than the "big" companies in another. The interesting feature is that, notwithstanding their absolute sizes, the problems confronting SME's appear to be similar in most countries whether developing or developed. It is these features, which set them apart as a distinct group and it is these factors, and not the quantitative definition, which are common and have universal applicability.

A quantitative definition of SME's in each national context is, however, advantageous, as it makes it easier to target macro-policies to a specific group of enterprises. It facilitates the provision of technical assistance and the channeling of benefits under various policies, fiscal and financial concession, and other incentives. It makes possible the physical identification of SMEs on the micro-level, encourages the formation of SMEs associations at the macro-level, and facilitates better articulation of the problems and prospects of the sector. The European Commission currently defines SMEs as one with up to 250 staff.

In much of the developing world, SMEs are the only realistic employment opportunity for millions of impoverished communities. A significant proportion of SMEs in developing countries are involved in traditional activities serving small, localised markets with little or no technological dynamism. In reality, few 'graduate' into larger or more modern technologies. SMEs are officially defined and exclusively identified for promotion in the manufacturing sector of most national economies. The most important justification for the exclusive promotion of SMEs s their potential for employment intensity. In general, an SME generates more jobs per unit of capital investment than a large enterprise. The role off SMEs in the economic growth need not be over-emphasised and their vibrancy is a clear pointer to the health of the economy. In this connection, the present scenario is summarised here under.

SMEs in India

With the advent of planned economy from 1951 and the subsequent industrial policy followed by Government of India, both planners and government earmarked a special role for small-scale industries (SSIs) and medium scale industries in the Indian economy. Due protection was accorded to both sectors and particularly for small-scale industries from 1951 to 1991, till the nation adopted a policy of liberalisation and globalisation. Certain products were reserved for small-scale units for a long time, though this list of products is decreasing due to the change in industrial policies and climate.

SSIs always represented the model of socio-economic policies of Government of India, which emphasised judicious use of foreign exchange for import of capital goods and inputs, labour intensive mode of production, employment generation, non-concentration of diffusion of economic power in the hands of few (as in the case of big houses), discouraging monopolistic practices of production and marketing, and finally effective contribution to foreign exchange earning of the nation with low import-intensive operations.

The small-scale industrial sector of the Indian economy encompasses in itself almost all of the products (including a large number of services) produced by the Indian industries within the economy. Most of the times the products produced by the small and medium enterprises comprise of the intermediary products produced by the large-scale industries. They also include semi processing units and processing units, which are an important link between exports and re-exports. Thus, SMEs act both as a backward and forward linkage to the overall industrial sector of the Indian economy. Interestingly, the segment plays a crucial role in spreading the benefits of economic growth among the masses by drawing surplus workforce from the farm.

SMEs exist in almost all-major sectors in the Indian industry such as food processing, agricultural inputs, chemicals and pharmaceuticals, electrical and electronics, medical and surgical equipment, textiles and garments, gems and jewellery, leather and leather goods eat products, bioengineering, sports gods, plastics products, computer software, etc.

Classification of SMEs

This classification follows the global trend in defining SMEs. The above definitions are to be compared with the old definition of small-scale industries. It's an industrial undertaking in which the investment in fixed assets in plant and machinery, whether held on ownership terms or on lease or by hire-purchase that does not exceed rupees one crore. According to the old definition, the numbers of SSI were 3.572 million units in 2002-03 with almost 50 per cent of industrial output attributable to SSIs. 45 per cent to 50 per cent of the Indian exports are contributed by SSIs.

The size and scale of India's SME sector as per the new SMED Act 2006 is a matter of guesswork, ranging from 7.8 million to 13 million in number, the share in GDP of SMEs may be more than 80 per cent and if the global trend is true for

Table 1: Statement of Exports Performance / Share of SSIs in Country's Exports during 2002-2003

S.No	*Product Group*	*Total Exports 2002-2003**	*Share of SSI Sector for 2002-2003*	*% Share of SSIs*
(A)	**Non Traditional**			
1.	Engineering Goods	38093.00	12500.00	32.81
2.	Basic Chemicals	21701.00	9659.12	44.51
	Pharmaceutical & Cosmetic products			
3.	Chemical and Allied products	10026.75	3354.67	33.46
4.	Plastic products,	4469.78	1862.56	41.67
5.	Finished Leather & Leather products	8779.78	6108.24	69.57
6.	Marine products	6881.31	3251.40	47.25
7.	Processed Foods	13827.95	9679.57	70.00
8.	Wool & Woolen Products	1289.17	1224.71	95.00
9.	Sports Goods	317.51	317.51	100.00
10.	Ready made Garments	26005.39	23404.85	90.00
11.	Synthetic & Rayon Textile	7811.53	1484.19	19.00
12.	Processed Tobacco, Bidi & Snuff	1066.10	675.19	63.33

(Contd.)

(Contd. Table 1)

S.No	Product Group	Total Exports 2002-2003*	Share of SSI Sector for 2002-2003	% Share of SSIs
13.	Electronics & Computers	52100.00	9860.0	18.93
	Total of Non-Traditional Products (A)	192369.27	83382.01	43.34
(B)	**Traditional Items**			
	Cashew	2014.77	2014.77	100.00
	Lac	100.69	100.59	100.00
	Spices	1790.00	515.05	28.77
	Total of Traditional Products (B)	3905.46	2630.51	67.35
A + B	Total of {A} and {B} (Rs. 1 Crore = Rs. 10 million)	196274.73	86012.52	43.82
	Total Exports of the Country		Rs. 196274.73 Crores*	
	Share of SSI Sector		Rs. 86012.52 Crores	
	% share of SSI to of the total exports		43.82 per cent	
	Country's Growth Rate		20.73 per cent	

India, more than 90 per cent of all the enterprises are SMEs. Also every enterprise in its infant years is an SME.

Major Industries of SMEs

In spite of their limitations, the SMEs have made a significant contribution toward technological development and exports. They are established in almost all major sectors in the Indian industry such as:

- Food processing
- Textiles and Garments
- Agricultural Inputs
- Leather and leather goods
- Chemicals and Pharmaceuticals
- Bio engineering
- Engineering, Electrical, Electronics
- Sports goods
- Plastics products
- Electro-medical equipment
- Computer software, etc

The following table briefly explains about the export performance / share of SSIs in Country's Exports during 2002-2003.

Inter-linkages of Forests and SMEs

There is a high rate of attention among SMEs in this sector (Vermeulen et.al. 2003), with most of the SMEs being low-return NTFPs based activities that scarcely have prospects beyond short-term existence. Profitability of SMEs in this sector is generally not viewed by the participants in the traditional sense of income off set against costs such as labour etc., Due to the limited income earning opportunities in rural areas, any cash earned is often perceived and the enterprise is continued. Some of the main constrains to the development of these SMEs include.

(i) difficulty in securing legal access to harvesting the NTFPs. For example, most of the medicinal plant harvesting operations take place without the permits required for the harvesting of indigenous, often protected, medicinal plants.

(ii) most NTFP enterprise opportunities are characterised by ease of entry, i.e., access to the "free NTFP resources". However, in the case of those activities that do require some access to skills, technology or capital, the poor find it difficult to take advantage of market opportunities.

(iii) small-scale forest product enterprises are prominent where there are dispersed rural markets for simple, low cost products and where high transport costs protect them against competition from urban suppliers.

(iv) proximity to markets is one of the most important factors determining the profitability or SMEs based on NTFPs, and therefore one of the most limiting factors for commercialisation initiatives.

(v) the profitability of SMEs based on NTFP extraction is highly dependent on multiple costs including labour and transport, which are rarely fully quantified in project studies.

(vi) rising NTFP prices can have a variety of ecological consequences, including resource depletion, changes (positive or negative) in biodiversity and changes in resource quality.

(vii) since demand curves for NTFPs are often extremely elastic models assuming an inelastic demand curve can result in misleading predictions, and many SME developments overestimate the potential value of NTFPs because they assume an unlimited market demand.

Most emerging forest based small businesses face similar challenges and constraints. Whether they are manufacturing crafts, selling firewood, or supplying raw resources (e.g. medicinal plants), they all struggle with accessing the market and increasing their productivity to meet the growing demand. The latter implies that they are facing operational constraints such as technical know how, infrastructure limitations, inadequate business knowledge / information, problems with accessing finance, etc., This is largely why government, donors and NGOs adopted a supply oriented and subsidy driven approach in their efforts to stimulate the growth of the SME sector. Focus is largely on the inputs (skills and finance, etc.), and outputs (sales and market growth) are commonly neglected. For example, it is reported that the success rate of promoting new SMEs by providing the unemployed with training in basic business skills alone is one in one hundred (Vermeulen, etal. 2003).

NTFP based SMEs: A Sky Boat for Poverty

The vast majority of India's poor people live in rural areas. Rural poverty is estimated at 42.7 per cent, with 43.3 per cent of India's rural poor people belonging to scheduled tribes and scheduled castes (Mukherjee, 2006). SMEs aim to contribute to the reduction of rural poverty and seasonal food insecurity through exploring and developing the role which non-timber forest products (NTFPs) can play in the livelihoods of the rural poor.

Small and medium enterprises are small companies, community groups and collectives involved in the growing, harvesting, processing and marketing of timber and non-timber forest products. They play a significant role in India's forestry sector, supporting the livelihoods of millions of people in rural areas and generating revenue and foreign exchange for the country. But exactly how significant is their role, and how can national and sub-national policies best facilitate them? We believe that answering such questions should be a research priority.

In India, NTFPs provide about 40 per cent of total official forest revenues and 55 per cent of forest-based employment.

Nearly 500 million people living in and around forests in India rely on NTFPs as a critical component for their sustenance. In Madhya Pradesh, the NTFPs which are primarily collected by tribal (i.e. members of local indigenous groups) women are worth more than Rs. 21 billion (US$ 700 million) annually (World Watch Institute, 1991). Based on a study of ten forest protection committees under the joint forest management programme, it was fond that the income from NTFPs ranges from Rs. 234 to Rs. 5569 (US $6-$139) per hectare per year with a mean of Rs. 2299 (US $57) (Malhotra etal. 1991).

Furthermore, revenues from NTFPs have been growing faster than revenues from timbre in the past. For example, compound growth rates in revenue from NTFPs in India during the 1968/69 to 1976/77 period were 40 per cent higher than those for timber. Export earnings from NTFPs on an average account for about 60 to 70 per cent of total export earnings from forest products, and this proportion has been rising. Moreover, there is considerable scope for increasing exports further by exploiting untapped resources as the current production of most NTFPs is estimated to be about 60 per cent of the potential production. In the case of non-edible fibers and flowers, production is only 7 and 12 per cent, respectively, of the potential production (Gupta, Banerji and Guleria 1982).

Small and Medium Enterprises Associations in Poverty Alleviation

Difficulties in business associations, outside the community setting, on-farm tree planting (primarily for subsistence), harvesting of NTFP such as medicinal plants, honey, and shea butter and collaborative management of forest reserves and national parks are the most common forestry focus of the associations reviewed in this study. These are the kinds of activities most frequently associated with poverty alleviation in the forest policy and the national forest plan.

It is important to explore how the spirit and evident success of association at grassroots level can be taken a step further than social cohesion and meeting household subsistence needs. Human development and social empowerment are extremely important, as emphasised under Pillar 5 "human development" of the PEAP and the MDGs. But activities of social development organisations are often focused on coping with the day to day stresses of poverty and less on escaping it in the long term through economic empowerment.

Going beyond social empowerment how can community based associations be supported to increasingly tackle some of the more economic development objectives outlined under Pillar 2 "Enhancing production competitiveness and incomes" where SMEs are primarily targeted? There is evidence that even associations that form primarily for social objectives often achieve better market access (26% of members raised this as the main benefit of association). They also remarked on improved product prices (33%) with corresponding improvements in income for their members. These benefits are unanticipated – only two per cent of leaders / founding members quoted market access as a motivation for association. The main source of income for these associations (as distinct from their members) has been donor grants and technical assistance. Some 65 per cent do not charge any membership fees.

There are clearly some exceptions – the fuel wood growers have been able to form strong associations to meet a commercial demand, and the Kamusime Memorial Rural Development Association has successfully established timber plantations. Perhaps what distinguishes these two case studies from many other markets is that they remain local (growers can sell directly to end users missing out the middle man) and the growers remain closely tied in social terms – they are still from the same families and villages. When markets become more remote, or less homogenous, and SMEs are run by individuals without strong social ties (such as urban-based carpenters), then it seems to be much more difficult for them to associate and / or remain cohesive.

There are some outstanding conundrums. For example, commercial enterprises, which better match the definitions of small to medium scale, are typically not owned by the poor. Entrepreneurs are almost by definition better off than most. They have already ascended out of the subsistence rural economy, even if they remain farmers albeit successful commercial ones. These commercial forestry enterprises are relevant because the estimated 800,000 SMEs in Uganda (across all sectors) do employ about 90 per cent of the non-farming workforce and contribute more than 20 per cent of GDP. Thus they are a crucial engine for economic development: they are growing fast and generate more and more jobs, but in the context of widespread under-employment, they are give away their labour at very low rates.

The government turns a blind eye to the fact that even 'large scale' enterprises pay less than the recommended 'minimum wage' per month and do not provide health and safety measures for workers to officially required standards. Owners readily tell their employees that there is an unending supply of people ready to workforce the same amount, and argue to the outside world that paying more for labour than the competition would be counter-productive. The participatory poverty analysis revealed that while there is a steady increase in GDP, there is an ever-widening gap in wealth equity (MoFPED 2002). A few entrepreneurs are capturing most of the gains. The question is then how to ensure that successful SMEs benefit not only their owners, but also their employees?

This is a serious problem that some believe can only be solved when government regulatory system and watchdog organisation are functioning properly and level the playing field for all employers (SMEs included). The problem is especially acute in developing countries, such as Uganda, which suffer from chronic dysfunction in many parts of the public service. Government imposed employment standards are widely considered to be still some way off.

Conclusion

The Small and Medium Enterprises, many of which rely on NTFPs, provide up to 50 per cent of the income for about 25 per cent of India's rural labour force. The forestry sector provides about 2.3 million man-years of employment. Of this about 1.6 million man-years are related to NTFPs. It is estimated that NTFPs are capable of generating 4 million man-years of employment annually. Most of the NTFPs are collected in a particular season although they are utilised all year round and as much as 50 per cent spoil during storage. Most NTFPs currently provide employment only part of the year because processing of these NTFPs is still poorly developed. Since these products occupy an integral place in the international market, ample opportunities exist for enhancing export earnings by developing suitable facilities for processing, drying, storage, packaging and marketing. Improved labour intensive technologies for processing NTFPs could increase the employment opportunities for longer periods of the year and ensure high prices for the product(s).

References

1. **Mukherjee, A.K. (1994),** "India's Forests: A Status Report: Concepts, Definitions, Trends, Controversies", *International Workshop on India's Forests Management and Ecological revival,* New Delhi, 10-12 February.
2. **Anon (1995),** *Non-wood Forest Products 7: Non-wood Forest Products for Rural Income and Sustainable Forestry*, FAO, Rome, Italy.
3. **Kim Wilkinson and Craig Elevitch (2006),** "Non-timber Forest Products: An Introduction: Over Story", Internet Material.
4. **Mukherjee, R. (2006),** "The Current Status of Mariculture in India and Livelihood Opportunities for Coastal Communities". The Future of Mariculture: A Regional Approach for Responsible

Development of Marine Farming in the Asia-Pacific Region, Bangkok: STREAM.

5. **Malhotra, K.C., et.al., (1991),** *Role of Non-timber Forest Products in Village Economy: A Household Survey in Jamboni Range", Midnapore, West Bengal, India,* Indian Institute of Bio-social Research and Development.
6. **Gupta, R., Banerjee, P. & Guleria, A. (1982),** "Tribal Unrest and Forestry Management in Bihar". *CMA Monograph No.98*, Indian Institute of Management: Ahmedabad: 88.
7. **Edgar Hibbert, (2000),** "The Globalisation of markets – how can SMEs Compete?"
8. **Fonda Lewis, et.al., (2004),** "Small and Medium Scale Enterprises in the Forestry sector in South Africa: An Analysis of Key Issues", Institute of Natural Resources, Forestry South Africa and Fractal Forests.
9. **Vermeulen, J. Burke, M and Ngwenya, A. (2003),** "Options Study for Department of Water Affair and Forestry: Enterprise and Public Private Partnership Opportunities". *Draft Unpublished Report*. ITSD Consulting, Johannesburg, South Africa.

10

Status and Achievements of Wind Power Industry in Tamil Nadu

Dhulashi Birunda Varadharajan and M. Murugan

Abstract

This chapter makes an attempt to analyse the current status and the achievements made by the Wind Power Industry in Tamil Nadu. India's Wind Power potential is assessed at 45,000 MW. Of the total available wind power generation potential, the contribution of Tamil Nadu is estimated at 3050 MW. In Tamil Nadu four potential areas have been identified as suitable for wind power generation. As Tamil Nadu is one of the best Windy States in our Country the Wind Power Industry of Tamil Nadu is taken up for the present analysis. As on 30.06.2003 the total Wind Power Generation of the Wind Power Industry of Tamil Nadu was 8186.79 MU. There is an increasing trend in this industry as private investment and Foreign Direct Investment (FDI) are coming at a faster rate to this industry. This chapter suggests that the government has to concentrate much on this industry to overcome power shortage in our country, as power is one of the powerful components of infrastructure. In the study area, the state owned wind turbines are very less in number. There is no improvement in the establishment of wind turbines. This situation should be changed. Government should also work like the private investors to exploit the fullest potentiality of the wind power, which is a clean and environmental friendly source of power.

Introduction

Tamil Nadu is one of the best windy states in India. The following areas in Tamil Nadu have been identified as suitable place for wind power generation.

(a) Aralvoimozhi pass covering Kanyakumari and Tirunelveli Districts.

(b) Shengottai pass covering Tirunelveli and Thoothukudi District.

(c) Palghat pass covering Coimbatore and Erode Districts.

(d) Coastal area of Rameswaram in Ramnad Districts (Mani, A., and D.A. Mooley, 1990).

The largest installation of wind turbines in the country so far has been in Muppandal – Perungudi near Kanyakumari in Tamil Nadu. It is one of the largest concentrations of wind power capacity in the world at a single location (Thomas, E.C., 2002).

The wind abounding sites like Muppandal has made Tamil Nadu achieve a lot in wind power installed capacity. Therefore, an attempt is made to study about the status and achievements of wind power industry in Tamilnadu.

Wind Power Installed Capacity of the Various States in India and the Position of Tamil Nadu

India's wind power potential estimated by the Ministry of Non-conventional Energy Sources (MNES) is 46092 MW (C-WET). India is one of the major countries harnessing wind

Table - 1

State – Wise Wind Power Installed Capacity

(as on 31.5.2005)

State	*Demonstration Projects (in MW)*	*Private Sector Projects (in MW)*	*Total Installed Capacity (in MW)*	* *Percentage*	* *Rank*
Andhra Pradesh	5.40	115.2	120.6	3.35	6
Gujarat	17.30	236.2	253.5	7.04	5
Karnataka	7.10	403.6	410.7	11.42	3
Kerala	2.00	0.0	2.0	0.06	8
Madhya Pradesh	0.60	29.3	29.9	0.83	7
Maharashtra	12.20	444.1	456.3	12.69	2
Rajasthan	6.40	279.4	285.8	7.95	4
Tamil Nadu	19.40	2017.5	2036.9	56.63	1
West Bengal	1.10	0.0	1.1	0.03	9
Total	71.50	3525.3	3596.8	100.00	

Source : Ministry of Non-Conventional Energy Sources, New Delhi

* Calculation made by the Researcher.

energy. It has been able to achieve significant capacity addition of 3596.8 MW through wind farms and ranks fourth in the world after Germany, Spain and the U.S.A. (MNES). Tamil Nadu plays a crucial role in harnessing wind power in India. The state-wise wind power installed capacity and the position of Tamil Nadu in wind power installed capacity is presented in Table 1.

From Table 1, it is very clear that Tamil Nadu has played a significant role in wind power installed capacity of India. It has contributed a very big share of 2036.9 MW to the nation. It accounts for 56.63 per cent. The performance of other states are very poor. Though Gujarat was the first state in the country to undertake a major wind assessment programme in preparing a detailed wind atlas of the state to identify the wind energy potential for power generation and to install wind turbine (GEDA, 1995) the performance is not upto the level. Its share to the total installed capacity of India is only 7.04 per cent. One can infer from table 1 that Tamil Nadu has been able to achieve a significant additional capacity through wind farms and ranks first in India. Other states can follow Tamil Nadu, to exploit wind power at a faster pace to raise the installed capacity of India.

Wind Power Capacity Utilisation and the Position of Tamil Nadu in India

As far as wind power installed capacity is concerned, India ranks fourth in the world (GWEC). But as far as potential exploitation is concerned its position is not worth mentioning. It has utilised only 7.80 per cent of its exploitable potential. So as to explore the position of Tamil Nadu in wind power exploitation, the state-wise wind power capacity utilisation figures are given in Table 2.

Table 2 elucidates data related to the wind power potential utilisation of various States in India. Tamil Nadu, which ranks first has utilised 48.98 per cent of its installed capacity. From this table, it is clear that a very considerable achievement has

Table - 2

State-Wise Wind Power Capacity Utilisation and the Position of Tamil Nadu

State	*Exploitable potential (in MW)*	*Installed Capacity (in MW)*	** Potential unexploited*	*** Percentage of utilise potential*	****Rank*
	(A)	*(B)*	*(C = A-B)*	*D=B/Ax100*	
Andhra Pradesh	9063	120.6	8942.4	1.33	7
Gujarat	7362	253.5	7108.5	3.44	5
Karnataka	7161	410.7	6750.3	5.74	3
Kerala	1026	2.0	1024.0	0.19	9
Madhya Pradesh	4978	29.9	4948.1	0.66	8
Maharashtra	4519	456.3	4062.7	10.10	2
Orissa	1120	0.0	1120.0	0.00	10
Rajasthan	6672	285.8	6386.2	4.28	4
Tamil Nadu	4159	2036.9	2122.1	48.98	1
West Bengal	32	1.1	30.9	3.43	6
Total	46092	3596.8	42495.2	7.80	

Source : Ministry of Non-Conventional Energy Sources, New Delhi.

*, **, *** Calculation made by the Researcher.

been made in Tamil Nadu in wind power potential utilisation. Though Andhra Pradesh has the largest wind power potential of 9063 MW, it has been in a position to utilise 120.6 MW only. Wind power potential in Tamil Nadu is below the wind power potential of some of the other states in India. But the potential utilisation is at the highest level. Though, its achievement is considerable in comparison with other states, it has miles to go to tap the fullest potentiality. It has miles to go to find out the uncovered possible potential sites and to use the available potential in an efficient manner.

Wind Power Generation in Tamil Nadu

Tamil Nadu is one of the best windy states in the country. The seasonal pattern of wind in Tamil Nadu is dominated by the monsoons. Wind is influenced by the strong south-west summer monsoon, when the cool humid air moves towards the land and the North-East winter monsoon, when the cool dry air moves towards the ocean. This acts as a source as well as impetus to wind power generation in Tamil Nadu (TNEB, 1993).

The wind farms so far commissioned in Tamil Nadu are functioning very well and beyond expectations. The wind power generation in Tamil Nadu was started in coastal area first during January 1986 at Thoothukudi. Then it was followed by installation of series of demonstration wind farms with different capacities and makes of Wind Electric Generators (WEGs) in different parts of the state to the tune of 19.355 MW in the government sector (Tamil Nadu – An Economic Appraisal, 1996-1997). Motivated by the success of the wind mills under demonstration programme and conducive policies of the TNEB, State Government and the Ministry of Non-conventional Energy Sources, private investments came in a big way, which has made Tamil Nadu the No. 1 state in the country in wind power generation (Tamil Nadu – An Economic Appraisal, 2002-2003). With 2036.9 MW installed capacity wind power Tamil Nadu is now 18.41 per cent of total installed capacity of 11113 MW by all sources as on 31.3.2005.

Yearly Power Generation of TNEB Wind Farms from 1990-2003

Even before the commencement of wind survey study in Tamil Nadu scientifically, the first demonstration wind farm was established at Thoothukudi, based on the wind data obtained from Indian Meteorological Department (IMD). The successful commissioning of the first project followed by the encouraging results received from the first batch of nine wind monitoring stations, gave confidence to establish a chain of new demonstration wind farm projects (TEDA 1995). From the date of inception of the first wind turbine, wind power generation started in Tamil Nadu. The following table shows the yearly power generation of TNEB wind farm from 1990-2003.

Table - 3

Yearly Power Generation of TNEB Wind Farms from 1990-2003

Year	*Power Generation (in MU)*
1990	28.6364
1991	23.2914
1992	28.6203
1993	32.6765
1994	30.0258
1995	23.2147
1996	18.3599
1997	18.3247
1998	23.7561
1999	27.2267
2000	18.2972
2001	16.7745
2002	20.0602
2003	24.1747

Source : Tamil Nadu Energy Development Agency, Chennai.

Table 3 reveals the annual power generation of TNEB wind farms in Tamil Nadu. It is clear from table 3 that there has been much variation in power generation as far as TNEB wind farms are concerned. From the year 1993, there is no change in the wind power installed capacity of TNEB wind farms. But, there has been a decline in power generation. Much variation in power generation has been observed from Table 3.

The regression equation for the yearly power generation of Tamil Nadu Electricity Board wind farms from 1990 to 2003 is calculated as Y = 28.98-0.69x. The coefficient of x reveals the direction of the yearly power generation. Since the coefficient of x is –0.69, the yearly power generation shows a downward trend. The annual decline in the power generation is to the tune of 0.69 million units.

Yearly power generation of private wind farms in Tamil Nadu from 1990-2003

Demonstration projects have triggered private sector entry into wind power generation. Since then, the wind power generation has been increasing at a faster pace in Tamil Nadu. The yearly power generation of private wind mills from 1990 to 2003 is shown in Table 4.

Table - 4
Yearly Power Generation of Private Wind Forms in Tamil Nadu from 1990-2003

Year	*Power Generation (in MU)*
1990	2.6222
1991	7.072
1992	12.1209
1993	34.1476
1994	103.3513

(Contd.)

(Contd. Table 4)

Year	*Power Generation (in MU)*
1995	346.4346
1996	710.4209
1997	771.8439
1998	944.1034
1999	1111.3030
2000	1090.6177
2001	1168.7762
2002	1280.2879
2003	1627.7333

Source : Tamil Nadu Energy Development Agency, Chennai.

From table 4 it is clear that there is a continuous rise in power generation, say the year 2000, as far as private wind farms are concerned. As the private wind farms carry out proper maintenance works, the power generation is kept at a higher level than that of the demonstration projects.

The regression equation for the yearly power generation of private wind farms from 1990 to 2003 is calculated as Y = -328.31 + 131.5x. It is clear from the above equation that the yearly power generation of private wind farms from 1990 to 2003 shows an upward trend. The annual increase in the power generation is to the tune of 131.5 million units.

Trend Analysis of Wind Power Generation of Various States in India and the Position of Tamil Nadu

To know about the performance of Tamil Nadu in wind power generation, trend analysis is carried out for the wind power generation of selected states, where wind power generation is done for more than 7 years in India, using linear regression equation. The trend values of the selected states are presented in table 5.

The results of trend equations obtained for the wind power generation of various potential states where wind power projects have been installed, during the study period are shown in Table 5.

Table - 5

Trend Analysis for State-wise Wind Power Generation in India

Model Y = a + bt, Y = Wind Power Generation in MU t = time (1,2,3,......)

State	*Co-efficient*	*Estimated Value*	*T Value*	*F Value*	*SE*	*DW*	*R*	R^2
Andhra Pradesh	(i) a	-25.68	-2.93	83.09	8.29	1.76	0.95	0.90
	(ii) b	11.77	9.12		1.29			
Gujarat	(i) a	10.80	0.77	43.64	14.09	1.42	0.91	0.83
	(ii) b	13.73	6.61		2.08			
Karnataka	(i) a	-45.70	-2.26	30.16	20.21	1.09	0.91	0.83
	(ii) b	21.98	5.49		4.00			
Kerala	(i) a	1.41	2.18	0.37	0.65	1.47	0.22	0.05
	(ii) b	0.07	0.60		0.12			
Madhya Pradesh	(i) a	-9.65	-3.36	76.92	2.87	0.87	0.95	0.90
	(ii) b	3.71	8.77		14.26			
Maharastra	(i) a	-172.95	-1.79	10.91	96.71	0.59	0.74	0.55
	(ii) b	47.10	3.30		14.26			
Tamil Nadu	(i) a	-22.17	-0.29	164.92	77.58	1.17	0.97	0.95
	(ii) b	146.91	12.84		14.45			
India	(i) a	-370.59	-3.78	258.18	98.03	1.21	0.98	0.97
	(ii) b	232.24	16.07		14.45			

Source : Computed Data. MU - Million Units.

R^2 value is satisfactory for all other states and for the total of India's wind power generation except Kerala and Maharastra. In the case of Andhra Pradesh and Madhya Pradesh 90 percent of the dependent variable is explained by the independent variable. As far as Gujarat and Karnataka are concerned, the independent variable explains 83 per cent of the dependent variable. In the trend equation for the wind power generation of Tamil Nadu, 95 per cent of the dependent variable is explained by the independent variable. As far as the regression equation for the wind power generation of India is concerned, 97 per cent of the dependent variable is explained by the independent variable.

The trend co-efficient were found to be statistically significant for the trend equations estimated for the wind power generation of Andhra Pradesh, Gujarat, Karnataha, Madhya Pradesh, Maharashtra, Tamil Nadu and over all India. But it is statistically insignificant for the wind power generation of Kerala. Among the trend co-efficient for the wind power generation of the various wind power potential states, Tamil Nadu topped the list and the wind power generation from Tamil Nadu from 1993 to 2003 increased by 146.91 MU per annum on an average. This increasing trend with regard to the wind power generation of Tamil Nadu is due to the conducive environment prevailing in the state. The well conceived policies announced and the facilities offered by the Government of Tamil Nadu for harnessing the vast wind potential in Tamil Nadu has made it possible for Tamil Nadu to be in the forefront in the country in the field of wind power generation. Tamil Nadu Energy Development Agency is also taking strenuous steps to popularise this clean energy technology in Tamil Nadu. That is the reason why Tamil Nadu is on the topmost position in wind power generation.

The wind power generation of Andhra Pradesh on an average has increased by 11.77 MU annually. On an average the annual wind power generation has been increase by 13.73

MU in Gujarat, 21.98 MU in Karnataka. But very megre power is generated from Kerala (0.07 MU), Madhya Pradesh (3.71 MU) and Maharashtra (47.10 MU). The total wind power generation of India has shown an upward trend every year by a sum of 232.24 MU. Among the various wind power potential states considered in this study, Tamil Nadu showed the highest positive increase of 146.91 MU every year on an average. This analysis shows that, Tamil Nadu plays a predominant role as far as the wind power generation of India is concerned. The performance of Tamil Nadu in wind power generation as compared with other wind power potential states is very remarkable.

Conclusion

Wind power is one of the important sources of the renewable energy technology. When wind power is exploited at a faster pace, that solves two important problems viz., fast depletion of fossil fuels and environmental problem of air pollution. India is one of the countries, which has achieved something remarkable in wind power development and ranks fourth in the world. In taking the fourth place, the role of Tamil Nadu is of greater importance. Tamil Nadu has performed extremely good in wind power installation, wind power potential utilisation and wind power generation. Tamil Nadu has attracted a large number of private entrepreneurs to this new form of power sector. So, it can be said that Tamil Nadu is the role model for other states in wind power development. If all the states, where wind power potential is identified, developed the wind power sector like Tamil Nadu, definitely India will be in the first place as far as wind power exploitation is concerned.

References

1. Anon (1993), *A Profile of Wind Farms in Tamil Nadu,* TNEB: 2-3.

2. *Global Wind Energy Council*, www.gwec.com
3. Gujarat Energy Development Agency (GEDA 1995), "Wind Power Generation: The Status in Gujarat", ***Energy Environment Monitor***, 11(1): 77-78.
4. Jagadeesh, A., 2000, Wind Energy Development in Tamil Nadu and Andhra Pradesh, India Institutional Dynamics and Barriers – A case Study, ***Energy Policy,*** 28(3): 157-168.
5. Mani A. and D.A. Mooley, (1990), ***Wind Energy Resources Surveys in India***, Allied Publishers, New Delhi: 7.
6. Monga, P., (1997), Barriers to Renewable Energy Development, ***IREDA News***, 8(3): 31-37.
7. Anon, *Report of the Centre for Wind Energy Technology (C-WET)*, Chennai.
8. Anon (2006), Ministry of Non-Conventional Energy, New Delhi: www.windpwoerindia.com
9. Suresh R., (1995), "Key Issues in Wind Power Generation", ***Energy Environment Monitor,*** 11(1): 79.
10. Anon (1996), *Tamil Nadu – An Economic Appraisal, 1996-97*, Chennai: 137.
11. Anon (2002), *Tamil Nadu – An Economic Appraisal, 2002-2003*, Energy, Chennai: 96.
12. Anon (1995), Wind Energy Activities in Tamil Nadu and Tamil Nadu Energy Development Agency's (TEDA's) Role, ***Energy Environment Monitor,*** 11(1): 71-73.
13. Thomas E.C , 2002, "Renewable Energy in India", ***Yojana,*** Vol. 46: 48.
14. www.windpowerindia.com.

Part – III Food Processing Industry Under Globalisation

11

Performance of Small Enterprises in Dairying – A Study with Reference to Madurai District

Haridoss, R. and I. Jeyaraj

Abstract

Dairy is an important supportive occupation to millions of resource poor families in India. Many of these families opt for dairy farming as it offers economic, food and social securities to them. Experiences of small enterprises in dairying are a unique success in India. An attempt has been made in this chapter to analyse the performance of small enterprises in dairying. For this, Madurai district has been taken into consideration. There are two animal husbandry divisions in Madurai district namely Madurai and Thirumangalam. Madurai Animal Husbandry division has six blocks and Thirumangalam Animal Husbandry division have eight blocks. For the present study, six blocks in Madurai Animal Husbandry division have been taken. From these 120 sample dairy enterprises were taken. Primary data collection was made from 20 samples from each block during the period from September 2005 to December 2005. In order to analyse the performance of small enterprises in dairying the following specific objectives have been formulated. They are, to analyse the cost and returns structure of milk production among cows and buffaloes and to examine and compare the break-even output of milk for cows and buffaloes. As far as the cost of milk production is concerned, the cost per litre is higher in the case of buffaloes than cows. Even though gross returns are higher in the case of buffaloes, the rate of returns per rupee is higher in the case of cows only. Another observation made in the break-even output analysis is the margin of safety is higher in the case of cows than buffaloes. Therefore milk production with cows is economically viable for the small enterprises because of high margin of safety.

Introduction

India is a country of villages. Almost 70 per cent of Indians live in villages and a majority of them are engaged in agricultural and allied activities. The green revolution in the early 70s is a milestone in the history of Indian agriculture. Dairying, one of the expanding branches came out of the green revolution. It is an agro-based industry, expanding fastest throughout the world. A decade ago only 5 per cent of the milk produce came into the dairies, whereas today it is 10 per cent and it is increasing.

Dairy is an important supportive occupation to millions of resource poor families in India. Many of these families opt for dairy farming as it offers economic, food and social securities to them. Approximately one million persons are employed in this sector in principal states whereas another 9 million persons are provided subsidiary status employment. Livestock assets are particularly important among the landless, small and marginal farmers as well as women.

For small farmers, cattle are perhaps the only tangible asset and mainstay for their socio-economic security. Dairy sector provides draught power, manure and cash income, which augments the crop production. Further animals produce milk by converting the crop residues and by-products which other wise would be wasted. Thus, dairying, since time immemorial has provided a means of livelihood for our rural masses but it is only over the last half century that its role in contributing to their socio-economic betterment became recognised.

Dairy Enterprises in India

Indian dairy industry has grown phenomenally since 1971, with an annual increase of 4.7 per cent in milk production and has increased from 17 million tonnes in 1971 to 94 million tonnes in 2004-05. Dairy development in India has emerged as one of the modern India's most successful development programmes. The strength of Indian dairy enterprises lies in the fact that despite limited investments, it has shown consistent and sustainable growth Planning Commission estimate suggests that by the end of X plan, milk production will touch 100 million tonnes, growing at 4.2 per cent. Currently, consumption of liquid milk accounts for about 46 per cent of the total milk production and percapita availability of milk is 226 grams/day, which is greater than the recommended 200 grams/day, by Indian Council of Medical Research. The remaining 54 per cent is utilised for conversion of milk products.

Unique Features of Indian Dairy Enterprises

The unique feature of our dairy enterprises is production by masses rather than mass production system. This is evident from the fact that India's 94 million tonnes plus milk production comes from a milk herd of around 100 million comprising 60 million cows and 40 million buffaloes involving 70 million dairy farmers. Further, though scale of milk production is small in our country yet marketing is of large scale; consequently the difference arises with the scale of production, which cannot easily compete with products resulting from mass production technologies until the power of scale both at the production and marketing ends is conferred on small production units, as has been done successfully in the cooperative dairy sector.

Another special feature of Indian dairy industry is that buffalo's milk constitutes about 55 per cent of the total milk production in the country, which is considered to be commercially viable than cow milk for the manufacture of fat and SNF based milk production such as butter, ghee and milk powders, because of its higher fat and lesser moisture content.

Economics of Dairy Enterprises

- Socio-economic developments are substantially influenced by the dairy sector, which contributes to about 10 per cent of its GDP.
- Dairying with cross-bred cattle and high – yielding buffaloes is a remunerative business, with higher profits than crop growing, in marginal, small and medium sized holdings.
- For small farmers having irrigated land, dairying activity, when done hand in hand with crop production, is more profitable than crop production alone.
- The returns from dairy sector and mixed farming in small and medium farm holdings are larger and highly sustainable.
- Scale of milk production is small but marketing is of large scale.

Dairying is an economic activity, which evens out cash flows to households. It is not only a source of employment and income but also a storehouse of wealth, an asset that often helps tide over unforeseen demands for liquid cash. Due to the growing importance of dairy enterprises, an attempt has been made in this paper to analyse the performance of small scale enterprises in dairying in Madurai.

Objectives

In order to analyse the performance of small enterprises of dairying in Madurai, the following specific objectives have been formulated. They are :

- to analyse the cost and returns structure of milk production among cows and buffaloes, and
- to examine and compare the break even output of milk for cows and buffaloes.

Methodology

An attempt has been made in this paper to analyse the performance of small enterprises in dairying. In the present study, Madurai district has been taken. Two animal husbandry division are there in Madurai district namely Madurai and Thirumangalam, which consist of six and eight blocks respectively. 120 sample dairy enterprises are taken for analysing the performance on the basis of cost and returns from the Madurai Animal husbandry division 20 samples were selected from six blocks, from which primary data collection was made during the period from September 2005 to December 2005.

Results and Discussion

In order to analyse the performance of small enterprises in dairying, milk yield of cows and buffaloes in the lactation period owned by the sample respondents is taken. The lactation period and milk yield are the two important elements to measure the productivity of milk. The life period of the animals varies from 10-12 years, irrespective of the breed. The fertility period may be treated as ending at the seventh lactation; and beginning from the first lactation the owners of the animal prefer to keep the animals only up to the fourth lactation because only during this period the milk yield would be higher and there will be appreciation in the value of the animals. Milk yield of an animal may be calculated in the lactation period and in the inter-calving period. The lactation period is the period in which the animals are in milk. Whereas, the inter-calving period is the sum of lactation and dry periods. For the present study, only lactation period was taken for the calculation of milk yield, costs, returns etc.

Table 1: Average Cost of Milk Production Per Animal

(In Rupees)

	Lactation Period	
	Cow	*Buffalo*
A. VARIABLE COST		
Feed Cost		
Green Fodder	1723.11 (13.89)	3448.57 (16.33)
Dry Fodder	2431.46 (19.60)	4189.81 (19.84)
Concentrates	2709.34 (21.84)	5159.12 (24.43)
Total Feed Cost	6863.91 (55.33)	12797.50 (60.60)
Human Labour		
Family Labour	1843.44 (14.86)	2910.06 (13.78)
Hired Labour	1087.95 (8.77)	1649.31 (7.81)
Total	2931.39 (23.63)	4559.37 (21.59)
Miscellaneous Expenditure	214.61 (1.73)	365.34 (1.73)
Total Variable Cost	10009.91 (80.69)	17722.21 (83.92)

(Contd)

(Contd Table 1)

	Lactation Period	
	Cow	*Buffalo*
B. FIXED COST		
Depreciation on cattle shed and Dairy Equipment	199.73 (1.61)	259.75 (1.23)
Depreciation on Animals	1247.98 (10.06)	1533.17 (7.26)
Interest on fixed capital	947.77 (7.64)	1602.85 (7.59)
Total fixed cost	2395.48 (19.31)	3395.77 (16.08)
Total cost (A+B)	12405.39 (100)	21117.98 (100)
Income from dung	794.97	828.73
Net Cost of Milk Production	11610.42	20289.25
Average milk production (litres)	1412.46	1962.21
Cost of milk production per litre	8.22	10.34

Note: Figures in brackets are percentages of total.

Cost Analysis

The cost of milk production is classified into variable cost and fixed cost. The variable cost consists of feed cost and labour cost. The feed cost includes the cost of green fodder, dry fodder and concentrates, while labour cost includes the cost of hired labour and family labour. The fixed cost includes depreciation on cattle shed and dairy equipments, depreciation on animals and interest on fixed capital.

Table 2: Average Cost of Milk Production Per Litre in Lactation Period

(In Rupees)

	Cow	*Buffalo*
A. VARIABLE COST		
(i) Feed Cost		
Green Fodder	1.22	1.76
Dry Fodder	1.72	2.13
Concentrates	1.92	2.63
Total Feed Cost	4.86	6.52
(ii) Human Labour		
Family Labour	1.31	1.48
Hired Labour	0.77	0.84
Total	2.08	2.32
(iii) Miscellaneous Expenditure	0.15	0.19
Total Variable Cost	7.09	9.03
B. FIXED COST		
Depreciation on cattle shed and Dairy Equipment	0.14	0.13
Depreciation on Animals	0.88	0.78
Interest on fixed capital	0.67	0.82
Total fixed cost	1.69	1.73
TOTAL COST (A+B)	8.78	10.76
Income from dung	0.56	0.42
Net Cost of Milk Production	8.22	10.34

Table 2 shows that the variable costs constitute 80.69 per cent and 83.92 per cent of total cost for the cows and buffaloes respectively during the lactation period. It is found that buffaloes have a higher variable cost than cows. The difference is due to the fact that the buffaloes require more feeds than the cows. As far as labour cost is concerned, it contributes 23.63 per cent and 21.59 per cent for cows and buffaloes respectively. Among the labour cost family labour dominates with 14.86 per cent and 13.78 per cent.

Among the fixed costs, cost due to depreciation on animals takes the major share especially for cows, that is 10.06 per cent while for buffaloes it is 7.26 per cent. But total fixed cost in terms of rupees is high for buffaloes. The net cost of production of milk of cows is Rs.11610.42 and for buffaloes it is Rs.20289.25 and the cost per litre is worked out at Rs. 8.22 for cows and Rs.10.34 for buffaloes.

In table 2, the average cost of production of milk per litre is calculated by dividing the total net cost of production per animal with the average yield of milk per animal in order to measure the relative importance of each cost component in the cost structure of cows and buffaloes milk production. This table reveals the respective cost of milk production per litre for cows and buffaloes. The total net cost of milk production per litre in lactation period is Rs. 8.22 and Rs. 10.34 for cows and buffaloes respectively.

The feed costs per litre dominate by Rs. 4.86 and Rs.6.52 for cows and buffaloes respectively. It is comparatively high for buffaloes than cows. The labour cost per litre is Rs. 2.08 and Rs. 2.32 for cows and buffaloes respectively. Total fixed cost is Rs.1.69 and Rs.1.73 for cows and buffaloes respectively. The average net cost of production of milk per litre is found to be greater for buffaloes than cows because the yield of buffaloes is higher than cows.

Among various costs incurred on milk production, variable cost is recorded as high in both the cases of cows and buffaloes.

Table 3: Return on Investment

	Cow	*Buffalo*
A. ANNUAL RETURNS		
Quantum of milk yield (in litres)	1412.46	1962.21
Value of milk yield (in Rs)	15791.30	25744.20
Value of dung (in Rs)	794.97	828.73
B. GROSS RETURNS	16586.27	26572.93
C. NET RETURNS		
Net returns over variable cost	6576.36	8850.72
Net returns over total cost (Excluding family labour)	6024.32	8365.01
Net returns over total cost (including family labour)	4180.88	5454.95
D. RATE OF RETURNS PER RUPEE		
Gross return/variable cost ratio	1.66	1.50
Gross return/total cost ratio (excluding family labour)	1.57	1.46
Gross return/total cost (including family labour)	1.34	1.26

That is Rs.7.09 out of Rs. 8.78 in the case of cows and Rs. 9.03 out of Rs.10.76 in the case of buffaloes.

The rate of returns measures the returns per rupee on the basis of expenditure on various input items of milk animals. For this, the gross returns are calculated by adding the value of milk yield in rupees with the value of dung. The net returns are measured in three ways namely net returns over variable cost, net returns over total cost excluding family labour and net returns over total cost including family labour..

Table 3 shows that the gross returns are higher in the case of buffaloes than cows. This difference is due to the variation in quantum of milk yield. It is inferred from the results of net returns over total cost that the buffalo is found the most remunerative milk animal compared to cow. Even though gross returns are higher in the case of buffaloes than cows the rate of return per rupee over total and variable costs is higher in case of cows than buffaloes.

Break-Even Output

Break even analysis has been used to find out the break even output for milk animals, namely cows and buffaloes. Break even output is an output at which the total revenue and total cost are equal. It can also be defined as the point at which the total revenue curve breaks through the total cost curve where total revenue is greater than total cost. The following is the formula to calculate break even output.

TFC

$$BEP = \frac{TFC}{ASP-AVC}$$ Where,

ASP-AVC

BEP = Break-Even Output of Milk in Litres

TFC = Total Fixed Cost of Milk

ASP = Average Selling Price of Milk Per Litre

AVC = Average Variables Cost Per Litre of Milk

The percentage of break even output to the total output is calculated, which is reverse of margin of safety. Margin of safety is the cushion owned by the enterprise even when there is a decline in production of milk per animal, but the enterprise will not incur any loss. The percentage of safety margin is calculated by

$$\text{Margin of Safety} = \frac{\text{Actual output - BEP output}}{\text{Actual Output}} \text{ X } 100$$

Table 4: Break-Even Output for Milk Animals in Lactation Period

	Cow	*Buffalo*
Average yield (in litres)	1412.46	1962.21
Fixed cost per animal (in Rs.)	2395.48	3395.77
Variable cost per animal (in Rs.)	1009.91	17722.21
Total cost per animal (in Rs.)	12405.39	21117.98
Selling price per litre (in Rs.)	11.18	13.12
Average variable cost per litre (in litres)	7.09	9.03
BEP output (in litres)	585.69	830.26
Margin of safety (in percentage)	58.53	57.69
Percentage of BEP output to total output	41.47	42.31

Table 4 shows that the break – even output of milk is low (585.69 litres) in the case of cows while it is found to be high (830.26 litres) in case of buffaloes. In the case of variable cost per litre, it is lesser (Rs. 7.09) for cows than for buffaloes (Rs. 9.03).

The margin of safety is recorded high in the case of cows that are 58.53 percent, while in the case of buffaloes it is recorded as 57.69 per cent. Thus it is inferred that milk production with cows is economically viable for the small enterprises.

Conclusion

Experiences of small enterprises in dairying are a unique success not only in the study area, Madurai but also in India. This has been widely accepted world over as a model for the developing countries. Particularly, dairy is an instrument of silent socio-economic revolution among the resources poor rural people. People working in small enterprises in dairying have demonstrated their commitment and devotion to bring India the honour of being the number one milk producer in the world. The next phase of battle is on. They have to work for more effectiveness and efficiency in per unit milk production, which is much harder, a challenge to be won. Therefore, a good dairy enterprise network is sure to change the socio-economic scenario of the country.

References

1. Bhanja, S.K. and Vekatadri (1988), *Milk Animals in IRDP*, Published by NIRD, Hydrabad.
2. Balaraman, N. (2003), "Status and Prospects – Milk Production Systems", *Indian Dairy Man*, 55(3): 29-32.
3. Anon (2002), *Economic Survey 2002-2003*, Government of India, Ministry of Finance and Company Affairs, Economic Division.
4. Sah A.K. (1998), "Dairy Scenario: Rising Hope", *Yojana* 11:42-43.
5. Sushil Kumar (25), "Role of Dairy Development in Employment Generation", Poverty Alleviation and Food Security in India", *Indian Food Industry*, 24(3): 65-67.

12

Impact of Globalisation – Opportunities and Challenges in the Dairy Sector

Seethalakshmi, M and M.Sankar

Abstract

India possesses over 16 per cent of world cattle and some 57 per cent of buffalo population but it stands for only 14 per cent of world milk production. The sector is livelihood intensive and provides supplementary income to 60 to 70 per cent of rural households. The small and marginal farmers and landless constitute the core milk producer group, owning over 60 per cent of milch animal. The present system of milk production offers many challenges. The systems is characterised by low milk production per milch animal; and the households widely scattered, the quality of milk, existing pricing policy, lack of public awareness and ineffective regulatory mechanism are the greatest challenge to this sector. The next two decades would offer immense opportunities for dairy sector together with associated challenges. The dairy sector hopefully would capitalise on the opportunities for the welfare of millions of families engaged in dairy farming and associated activities.

Introduction

India possesses over 16 per cent of world cattle and some 57 per cent of buffalo population but account for 14.20 per cent of world milk production. The sector is highly livelihood intensive and provides supplementary income to 60 to 70 per cent of rural households. Milk production takes place in millions of small and very small holdings; approximately 7 million households (HH) scattered throughout the country are involved. The small and marginal farmers and landless constitute the core milk producer group, owing over 60 per cent of milch animal.

From chronic shortages of milk, India has emerged today as the largest producer of milk in the world crossing 80 million tonnes (GOI 2002). This success story of Indian milk production has been written primarily by millions of small farm holder producers. Although the yields have remained quite low compared to the world standards, yet it has not only survived but also flourished. Several factors appear to have helped it flourish. The "Operation Flood", one of the world's largest dairy development programmes, which helped to create strong network and linkages among millions of smallholder producers, processors and urban consumers, was an important instrument in achieving this success. The commercial imports and exports of almost all dairy products had been banned and processing activity had been controlled through licensing, which favoured cooperative societies over private entrepreneurs. Since early 1990s, India embarked upon liberal policy framework, which got reinforced with the signing of Uruguay Round Agreement on Agriculture (URAA) in 1994. The dairy industry was delicensed in 1991 and the private sector including multinational companies (MNCs) was allowed to set up milk processing and product manufacturing plants. However, in 1992, controls were brought back through the 'Milk and Milk products Order' (MMPO) with a view to have 'orderly growth' of dairy industry in India.

Opportunities of Milk Production

The world milk production is growing at 0.5 to 1.0 per cent per annum and is likely to be 600 million tonnes by 2020. With production of 200 million tonnes, India would account for one-third of global milk production. The structure of milk production at farm level is not going to change and small and marginal farmers would continue to play dominant role.

The productivity enhancement programme would provide opportunities for the dairy sector. Some of the areas are listed below:

- Breeding and providing First Class services including Biotechnology and Embryo Transfer Technology for production of breeding bulls.
- Fodder seeds production of legume, grasses, trees
- Green fodder drying and briqueting
- Straw treatment and supply of minerals and briqueting of roughages for scarcity periods and deficit feed / fodder production regions.
- Milking machines and parlours
- Animal housing for individual farmers

The changes likely to offer opportunities are in production of cheese and various value added milk products, cultured products, desserts, ice cream, long shelf-life milk products. This would also offer opportunities for production and marketing of equipments for such products and milk and milk product packaging. India is likely to become 'Hub of Dairying in Asia'. Many multinationals would target / source India for Gulf, Middle East and Asian markets.

The demand for milk and its products depend on the income level. It would therefore be influenced by GDP growth. Milk and Milk products are income and price elastic, elasticity of demand being between 1.15 – 1.65. A demand supply analysis mode at different levels of growth shows that 5 percent growth in milk would be sufficient to meet the national demand in 2010 as well as 2020. Achieving a growth of 7 per cent in production is likely to result in large surpluses requiring creation of large infrastructure for procurement, processing, marketing and exports.

Table 1: Demand and Supply of Milk Production in India

Product	*GDP Growth (%)*	*Demand* 2010	*Demand* 2020	*Milk Production* 2010	*Milk Production* 2020
Milk	4	95.60	126.00	111.65	159.20
Milk	5	103.70	142.70	119.60	194.82
Milk	7	122.00	182.80	136.49	250.94

Source : Bhasin N.R (2004)

Table 2: Export Scenario of Dairy Products

Year	*Quantity (in mts)*	*Value Rs. Crore (US$ in million)*
1997-1998	2378.24	13.39 (2.92)
1998 – 1999	2568.42	13.65 (2.92)
1999 – 2000	6134.42	37.21 (8.12)
2001 – 2002	24774.13	182.45 (39.83)

Source : Bhasin N.R (2004)

About 47 per cent of milk produced is retained in the house for household consumption and the surplus sold to available marketing channel. Organised sector (both cooperative and private dairy plants) handle about 20 per cent of the marketable milk and the balance is handled by unorganised sector.

Challenges of Dairy Industry in the Globalisation Scenario

The present system of milk production offers many challenges. The system is characterised by low milk production per milch animal and households are widely scattered, milk production are seasonal, and these seem regional imbalances. The Government policies to promote dairying in non-viable areas offers challenge to dairy sector. The lack of zoning of livestock production makes optimum utilisation of resources difficult. The quality of milk pose greatest challenge to the system due to poor infrastructure. Existing pricing policy which does not provide incentive to quality, lack of public awareness and ineffective regulatory mechanism are some of the challenges faced by Indian dairy sector. The major challenges to future development arise on account of Quality Assurance. To meet the challenge, the national Quality Standards require harmonisation with international standards. The existing inadequate infrastructure for quality of milk should be upgraded.

Much needs to be done to improve the quality of the milk. One cannot make good quality products from bad quality milk. One has to adopt clean milk production techniques. Milk should be chilled instantly at the village level and transported to the dairy plants in chilled condition rather than at ambient condition. Everyone knows that milk is the ideal medium for the growth of bacteria and the bacteria multiply at much faster rate at room temperature as compared to 4 degree C. So, one has to go for VLCC system with farm bulk coolers installed as many as possible to improve the quality of milk.

Bactofugation technology will have to be adopted as much as possible. The technology to improve productivity is available and is being made use of in the development programme. High producing animals would require better management and feeding practices requiring change in production system. The small commercial milk productions have to be developed and attempts are to be made to diversify agriculture land for cultivation of fodder crops leading to integrated milk production with crop farming.

Policy and Strategy

Steps to improve supply system should include

Training and extension to enhance milk production per animal

- Provision of technical inputs
- Price incentive on the basis of quality of milk
- Re-designing of the existing milk collection routes and addition of new economic routes.
- Introduction of bulk cooling / chilling
- Introduction of stricter quality norms
- Improved communication system.

Strategy

The focus of the strategy should be:

- A sustainable and financially viable livestock and dairy farming.
- Technology support not only for enhancement of productivity but also for reduction of per unit cost,
- Ensure policy environment influencing a wide range of services and service providers which have large employment potential,
- Recognising institutional lending and remunerative price for rapid growth in livestock sector,
- Supplement the impact of growth with special programmes aimed at special target groups, which may not benefit sufficiently from the normal growth process.

At the national level the strategy should include

- Greater budgetary and incentive oriented policy support to enhance productivity as well as impact quality at all levels in the dairy sector.
- To overcome the quality constraints, special incentives are to be given for clean and quality milk production.
- Enforcement of disease control measures to combat the prevailing diseases which have been acting as a deterrent to the animal health vis-à-vis the growth prospects of the livestock and dairy sector.
- The policies related to quality are implemented at present primarily by the State and parastatial bodies, which are lesser effective. Therefore, time bound action-oriented

implementation policies are required in quality enhancement by involving NGOs, cooperatives and private investors.

The strategy at regional level should include

- Creation of a common forum to deal with the quality issues especially at the regional and the global levels.
- The forum could be of a federation type for milk production at the regional level.
- The forum should primarily identify mutual beneficial areas, keeping in view of the national and regional interests.
- The forum might join hands with the other developing countries, to deal with the quality and other issues connected with the dairy sector, to enforce a level playing field for all stakeholders.

Conclusion

The next two decades would offer immense opportunities for dairy sector together with associated challenges. The dairy sector hopefully would capitalise on the opportunities for the welfare of millions of families engaged in dairy farming and associated activities.

References

1. Ashokchoudhery (2004), "Vision of Dairy Technology and the Opportunities and Challenges in the Field of Technology", *Journal of Indian Dairy Man*, 56(10): 26.
2. Bhasin N.R (2004), "Dairy Vision 2020 Opportunities and Challenges", *Journal of Indian Dairyman*, 56, 10.
3. Vijay Paul, Sharma and Ashok Gulati (2003), Trade Liberalisation, Market Reforms and Competitiveness of Indian Dairy Sector International Food Policy Research Institute, Washington, U.S.A., www.ifpri.org.

4. Vijay Sardana (2002), "Future of Global Dairy Industry and Opportunities for India", *Journal of Indian Dairy Man*, 54(2).
5. Deepak Jain (2002), "Global opportunities for Indian Dairy Industry", *Journal of Indian Dairy Man,* 54(2).

13

Globalisation and Cashew Processing Industry: Prospects and Problems

Nehru, S

Abstract

Cashew processing initially started as a cottage industry has developed into a highly organised labour intensive industry. As cashew processing involves many steps, the industry is naturally labour intensive. As cashew is highly nutritious, it has vast demand in America, Europe, South and Far East Asia and Africa. The nature of work in cashew processing is highly suitable for women workers.

Introduction

An American archeologist has found evidence, which suggests that over 10,000 years ago the first permanent villages of the world possibly were based in nut groves. The inhabitants ate the nuts and legumes and raised the first domestic animals. About four hundred years ago the Portuguese introduced cashew wild growth in jungles in India. The nut (kernal) came to be known by the name parangiandi, since it was brought by the Portuguese (Krishnaswami 1980). In the early period cashew tree was mainly cultivated to prevent soil erosion and its soft wood was used for packing and other purposes. These tree nuts formed the basis of a life sustaining diet-a clear indication that tree nuts are a fairly complete food. Nut has evolved for centuries as festive, mysterious, symbolic and supremely versatile. In prehistoric times nuts were a dietary staple, and they still are, in some places, but the changed view of people that to grow and market them takes a lot of work has turned nuts into a luxury food in the western world.

Nuts loomed large in the diet of the anthropoid that preceded the human race and are therefore a natural food. Nuts are exceptionally nutritious. The mystique of nuts is greatly enhanced by their aesthetic qualities. Scientists speculate that the type of the fat found in nuts may be at work in their present popularity. Nuts contain mostly unsaturated fats, which have been shown to lower cholesterol, says a physician named Dr. Charles Heinekens, an associate editor of Health News. "Some nuts are abundant in alphalinolenic acid, a fatty acid that has been linked to a reduced risk of health diseases". And nuts contain other nutrients, such as vitamin E and fiber. Cashew is referred to as "poor man's crop and rich man's food". It is one of the most important cash crops in India. The country produces around 42 per cent of the total world production of 10 lakh M.T. of raw cashew nuts. From the export of cashew kernels, on an average, the country earns a foreign exchange of rupees 535 crore per year.

Cashew Processing Industry in India

In India, cashew processing was initially started as a cottage industry, but with the passage of time it has developed into a highly organised labour intensive industry. As the world demand for cashew kernels has been rising steadily, the processing of cashew has become a highly profitable industry. Once the largest exporter of raw nuts, Mozambique, began importing raw nuts from Tanzania to meet the requirements of her increased processing capacity. The emergence of China and Brazil as importers of raw nuts from East African countries also affected the imports into India.

In India, there are about 1132 cashew processing factories employing more than 3.5 lakhs workers. The prohibition of cottage processing and the revision of minimum wages in 1967 induced the processors to close down the factories in Kerala and to shift the processing to the neighboring Kanyakumari district of Tamil Nadu. In 1959, Kerala state had all the 170 cashew factories in India. In the year 1972, the number of factories in India increased to 390. Out of the, 220 new factories established in the country 107 were in Tamil Nadu alone and only 44 factories were added in Kerala, between 1966 and 1972. Tamil Nadu established 95 new factories, (i.e. from 12 in 1966 to 107 in 1972). From the data, it is clear that the diversion took place mainly after 1967 when cottage processing was abolished in Kerala. Between 1966 and 1974, the number of factories in Tamil Nadu increased by 20, the quantity of nuts processed seventy times, and the number of workers 12 times. The process of shifting accelerated further after 1975 when the minimum wages were revised.

Characteristics of Cashew Processing Industry

The cashew kernel, which is the product of the cashew processing industry, is derived out of the raw cashew nut. To understand the characteristic of the industry, particularly in terms of the domination of women in cashew processing, we need to examine the different stages in the production of cashew kernels. The processing of cashew nut involves following steps, namely roasting, shelling, drying, peeling, grading and packaging.

Production of Raw Cashew Nuts

Domestic Production of Raw Cashew Nuts

India is the largest producer of raw cashewnuts in the world followed by Brazil and Vietnam. According to preliminary estimates made by the Directorate of Cashewnut and Cocoa Development, Department of Agriculture and Co-operation, Ministry of Agriculture, Government of India, Cochin, the production of raw cashew nuts during 1998-99 was 3,50,000 m.tonnes. As such, Kerala is the largest producer of raw cashew nuts followed by Maharashtra, Andhra Pradesh, Orissa, Karnataka and Tamil Nadu. The contribution of raw cashew nut from Tamil Nadu is only 25000 m. tonnnes.

Table 1: Production of Raw Cashewnuts in India: Share of Different States

State	*Production (M.T)*	*Percentage*
Kerala	100000	28.57
Maharastra	65000	18.57
Andhra pradesh	60000	17.14
Orissa	40000	11.43
Karnataka	30000	8.57
Tamil nadu	25000	7.14
Goa	15000	4.29
Others	15000	4.29
Total	3,50,000	100.0

Exports of Cashew Kernels to Different Zones

During 1998-99, more than 45 per cent of our exports of cashew kernels were to the American zone. The European zone accounted for 34.2 per cent, the South East and Far East Asian zones for 9.6 per cent, the West Asian zone for 7.7 per cent, the Oceanic zone for 2.9 per cent and the African zone for 0.2 per cent. There was considerable increase in our exports to American zone (12.02 per cent) and the West Asian zone (*7.46 per cent) whereas our exports to other zone declined.

American zone

Exports to the American zone was 34082 m.tonnes valued at Rs.727.10 crore, compared to 30426 m.tonnes valued at Rs. 549.4 crore, exported during 1997-98. Exports to the USA increased by 13 per cent in terms of quantity and 33 per cent in terms of value, while exports to Canada decreased by 40 per cent in quantity and 23 per cent in value. During the period 45.4 per cent of India's total exports of cashew kernel exports was to the American zone.

European zone

The European zone accounted for 34.2 per cent of India's total exports of cashew kernels during 1998-99 in terms of quantity. Exports to the East European zone was 534 m.tonnes valued at Rs. 7.6 crore, which is 63 per cent less in terms of quantity and 61 per cent less in terms of value when compared with the previous year's exports of 1446 m.tonnes valued at Rs. 19.7 crore.

West Europe

There was a decrease of 14 per cent in quantity and 1.3 per cent in value in the exports of cashew kernels to the West European region. The total cashew kernels exported to the West Europe during 1998-99 was 25109 m.tonnes valued at Rs. 536

Table 2: Exports of Cashew Nut

Region	*Cashew Exports (in M.T)*	*Percentage*
America	34082	45
Europe	25643	34
South East & Far East Asia	7227	10
West Asia & Africa	5879	8
Oceania	2195	3
Total	**75026**	**100**

crore, as against 29133 m.tonnes valued at 543 crore, exported during 1997-98. There was considerable increase in the exports of cashew kernels to France. As against 1939 m.tonnes valued at Rs. 35.1 crore were exported during 1997-98, 2305 m.tonnes valued at Rs. 45.7 crore were exported during 1998-99, recording an increase of 19 per cent in quantity and 30 per cent in value. Netherlands, Germany, Spain and Greece were some of the major markets to which the exports during the year went down considerably.

West Asian Zone

Exports to the West Asian zone was 7.7 per cent in terms of quantity of India's total cashew kernel exports during the year. During the period 1998-99, exports to the West Asian zone was 5765 m.tonnes valued at Rs. 130 crore, which is 7.5 per cent more in quantity and 27.6 per cent more in value when compared to the exports of 5365 m.tonnes valued at Rs.101.6 crore during 1997-98. Exports to most of the major markets like Saudi Arabia, UAE, Oman, Turkey etc. recorded an increase while those to Bahrain and Kuwait showed a slight decrease.

South East and Far East Asia

South East and Far East Asia accounted for 10 per cent of India's total exports of cashew kernels during 1998-99 in terms of quantity. In the case of the South East and Far East Asian zone, exports decreased by 8 per cent in quantity and 11 per cent in value. Total exports to this region during 1998-99 was 7227 m.tonnes valued at Rs. 160.1 crore compared to 7866 m.tonnes valued at Rs. 144.3 crore during 1997-98. Exports to Japan and Singapore, the two major markets in the region, recorded a decrease of 8.6 per cent and 13 per cent respectively in terms of quantity. Exports to Hong Kong went up by 14.7 per cent in terms of quantity.

African zone

The African zone accounted for only 0.3 per cent of India's exports during the year in terms of quantity. During the year

1998-99 exports to the African zone was 114 m.tonnes valued at Rs. 2.8 crore compared to the exports of 113 m.tonnes valued at Rs. 2.1 crore during 1997-98. Egypt, importing 40 m.tonnes valued at 0.7 crores, and South Africa, importing 32 m.tonnes valued at 1.0 crore, were the major buyers.

Oceanic zone

The oceanic zone accounted for 3 per cent of the total exports from India during 1998-99 in terms of quantity. Exports to the Oceanic zone was 2195 m.tonnes valued at 47.1 crore during 1998-99 as against 2214 m.tonnes valued at Rs. 36.2 crore exported during 1997-98. This was 0.9 per cent less in terms of quantity and 30 per cent in terms of value. During the year, exports to Australia decreased by 2.89 per cent and that to New Zealand increased by 9.5 per cent in terms of quantity.

Major Markets for Cashew Kernels

The major markets for Indian cashew kernels during 1998-99 were the USA, the Netherlands, Japan, UK, UAE., France, Australia, Israel, Germany, Singapore, Hong Kong and Saudi Arabia.

Imports of Raw Cashew nuts

During the period 1998-99, the total raw cashewnuts imported into India for processing and exporting was 1,80,686 m.tonnes valued at Rs. 693.17 crore. This was 27 per cent less in quantity and 10 per cent less in value as against 2,47,181 m.tonnes of raw cashewnut valued at Rs.769.6 crore imported during 1997-98.

Import of raw cashewnut from Tanzania, Mozambique and Senegal increased by 29 per cent, 13 per cent respectively in respect of quantity, compared to that in 1997-98. import from Guinea Bissau, Indonesia, the Ivory Coast, Benin and Nigeria decreased considerably. Apart from African countries, Indonesia and the Philippines in the South East Asian region also supplied considerable quanity of raw cshewnuts to India during 1998-99.

Imports of Raw Cashewnuts into India

Table 3: Share of Different Regions 1998-99

Region	*Imports of raw cashew nuts (in M.T)*	*Percentage*
East Africa	98959	54.77
West Africa	59650	33.01
Sout East Asia	15320	8.48
Others	6757	3.74
Total	180686	100.0

Problems faced by the cashewnut processing industry workers

Personal problems

The workers working under the cashew processing industry face physical and psychological problems. As industry workers, they work for 9 hours in the factory. As women they have their household work both before going to their job and after returning. On account of this, they have hardly a few hours of rest, particularly the married women. In the factory, they have to sit on the floor throughout their 9 hours of work per day. The workers have severe dermatological problems and suffer back pain, nerve problems and headache. This adversely affects their health. Even though they are industry workers and are having independent economic status, they are not given their due place in major policy decision making regarding control over income, expenditure and family assets. Inspite of their economic independence, these women workers are not given due importance in decision making at family level with regard to income, expenditure and other family assets. Many workers prefer to continue in the job in spite of their health problems for want of money.

Family Problems

The workers have got a crucial role to play in family affairs. Being industry workers they are not able to spend many hours with their family members and take care of their needs. They are not able to pay attention to their babies and young children. They are not able to even pay attention to their children's educaton and the elder members in their families. Similarly, even on holidays they are not able to be in touch with their neighbours, friends, and relatives. They are not able to even attend functions celebrated by their relatives and co-workers.

Problems connected with the Nature of Work and the Place of Work

They have to reach their industry in time from distant place on foot or by bus and sometimes at unusual times. Their health is very much affected by severe dermatological problems and headache. As they are working in the cashew processing industry the women are affected by the smearing of oil over their hands to have a grip over the nut. Some times the married women are affected due to lack of backrest at the work site for leaning at they are also getting low level of wages.

Conclusion

The nature of work in the cashew processing industry is highly suitable to women workers. However, the women were paid low wages in this industry. The owners of the cashew processing industry exploit the women for getting more profit. Women are forced to work more than nine hours per day. Most of the women workers, suffer from mental tension and dermatological disease due to the bad environmental conditions of the cashew processing industry. Therefore, it is concluded that, even after sixty one year of independence, women's status is deplorable in general and most pitiable in the cashew processing industry in particular.

References

1. Arindampal, K.S. Somayaji, (1999), "A Status paper on Cashew Processing Industry", *State Bank of Indian Monthly Review:* 1247-1258.
2. Betty Friedam, (1995), "The North A Disturbing Independence", *The UNESCO courier*, September 8.
3. Devadas, R.P, (1990), Cited by Sithalakshmi, S. and Jothimani, G. (1994), "Organisational behaviour as a means of Empowerment", *Kurukshetra*, New Delhi, 13(12): 18-23.
4. Anon (2003), *Indian Cashew Journal,* 23(1): 5.
5. Rodgers, Janine (1991), "Women at Work in Western Europe", *Indian Journal of Labour Economics*, 341 (3).
6. Sita, S. and Kamalamma, N. (1999) "Occupational Health Problems of Women Workers in Cashew Industry", *Social Welfare:* 9-11.
7. Annon (1999), *The Hindu survey of Indian Agriculture:* 117-120.
8. Unni, (1984), "Female Employment and Occupational Diversification of Women in India", *ILO*, New Delhi.
9. Varghese N.V, (1991), "Women and Work: An Examination of the Female Marginalisation Thesis in the Indian Context, *Indian Journal of Labour Economic*, 34(3).

14

Dairy Cooperative Marketing Business Organisations in the Globalised Market Environment

Samwel Kakuko Lopoyetum

Abstract

The dairy co-operative marketing business organisations are facing high and stiff competition emanating from public, private, MNCs and quasi government sectors. Hence, there is an imperative need to improve their productivity, profitability, improve their procurement system, processing system, distribution management system and marketing system in order to enable them to participate fully in the global market environment. The chapter further highlights the essential strategies required for effective functioning of dairy co-operative marketing organisations in the globalised regime.

Introduction

Dairy Cooperative Marketing Business Organizations are facing insurmountable challenges, competition and threats in the global market environment. There are also huge opportunities, chances, and scope for penetrating deeply into the global market environment. The new economic environment characterised by liberalisation and globalisation policies have had tremendous impact on the growth and development of dairy cooperative marketing business organisations. The adoption of open market economy and economic liberalisation has motivated the Indian dairy industry, dairy trade and commerce to cope with unforeseen dynamic forces. In fact, it has encouraged the direct and indirect flow of technological benefits, socio-economic benefits and investment opportunities to various sectors of the economy including the entire gamut of cooperative sector. It is commonly known that, immediately after independence, the Indian Government embraced cooperative sector as an instrument of economic development, bringing about socio-economic changes and as a means of implementing socio-economic programmes / schemes to transform the rural masses and improve their livelihood system. But, the present scenario is completely different in the sense that dairy cooperative marketing business organisations are expected to compete and function in an atmosphere of liberalised, privatised, and globalised environment. The legal framework and legislation which are existing in this country are not even conducive for long-term development of dairy cooperatives, therefore it retards the growth and development of this sector in the long-run. Side by side, dairy cooperative institutions are poorly managed and riddled with insufficient professionalisation of operations and management of dairy cooperatives. While formulating the National Policy on cooperatives, it is essential to uphold the values, principles, objectives, autonomy and democratic values of dairy cooperative marketing business institutions. They are expected to maintain and accelerate their financial and non-financial capabilities (technical and marketing) to fully enter into the globalised market business environment. On introduction of new economic policies, dairy cooperative marketing business organisations are facing huge and stiff competition emanating from public, private sectors, MNC's and, quasi governmental sectors. Hence, there is an imperative need to improve their productivity, profitability, improve their procurement system, processing system, distribution management system, and marketing system to enable them to participate fully in the global market environment.

Current Status of Milk Production and Per Capita Availability

Table 1 discusses the current status of milk production and per capita availability of the milk in India.

Table – 1
Current Status of Milk Production and Per Capita Availability

Year	*Production (Million Tonnes)*	*Per Capita Availability (gms / day)*
1994-95	63.8 (----)	194 (----)
1995-96	66.2 (3.76)	197 (1.55)
1996-97	69.1 (4.38)	202 (2.54)
1997-98	72.1 (4.34)	207 (2.50)
1998-99	75.4 (4.58)	213 (2.90)
1999-2k	78.3 (3.85)	217 (1.90)
2000-01	80.6 (3.00)	220 (1.40)
2001-02	84.4 (4.71)	225 (2.30)
2002-03	86.2 (2.13)	230 (2.22)
2003-04	88.1 (2.20)	231 (0.43)
2004-05*	91.0 (3.30)	232 (0.43)

*Provisional; Figures in parentheses indicate growth rate
Source: State/UT Animal Husbandry Departments, 2004

It is heartening to note that, the milk production and per capita availability of milk is showing increasing trend. The effect and impact of White Revolution have been felt in many milk shed regions of the country. Due to the positive policy changes in the dairy sector, the country has attained self-sufficiency in milk production. There is an imperative need to enhance the marketing efficiency and strategies. But, the vital and moot issue shall remain as "Whether dairy cooperative marketing business organisations shall be pro-productive, viable, profitable and sustainable in the New Economic Environment?"

Dairy Cooperative Marketing Organisations in Global Dairy Trade

It is the highest time for dairy cooperative marketing business organizations to take appropriate measures for enhancing their efficiency and effectiveness by pursuing effective and innovative ways of doing dairy business and trade. They can first initiate local measures, strategies, form, capture and capitalise on the nicher market (Local, Regional, State, National, International markets) and eventually they can go for the new emerging global markets. They can even deal with inter-regional dairy trade, inter-intra local trade, international trade, global dairy trade and increase mass consumptions of milk and milk products. Infact, dairy business cooperatives organisations can specialise on certain specific dairy products to capture global market. In fact, of the 616 million tonnes of milk produced globally in 2004, India's share was 91.5 million tonnes. Moreover, it is anticipated that the global production is expected to be more than 626 million tonnes with India's contribution being estimated at over 95 millions tonnes. Around 12 per cent of the total production reaches the larger dairies for handling, processing and marketing. Hence, there is a need for dairy cooperative sector to enhance and expand its supply chain, adopt better strategies for Supply Chain Management (SCM), use of improved storage facilities (cold storage system), aim at cost focus strategy, apply product differentiation strategy, adoption of value addition techniques, professionalisation and improvement of human resource management and development, promotion of dairy business diversification, use of Information Technology and Modern Communication (ICT) System, use of improved technology by the dairy producers, transfer of technology, adoption of improved technology, imbibing the culture of creativity and innovative strategies, use of computerisation and automation of the processing and manufacturing system. They must organise themselves in this era of globalised market environment and export more milk and milk products. Moreover, by expanding the size of the local, regional, national, international (global) produce dairy market would become a source of prosperity, wealth, permanent employment and gainful income to the Indian dairy farmers. It becomes also imperative to constantly encourage domestic market and local consumption of milk and milk products and then go for global market. The overall level of money income and demand of different varieties of dairy products is constantly increasing, but the cutthroat competitive conditions prevailing at the local, regional and global market environment are influencing the performance of dairy cooperative marketing business organizations in the changing global business scenario.

WTO Regime, Globalised Market Environment and its Impact on Dairy Cooperative Business Organisations

The Uruguay Round of Multi-lateral Trade Negotiation in 1994 (India is signatory), made the dairy sector exposed to international competition and declared it as open market economy. The key components of "Agreement On Agriculture (AOA)" under WTO includes the following: (i) Improved market access for trading agricultural commodities in member countries, (ii) Reduction in domestic support given to agriculture in the member countries, (iii) Reduction in export subsidies and (iv) Implementing Trade Related Intellectual Property (TRIPS) for agricultural inventions. The major problem and fulcrum of WTO impact is that the variation in implementation process of WTO agreement. India is required to compete with major dairy products producers and processed milk products, by-products from countries located in European Union, USA, Australia and New Zealand. Probably, India will face additional and new competition from emerging African countries ın dairy products sector in the near future (East and Central African region can even pose threat to Indian cooperative dairying system).

It is evident that, the organised sector handles only 15 per cent, the rural producers retain 40 per cent, while 45 per cent is still handled by traditional sector. In India, 52 per cent of the milk is produced by buffaloes, 45 per cent by cows and only 3 per cent by other species, like goat, sheep and camel. The dairy sector provides additional income and generates job opportunities for 80 million farm families. There are about 63 million breedable cows and 42 million buffaloes in India. The crossbreed cows have good potential for milk production; this is not fully exploited due to lack of proper feeding habits and management of animals. The flow of dairy credit is highly concentrated in states such as UP, Punjab, Andhra Pradesh and Tamilnadu. The impact of liberalisation policy and open market economy has affected milk producers and dairy industry in many ways. Note that, there are more than 142 members of WTO, the fittest shall survive and Indian cooperative dairying can fit into the trading blocks if they are organisationally, technically, technologically, managerially, financially and administratively efficient in their business operations. Having this background in mind, the effect and impact of LPGs or globalisation environment of dairy sector can be analysed as (i) it has affected the dairy sector at the level of national economy, (ii) it has affected the business performance of milk products and milk production, (iii) it has affected the entire agricultural production system and agro-based commodities because milk producers are invariably practicing mixed farming system and they are based in the rural areas, (vi) it had both positive and negative effects on rural economy, (v) the de-licensing or deregulation policies of government has resulted in the higher capital inflow to the economy, (vi) numerous dairy plants have been set up in many places in India. This includes privately owned dairy factories, (vii) Increased competition, means improved effectiveness and efficiency of dairy cooperative sector, (viii) Small and marginal milk producers are affected because of multinational corporation's entry into dairy sector, moreover, they are also dealing with the consumer goods, (ix) there is a rise in price levels due to the removal of the subsidies and government support. So far, there is no proper agreement in the area of subsidy with WTO. Also, there is no proper definition, understanding and uniformity in the application of subsidy concept in developed and developing countries. This problem must be mitigated and resolved at the earliest.

Many other globalisation factors such as provisions for market access, removal of Quota Restriction, non-tariff barriers (Sanitary and phyto-sanitary regulations - SPS) and GMO issues may be the major cause of concern to the milk producers and dairy industry at large in the LPG's era.

Non-Tariff Barriers Directly Affecting Dairy Cooperative Sector

In addition to the tariffs barriers, there are many non-tariff barriers either under provisions of technical barriers to trade (TBT) or imposed by certain countries to make inroads into the open market economy of developed countries. In fact, the European Union (EU) insists that milking cows be fully mechanised to avoid contaminations, and portable water to be used in milk processing. It also, prescribes that only steel machinery and filtered air shall be used for processing. If this is the case, the Indian dairy industry is posed to face insurmountable problems and challenges in the globalisation environment. Moreover, suitable strategies must be laid down to enable the dairy sector meet the emerging challenges of globalisation and economic liberalisation.

Reformation of WTO and Dairy Cooperative Marketing Business Organisations

The leading world's major multi-lateral economic institutions namely the International Monetary Fund (IMF), World Bank in Washington DC and WTO in Geneva were created to build a strong, coordinated international set of economic measures contributing to the systems of cooperation between government to encourage global economic growth and development. There is an imperative need to start "Reformation process of WTO because it has created terrible fear ambivalence in developing countries because its operations, functioning and working are mainly based on industrially developed countries". It is only open and transparent to a few developing countries. Globalisation of trade, commerce, business, industries, technology, and investment has brought the trio multilateral economic institutions together. Many countries and ministers and their immediate subordinates spend endless time, hours negotiating and even reproducing and developing duplicative reports. There is a need to initiate reforms when things and operations are not working well. There is enormous scope for improvement in the global trading and commerce and economic development. WTO must focus and re-focus on issues and matters fundamental to securing fair and healthy globalised market environment. There is a need for enlarged scope and better leadership on the development of globalised market environment. It should not belong to super economic powers alone. Indian economic reforms must openly throw in new ideas. India needs to improve its competitiveness from poor ranking as indicated by the Global Competitiveness Report 2005 of the World Economic Forum, Geneva. It is ranked 50 among 117 countries. The mindset of the dairy farmers and SMEs must change and improve their management practices (informed, enlightened and holistic management approach). The tiny, micro, small and medium entrepreneurs should posseses an in-depth knowledge of management in 10 Ms viz Man (Manpower),

Machine, Market, Millieu, Materials (equipments), Money (Capital), Mind (intellectual Productivity), Motivation, Mood, and Management. The heart of India beats on micro, small and medium scale industries (MSME's). India to be more developed country MSME's must be given top priority, care and due concern. The WTO ministerial conference of 149 countries held at Hong Kong during December 13 – 18 2005 eventually succeeded in adopting a declaration, which drew mixed response especially with reference to agriculture. The commitment from them was to eliminate 7 – 8 billion dollar subsidy on agriculture exports by 2013! This is nothing but post dated cheque! They give domestic support to their farmers to the tune of 100 million dollars. They need to improve themselves, by denying remunerative price to Indian dairy farmers on export of their products on account of depressed global prices. We need a clear roadmap for WTO and India to tap global market. They must be competitive, efficient, eco-friendly, improve productivity, improve technology and productive investment etc., their agenda at Concun failed because of the unity of developing countries.

Quality of Milk and Milk Products in Globalised Market Environment

It is heartening to note the Indian Dairy Association (IDA) quality survey confirmed the global market enquires and status of 200 major dairies registered under Milk and Milk Products Authority (MMPA) and received responses from more than 160 having handling capacity of over 10,000 litres/day of milk or 500 tonnes of milk solids per annum. More than 100 responses were ISO 9000 series compatible and 80 had processed food quality namely the Hazard Analysis Critical Control Point (HACCP) Accreditation. The dairy industry sector must meet the global quality requirements and it is heartening to note that, the Gujarat Cooperative Milk Marketing Federation (Amul) is striving hard to attain the highest standards of quality of milk and milk products. The amendment of the Prevention of

Food Adulteration (PFA) Rules 1955, is highly essential in the globalised market environment. The Government of India also has taken measures towards this direction. The Union Health Ministry has issued notification modifying PFA rules to revise the standard of creams to harmonise it with codex standards. Also, there is need for exempting milk products from mandatory Bureau of Indian Standard (BIS) certification. In fact, certification for condensed milk sweetened, condensed skimmed milk sweetened, milk powder, skimmed milk powder, partly skimmed sweetened condensed milk is being dispensed with, as per the current notification (The Hindu, 30.6.2006). The food and beverage additives must be brought to the codex level, specification of expert committee of Food and Agricultural Organisation (FAO), World Health Organisation on Food Additives (considering the low acceptable daily intake-ADI). Moreover, in the WTO regime and Globalised market environment, there is vast and expanding scope for export of dairy products such as Skimmed Milk Powder (SMP), Ghee, Ultra Heated-Treated Milk (UHT), Cheese and Butter to numerous developing and developed countries, European Union Market (constituting more than 25 Countries) and America, even exported into the oil rich countries of Middle East. In this way, there is need for the Indian dairy sector to incorporate a world wide approach to comprehensively deal with export marketing management and must develop comprehensive export marketing plans, find export customers, increase the production and productivity, capacities of dairy cooperative manufacturing system, machines, equipment (processing), adapt to the changing export market, tastes and preferences, undertake export market research, produce the highest quality of dairy products at the lowest possible production cost and adopt better pricing system etc.

The export marketing opportunities for dairy cooperative marketing business organisations to serve a particular global market and buyers are extremely large in the globalised market environment. The global solidarity of cooperative movement can be treated as one of the most influential movements and organisation to deal with all dimensions of the WTO agreements on agriculture and dairy sector. It has greater bargaining power, pressure and indomitable force to negotiate with WTO functionaries. Also the apex level body of cooperatives namely ICA can champion the justifiable interest of dairy producers and cooperative sectors at large. It can protect and safeguard the interest of dairy farmers (small, marginal, medium) and their Dairy Cooperative Marketing Business Organisations in the context of liberal trade regime, which is currently tilted towards unfair and unjust treatment in the global market.

Even though WTO agreement and regime provide for a liberal approach to export and import of agricultural, dairy commodities, phasing out quantitative restrictions on commodities, adjustment of tariff rates within the boundary levels etc., dairy cooperative sectors still suffer under WTO regime. Under this scenario, the dairy market is faced with the problem of low cost import of dairy products such as butter oil, skimmed milk powder from several countries; hence affect the interest of domestic milk producers (dairy farmers) and processors. The sanitary and phyto- sanitary issues and anti-dumping measures continue to hound cooperative sector in most of the developing countries from developing effective and efficient diversification strategies of exports of milk products and meat products. The advanced (developed) countries are still providing high domestic support and subsidies to their farmers and tariffs are very high in certain sectors such as sugar, dairy products, export of fisheries and cereals etc., They block the value added products from developing countries. They even abuse anti-dumping procedures, health, safety measures/ standards etc., leading to unjust and unfair competition environment in global dairy market. Therefore, hard work and goodwill of the nation is necessary to make dairy cooperative sector more effective and efficient in global competitiveness of exports of their dairy products.

Essential Strategies for Dairy Cooperative Marketing Organisations

The most essential strategies propounded by the researcher are;

- Provision of efficient and effective methods of financing and financial services to dairy sector on long-term basis.
- Use of effective production and operations management in dairy cooperative marketing business organisations, particularly at the level of manufacturing plants.
- Inculcating the culture (habit) of effective and efficient management and administration of dairy marketing business organisations.
- Promotion of modern marketing and sales promotions methods and techniques in rural marketing of dairy cooperative marketing organisations.
- The rural dairy cooperatives marketing business organisations should take urgent measures for enhancing its efficiency and effectiveness by pursuing effective and innovative dairy trade and business. They can form and capitalise on the rural nicher market and new emerging rural markets. They can even increase their rural market share in many dairy products such as Skimmed Milk Powder (SMP), Ghee, Ultra Heated-Treated Milk (UHT), Cheese and Butter, in rural market.
- The Government (State and Central) and other dairy cooperative funding agencies/organisations must adequately provide both financial and non-financial assistance to promote rural dairy cooperative sector for ensuring sustainable growth and development of dairy sector in the new economic environment.
- The Board of Directors (BOD's) and concerned authorities of dairy cooperative business organisations should take suitable steps for admitting only active, effective, and efficient members in the rural dairy cooperative marketing business organisations.

- The government should reduce their inherent control on the rural dairy cooperative management affairs and administration and give maximum autonomy and independence to dairy cooperatives and encourage them to fix prices for their own dairy products.
- In the era of new economic environment, dairy cooperatives marketing business organizations must be given adequate autonomy and independence in fixing the prices of milk and milk products. This can be done with minimal interferences by the state government or any outside agencies.
- The government agencies may be treated as supervising authority only on the dairy business activities, trade, and development programmes, instead of involving themselves in the entire technical activities and decision-making process of dairy cooperative marketing business organisations.
- It is essential to take appropriate and suitable measures for linking of rural dairy cooperatives with other types of cooperatives like marketing cooperatives, employees cooperatives, consumers and multipurpose cooperative organisations. Through this approach dairy cooperative marketing business organisations can be innovative and create suitable opportunities to enhance the production of milk and milk products and capture larger market share in the open market economy.

Rural dairy cooperatives should take appropriate and immediate steps to make use of the available modern methods, advancement of science and technology, and by producing milk and milk products having high quality and thereby they can compete with private sector, public sector and even overtake the multinational corporations. They can capture domestic rural market and even the international market.

- Dairy cooperatives should take adequate measures for expanding procurement of milk, enhancing processing abilities and efficiency through modernisation of milk factories, enhancing their processing capacities, and finally they must increase their marketing efforts, particularly in the new economic environment.
- Use of appropriate and intermediate technology in dairy industry.
- NDDB, all federations and unions can have dairy business as joint ventures and collaboration basis.
- Promotions of inter cooperative dairy products export trade (SAARC & Non-SAARC Countries).
- Use of low cost packaging and effective labeling, practices.
- Application of product differentiation strategy as a rural – urban marketing strategy of dairy cooperative products and services.
- Propagation of the adoption of value addition techniques, especially in cooperative products and services.
- Mandatory adoption and promotion of dairy business diversification system in dairy cooperative sector.
- Use of information technology (IT) and communication system in all dairy societies.
- Use of creative and innovative strategies in manufacturing of dairy products.
- The NDDB's and federations (states) and dairy unions can adopt consultative strategies strictly based on business terms.
- There is imperative needs for Computerisation of dairy units and adopting collaborative strategy (strategic alliance) of dairy cooperative at local level, regional level, state level, national level and international level.

Conclusion

To sum-up, it is imperative to develop various new dimensions and approaches on WTO on the entire dairy cooperative sector and bring out some strategies/approaches for developing dairy sector and allied sectors to cope up with WTO Agreement. A study on "effect and impact of WTO on Dairy sector and Agriculture in developing countries such as India and Kenya can be sponsored and undertaken by the Government".

References

- Hage N.C., (2001), "WTO Challenges for Indian Dairy Farmers", Yojana.
- Koli P.A., (2000), "Can Milk Cooperative Sustain in the 21st Century", *Indian Cooperative Review,* 38(1): 30.
- Iyer L.L., (1973), " Fifty Years of Dairy Development in India Tasks Ahead", *Indian Dairyman*, 25(12): 29.
- Ravi Shankar, (2005), " Role and Vision of Dairy Cooperative in the New Millennium", *Tamilnadu Journal of Cooperation*, 2(4): 17 – 22.
- Shiyani R.L., (1996), "An Economic Inquiry into the Impact of Dairy Cooperative on Milk Production", *Indian Journal of Agricultural Economics*, 32(7): 29 –30.
- Samwel Kakuko Lopoyetum and Selvamani P., (2005), "Dairy Cooperative Marketing in the New Economic Environment", *Kissan World Journal*, 32(7): 29 – 30.
- Srinivasan Gowda M.V., (1994), "Cooperatives in the New Economic Scenario Agenda for Liberalisations", *Southern Economist*: 21.

Part – IV Women Entrepreneurship in the Midst of Globalisation

15

Access to Micro Finance and Women Entrepreneurship

Rathakrishnan, L, and V.P. Sriraman

Abstract

The first and conceivably the most critical Millennium Development Goals (MDGs) of all, is to make a critical difference in reducing the extreme poverty and hunger through out the globe by half within 2015. The United Nations Development Programme (UNDP) seeks to promote various approaches to reduce human poverty by emphasising the importance of social inclusion and equity, human rights and, women's empowerment towards achieving this goal. One of the powerful approaches is the formation of Self Help Groups (SHGs) especially among women, as the development of any country is inseparably linked with the status and development of women. This strategy had fetched noticeable results not only in Bangladesh and India but also the world over. Women are central to the entire development process and are the precursor of social transformation. This can be demonstrated with many examples that could include Grameen Bank's success, SHGs of ICICI Bank, Shakthi Ammas at HLL (now HUL), Cemex, Amul, the success of Avon, Mary Kay, and Tupperware in US and other parts of the world. Micro Finance as a tool of poverty alleviation and women empowerment has gained acceptance in development dialogue all over the world. There is an acute need among the poor for credit, both for consumption and production, which often forms the deciding line between the survival and succumbing to poverty. It has been found that besides food, credit is also needed for health, housing and education and critical for survival (Zeller, 2000). The success of SHGs as a development tool depends on the availability of Micro Finance. This chapter tries to link all the pertinent points related to Micro Finance, SHGs, Women Empowerment and Women Entrepreneurship. The paper discusses some of the interesting cases, news and occurrences.

Introduction

According to The World Bank, of the world's total population of over 6 billion, almost 20 per cent, ie. over 1.2 billion people live on wages of less than $1 per day; of which majority live in Asia. Close to 40 per cent of the population of South Asian region is poverty-stricken. While analysing the lifestyle of the rural poor, particular importance needs to be given to understand the status of women who contribute almost half of the world population and the development would be possible only if all sections of the society develop. The UN commission on status of women observed 'women who contribute half of the world's population by virtue of accident of birth, perform two-thirds of the world's work, receive one-tenth of its income and owns less than one-hundredth of its property'. In India, women produce 30 per cent of all food commodities consumed but get only 10 per cent of the property or wealth of the country. There is a growing realisation that rural women have been underestimated and discriminated in all walks of life, despite their substantial contribution to the household economy, and in turn, the national economy as such. As it is clear that the rights and protection of women from social inequalities in statute books are not good enough, some practical solutions are to be acknowledged and most importantly, implemented. Women have been deprived of economic independence. The empowerment of women and improvement of their status and economic role needs to be integrated into economic development programmes, as the development of any country is inseparably linked with the status and development of women. Given the gender division of labour that prevails in India, nutrition, child health, and related matters typically depend mostly on women's actions and decisions. Experience has shown that promotion of enterprise creation and income generating activities among women would transform them from 'being alive' to 'living with dignity'.

In most of the developing countries today, more and more emphasis is laid on the need for development of women and their active participation in the main stream of development process. It is also widely recognised that apart from managing household, bearing and caring children, rural women bring income with productive activities ranging from traditional work in the fields to working in factories or running small and petty businesses. They have also proven that they can be better entrepreneurs and development managers in any kind of human development activities. Therefore, it is important and utmost necessary to make rural women empowered in taking decisions to enable them to be in the centre of any human development process. Empowerment of women is also considered as an active process enabling them to realise their full identity and power in all spheres of life. Against the background of the patriarchal system of society, women need special attention to ensure their development and participation in the decision making process at home, in community and in governance.

Women are Critical for Development

In the book "The Fortune at the Bottom of the Pyramid", CK Prahlad comments, "A well-understood but poorly articulated reality of development is the role of women. Women are central to the entire development process. They are also at the vanguard of social transformation". For example, Grameen bank's success is based on lending only to women. There are adequate evidences from various studies undertaken so far that the role of women in building a new society is inevitable. The SHGs at ICICI bank are all women. The women entrepreneurs responsible for saving and accessing credit in the case of CEMEX, the company works only with women. Amul, a milk cooperative, depends on women for their milk origination from villages. Women also collect the cash for the milk and therefore have achieved a new social status. Access to economic independence can change the long tradition of suppression of women and denial of opportunities. The success of Avon, Mary Kay and Tupperware in US and other parts of the world are also based on the role of women entrepreneur. Although the evidence is overwhelming, very little explicit attention has been paid to actively co-opting women in the efforts to build markets and lead the development process.

When asked Muhammad Yunus, a nobel laurate, and a pioneer in the practice of micro credit lending, why loan was issued primarily to women? he replied, "It has to do with the decision to have a separate bank for the poor people. From the beginning, I had complained about the banking system on two grounds. One complaint was that the banking system was denying financial services to the poor people through certain rules it had set up. The second allegation was that the banking system also was not treating women fairly. If you look at the gender composition of all the borrowers of all the banks in Bangladesh, not even one per cent of the borrowers happen to be women. I said this is a very gender-biased organisation. So when I began, I wanted to make sure that half the borrowers in my programme are women so that they are even. I did that. It was not easy because women themselves didn't think that they could borrow money. I had to do a lot of convincing exercise with women. I encouraged them to believe that they can borrow money and make money. Part of that effort was to overcome fears, namely cultural fears as the women in Bangaladesh never had any experience with business. Soon we saw that money going to women brought much more benefit to the family than money going to the men. So we changed our policy and gave a higher priority to women. As a result, now 96 per cent of our four million borrowers in Grameen Bank are women".

Women Self Help Groups

One of the powerful approaches to women empowerment and rural entrepreneurship is the formation of Self Help Groups (SHGs) especially among women. This strategy had fetched noticeable results not only in India and Bangladesh but world over. Women self-help groups are increasingly being used as a tool for various developmental interventions. Credit and its delivery through self-help groups have also been taken as a means for empowerment of rural women. This integrated approach, whereby, credit is only an entry point, and an instrument to operationalise other aspects of group dynamics and management, also caters to the need for social intermediation of these groups. A self--help group is conceived as a sustainable people's institution that provides the poor rural women with space and support, necessary for them to take effective steps towards achieving greater control of their lives. The SHG approach has proved successful not only in improving the economic conditions through income generation but in creating awareness about health and hygiene, sanitation and cleanliness, environmental protection, importance of education and better response for development schemes.

Through organising informal self-help groups (SHGs), rural women in India are provided with credit and extension support for various production-oriented income-generating activities. These activities usually include garment making, embroidery, food processing, bee keeping, basketry, gem cutting, weaving, and knitting. SHGs are self-governed, with decisions about production and marketing taken collectively, although the group leader is responsible for identifying potential marketing centers and consumers. These groups represent a new culture in rural development, breaking the traditional bureaucracy and top-down management. Informal groups empower rural women to manage rural industries and make decisions collectively for their common economic interests. Studies on the development of informal women's groups in India, shows how it is possible to avoid the 'top-down management' and bureaucracy that often contribute to the failure of other schemes. Informal self-help groups in rural areas serve to empower women, and provide a basis for the provision of credit and other support for various production and income-generation activities.

The SHG Structure

A SHG is a group of about 10 to 20 people, usually women, from a similar class and region, who come together to form savings and credit organisation. They pool financial resources to make small interest bearing loans to their members. This process creates an ethic that focuses on savings first. The setting of terms and conditions and accounting of the loan were done in the group by designated members.

The SHG Federation

SHG Federations are a more sophisticated form of organisation that involve several SHGs forming into Village Organisations (VO) / Cluster Federations and then ultimately into higher level federations (called as Mandal Samakhya (MS) in AP or SHG Federation generally). SHG Federations are formal institutions while the SHGs are informal. Many of these

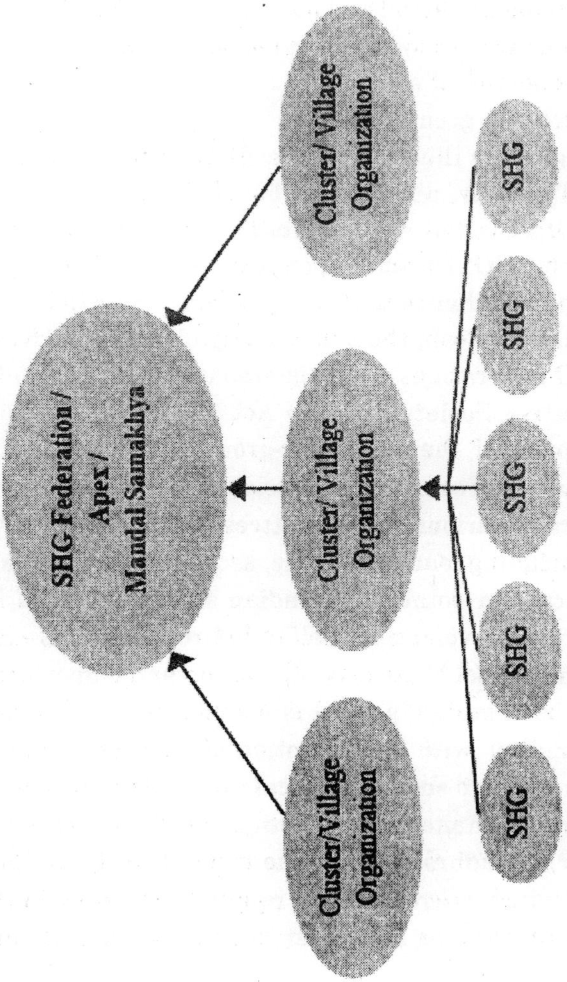

Figure 1: Structure of SHG federations

SHG Federations are registered as societies, mutual benefit trusts and mutually aided cooperative societies. SHG Federations brought in several key benefits including:

- Stronger political and advocacy capabilities
- Sharing of knowledge and experiences
- Economies of scale
- Access to greater capital

A graphic illustration of a SHG Federation is shown in Fig. 1. Typically, about 15 to 50 SHGs make up a Cluster / Village Organisation (VO) with either one or two representatives from each SHG. Depending on geography, several clusters or VOs come together to form an apex body or a SHG Federation. In Andhra Pradesh, the Village Organisations, SHG Clusters and SHG Federations are registered under the Mutually Aided Co-operative Society (MACS) Act 1995. At the cluster and federation level, there are inter-group borrowings, exchange of ideas, sharing of costs and discussion of common interests. There are typically various subcommittees that deal with a variety of issues including loan collections, accounting and social issues

A case in point is the Indian state of Andhra Pradesh, that has used development Self Help Groups (SHGs) extensively as a primary tool of poverty alleviation and empowerment. As already been stated, a SHG is a small group of persons who come together with the intention of finding a solution to a common problem such as medical issues, livelihood generation or watershed management, with a degree of self-sufficiency. However, in Andhra Pradesh, the groups largely are the conduit through which *micro credit* is routed to the poor in the belief that it will serve as a catalyst in helping them to pull out of poverty.

National and state Government initiatives, as well as NGO efforts, have used SHGs to implement poverty alleviation programmes in Andhra Pradesh since 1979. Self-help groups also empower poor women, more than 4.8 million of whom are mobilised into SHGs. Homogenous groups of women would choose and collectively undertake an economic activity suited to their skills and resources, supplemented by state matching grants. Following the successes of earlier programmes, the state government of Andhra Pradesh promoted the SHG concept significantly and through its state sponsored *Velugu* programme, which is working in more than 860 mandals (sub-district geographical units) in 22 districts aims to reach 2.9 million poorest of the rural poor in the state.

There is absolutely no doubt that SHGs have led to an expansion in the economic spaces of members. However, the composition of the members reveal that the coverage of the poorest of the poor is low, while the coverage of non-poor is considerable. The financial status of households and their savings capacities has improved due to improvement in access to formal credit, since SHGs are linked with banks. Access to credit has enabled the women to undertake economic activities, and tend to expand/strengthen the existing traditional activities. The diversification of occupation to non-agricultural activities has enhanced the quality of income of the households by reducing the dependency on risk-based agriculture. Increase in income have been spent on better nutrition for the children and on health care for the family.

Another case in point is the effort of a group of rural women belonging to the "Paraiya" caste in South India to initiate and build an organization of their own to stand up for their rights and to challenge their oppression. Rural Women's Social Education Center (RUWSEC) in Chingleput, South India, was initiated in 1981 by 10 women belonged to the villages of Chingleput. The women had come together because of the involvement in a nationwide literacy campaign in which the 10 village women worked as literacy teachers in their respective villages. Through their work, the women realised their own worth and potential and felt committed to working with other women in their communities to change their exploited situation.

There are many successful women forums and organisations that are trying to bring the rural women together for developmental works and to eradicate poverty. Some examples could be Working Women's Forum (WWF), SEWA, Shri Mahila Griha Udyog Lijjat Papad, or Lijjat, and Mann Deshi Mahila Sah Bank Ltd., Mhaswad, Maharashtra etc.

Major Initiatives for Women Entrepreneurship

Women in the rural areas are the catalyst of change and that is why its whole programme keeps women in progress. In the women's savings movement, rural women organised themselves into 'thrift and credit' groups with one rupee saving a day and this mass movement, in which 58 lakh members saved more than Rs.800 crore is rotated internally and lent amongst its members twice a year as per the interest rates fixed by the groups. While the savings were there among the SHGs, there was no proper channel of investment.

Hindustan Lever Limited (HLL now Hindustan Unilever Limited-HUL) "Project Shakti" - Through a combination of micro-credit and training in enterprise management, these women from SHGs have turned direct-to-home distributors of a range of HLL products and helping the company plump hitherto unexplored rural hinterlands. Project Shakti was piloted in Nalgonda district in 2001. The ambitious vision of this project is to create by 2010 about 11000 shakti entrepreneurs covering one lakh villages and touching the lives of 100 million rural consumers. On an average the shakti entrepreneur is earning a return of eight per cent. To get started the shakti women borrows from her SHG and the company itself chooses only one person. With training and hand-holding by the company for the first three months, she begins her door-to-door journey selling her wares. One of the plans of HLL is to allow other companies which do not directly compete with HLL to get onto the shakti network to sell their products. Talks are on with companies like Nippo, TVS Motors, and Insurance companies. HLL also operates I-Shakti an IT-based rural information service that will provide solutions to key rural needs in the areas of agriculture, education, vocational training, health and hygiene.

Hence, what is needed is an environment that is conducive to maximise the potential of rural women. This conducive environment should include basic amenities such as better health and nutrition, education and sensitisation to their rights and protection under the law and employment opportunities. Over the decades, various strategies have been adopted to empower rural women with some mixed results. One of the viable strategies, quite often talked about is the role of enterprise to empower rural women. For example, promotion of rural enterprise makes full use of family labour, requires less capital in production and uses locally available raw material. In addition, family ties and kinship linkages may help in promoting rural enterprise. Thus, enterprise development has been considered, among other factors, a powerful tool to eradicate poverty especially among rural women as they are at the lowest rung of poverty ladder.

Development experience shows that gender inequalities are a major factor impeding progress towards the Millennium Development Goals of poverty reduction. This is particularly true in rural areas, where women are generally highly involved in productive work but lack access to assets they need, to play that role effectively. As a result of this imbalance, rural women are often more vulnerable to poverty than men, and their limited ability to secure assets independently makes them more likely to be negatively affected.

According to a survey conducted by Centre for Bharatiya Marketing Development (CBMD), the highest number of SHGs are found in the southern states. On an average southern states constitutes 65 per cent SHGs, eastern 13 per cent, central 11 per cent, northern five per cent and western six per cent at the national scene. Andhra Pradesh, followed by Tamilnadu, has the highest number of women SHGs working independently and setting up a micro enterprise, which helps in income generation. The benefits that can be reaped by the grouping together of poor women in rural areas are many.

The Importance of 'Access to Finance'

For women to become a successful entrepreneur and to run a Micro and Small Scale Enterprise (MSE), she needs access to capital, technical and managerial know-how and market. The essence to empower rural women lies in catalysing appropriate economic activities at the grass root level and creating new opportunities for them to earn higher income in order to improve their standard of living. This objective could be accomplished by establishing enterprises that are based on the locally available resources and preferably indigenous knowledge. Of the many constraints on micro and small-scale enterprise (MSEs) growth and development, the most important constraint is lack of access to finance (Schmitz 1982; Anderson and Khambata 1985; Remenyi 1991; Levy 1993; Morewagae, Seemule et al. 1995). This is the leading constraint to MSE's growth and development since commercial or formal financial institutions are reluctant to grant them loans.

Why Banks are not Favoring Rural Poor?

There are at least three reasons why formal financial institutions are reluctant to lend loans to the MSEs.

- First, based on his study of small-scale manufacturing in developing countries, Schmitz (1982) points out that the formal financial institutions consider the security offered by small producers as inadequate. This happens because of the unstable and risky conditions of production by small producers that could cause repayment defaults.
- Second, the controls on interest rates and on the borrowings and lendings of financial intermediaries in most of the developing countries, apart from limiting capacities of these intermediaries to raise resources, have necessarily led them to concentrate their lending on low-risk, large-

scale, and corporate borrowers. In consequence, large number of efficient small-scale activities, which employ the majority of the labour force in mostof rhe developing countries, do not have any access to institutional finance (Anderson and Khambata 1985).

- Third, incentives for formal finance institutions (commercial banks) to lend to MSEs are weak (Levy 1993). Since loan sizes are small, the costs of processing are high in relation to loan amounts. Moreover, the track record and reputation of a MSE borrower is likely to be limited, which adds to the costs of loan processing. The probability of failure is high even for well-conceived new ventures.

Moregawe *etal.* (1995: 484) point out that the problem of access to credit is exacerbated by the fact that the majority of small-scale enterprises are run by people who either have no education or, attained only a few years of primary education. The author argues that "it is unlikely that people of this calibre would have the courage to approach lending institutions for financial assistance".

Approach to Micro Finance

In the literature, there has been a debate between two approaches concerning the best way to help low-income people such asmicro and small entrepreneurs through access to financial services provided by the institutions (Woller, Dunford etal. 1999; Morduch 2000).

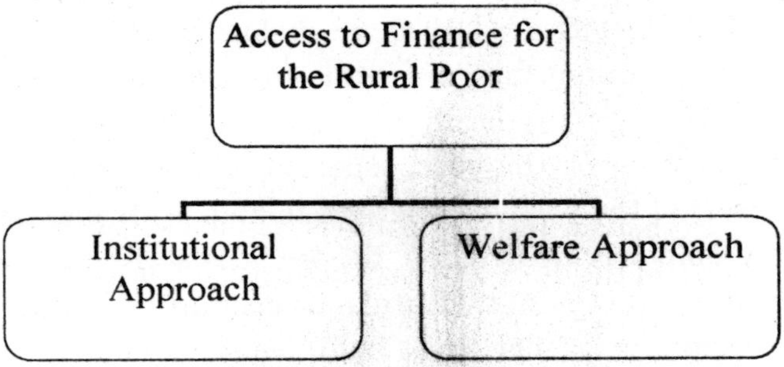

The first is the institutionist approach. This approach focuses on creating financial institutions to serve clients who either are not served or are underserved by the formal financial system (i.e. the commercial banks). The goal of this approach is to achieve institutional self-sufficiency through achieving financial self-sufficiency, breadth and depth of outreach, and positive client impacts. The central focus of this approach is the institution, and institutional success is generally gauged by the institution's progress toward achieving financial self-sufficiency. The institutionists argue that the primary objective of microfinance is financial deepening, that is, creating a separate system of sustainable financial intermediation for the poor. Theirs' is a "financial systems" approach to microfinance in which the future of microfinance is dominated by numerous large-scale, profit-seeking institutions that provide high quality financial services to large number of poor clients. The institutionists eschew subsidies of any kind, because they insist on financial self-sufficiency. This approach is rooted in the Ohio School of thought on microfinance (Hulme and Mosley 1996a). According to Woller *etal* (1999), the best-known examples of the institutionist approach are Bank Rakyat Indonesia (BRI), Banco Solidarion (BancoSol) in Bolivia, and the Association for Social Advancement (ASA) in Bangladesh.

The second approach is welfarist. This approach focuses on reducing poverty through credit, often provided together with complementary services such as skills training and teaching of literacy and numeracy, health, nutrition, family planning, and the like (Ledgerwood 1999: 63; Robinson 2001: 22). Robinson (2001) points out that under this approach credit is provided to poor borrowers, typically at below market interest rates. The goal is to reach the poor, especially the extremely poor - the poorest of the poor - with credit to help overcome poverty and gain empowerment. Thus, the welfarists are quite explicit in their focus on immediately improving the well-being of participants. Woller *etal.* (1999) point out that the welfarists are less interested in banking *per se* than in using financial services as a means to alleviate directly the worst effect of deep poverty among participants and communities, even if some of these services require subsidies. Their objective tends to be self-employment of the poorer of the economically active poor, especially women, whose control of modest increases of income and savings is assumed to empower them to improve the conditions of life for themselves and their children. The centre of attention is the "family".

Woller *etal.* (1999) point out that like the institutionists, welfarists have assumed more impact on poverty alleviation than they actually have been able to document. The most prominent examples of welfarist institutions are the Grameen Bank in Bangladesh and its replicas elsewhere, and FINCA (Foundation for International Community Assistance) village banking model in Latin America and, more recently, in Africa and Asia (Woller, Dunford et al. 1999).

In practice, Robinson (2001) notes that the two approaches have substantially contributed to the development of institutional microfinance. Some institutions using the welfarist approach have successfully reached poor people with donor- and government-subsidised credit services. This approach seems to be more suitable for the poorest of the poor. However, the successful institutions following the welfarist approach, in aggregate, can meet only a small portion of the demand for microfinance since most institutions following this approach (subsidised credit) are not sustainable (Robinson 2001:23 & 140-8). In contrast, the institutionist approach has proven that it is able to make financial services –both credit and savings- available to low-income clients on a large scale, and to do so profitably and sustainably. Institutions such as BRI *Unit Desa System* and BancoSol have demonstrated that broad outreach to economically active poor clients can be achieved without ongoing subsidies. Therefore, Robinson, as a proponent of the institutionist approach, argues that serving millions of clients on a long-term basis in multiple, competing institutions requires a financial system approach or institutionist approach (Robinson 2001, p.23).

Meaning of Microfinance

Robinson (2001) identified two reasons why microfinance is important. First microfinance provides the financial services not accessible through the traditional financial system, needed by many people to increase and diversify their economical activities. Secondly it builds the self-confidence of the poor.

In 1998 the General Assembly of the UN proclaimed the year of 2005 to be the international year of Microcredit. The UN claims that microcredit programmes have contributed to alleviate poverty or even lifting people out of poverty around the world "recognising that microcredit programmes have successfully contributed to lifting people out of poverty in many countries around the world" (UN 1998).

Ledgerwood (1999: 1) defines microfinance as the provision of financial services to low-income clients including small traders, street vendors, small farmers, service providers (hairdressers, rickshaw drivers), artisans and small producers. These clients are often classified as micro and small-scale enterprises (MSEs). He also claims that an estimate of 500 million economically active poor operate microenterprises in the world, of whom most have no access to formal credits.

The Consultative Group to Assist the Poorest (CGAP), an organisation consisting of public and private development agencies, defines microfinance as "the supply of loans, savings and other basic financial services to the poor". In the absence of micro credit, the poor normally acquires financial services from the informal sector, which often charge a very high interest. Savings and insurances were provided by different methods, which were normally erratic and insecure.

CGAP sees microfinance as a strategy that combines a possible huge outreach with far-reaching impact. CGAP claims that this together with the possibility to be financially sustainable makes micro finance unique among development interventions (CGAP (2005)). There are researchers, however, who do not share the certainty of the UN & CGAP. They claim that the microcredit programmes may not help the poorest of the poor. If you lend money to a borrower without food or a person who is sick might have no choice, but to use the loans for food or medicine. The loans will not be used for investment in the micro enterprise. These clients should be helped by government or donor subsidies and grants. Murdoch Jonathan (1999: 1609) finds that the claims of poverty alleviation are mostly unsubstantiated. Even so he argues that it's possible that microcredit may help other groups not extremely poor, but below the poverty line. If microcredit really helps, government grants could help the poorest to reach a level where they are reachable through the help of loans.

The Asian Development Bank (ADB: 2000:6) defines microfinance as the provision of a broad range of financial services such as deposits, loans, payment services, money transfers, and insurance to poor and low-income households and the micro-enterprises. The ADB definition includes low income households as well as those below the poverty line since there are a significant number of low-income households that are not below the poverty line, but have limited access to financial services, especially in rural areas.

Micro Finance and Women Empowerment

Links between microfinance and women's empowerment are viewed as optimistic, limited by design, cost effective in eliminating poverty, and a misplaced diversion of resources. Microfinance programmes range from small-scale self-help groups to large poverty-targeted banks. There could be three contrasting approaches to microfinance and women's empowerment namely the financial sustainability approach, the integrated community development approach, and the feminist empowerment approach. However, program evaluations revealed the need to question the assumptions underlying all three approaches. In most programmes, women benefited to a limited degree. Many women did not control the loan use. Most women were engaged in low paid, traditionally female activities, and their incomes were meagre. Resources and time invested in economic activity were limited due to the responsibility of looking after household work and unpaid domestic work. Microfinance programmes sometimes created domestic tension between spouses and loss of spousal income and support. Group repayment pressures sometimes created pressures between women. Many women focused on personal rather than social objectives.

Financial Services for the Rural Poor

While the fortunes of the many of India's biggest corporations are likely to shaped by 6,38,365 villages in India, the commercial sector has traditionally avoided the rural areas, deeming it as non-profitable and risky. This has led many of the 800 million poor to turn to local money lenders charging 36-72 per cent interest or suffer without capital. It is estimated that poor needs around Rs.2,000 billion.

Globally over a billion people are still without access to formal financial services and some 200 million of them live in India. Microfinance, the provision of a wide range of financial services to the poor on a sustainable basis, has proved to be immensely valuable. Access to financial services has allowed many families throughout the developing world (and, indeed, in poorer parts of the developed world) to make significant progress in their own efforts to escape poverty.

It has become clear that poor need access to money to send their children to school, to buy medicines; they need financial services to reduce their vulnerability. As a result, worldwide, MFIs have started developing and delivering a range of financial products. This reflects Millennium Development

Goals (MDGs) that offer broadly accepted, measurable indicators of poverty reduction that are focused on poverty, education, health and empowerment.

International year of Microcredit 2005's fact sheet, Microfinance and the Millennium Development Goals, notes that a review of microfinance literature points to several specific conclusions about its impact on poverty reduction and several other MDGs. Some of them are highlighted here:

(a) Shahidur R.Khandker's 1998 seminal study for the world bank notes that, 'In Bangladesh, 5 per cent of the grameen bank's clients graduated out of poverty every year by participating in microfinance programmes and, more importantly, households were able to sustain these gains over time.

(b) Save the Children's 1999 study in Honduras showed that microfinance clients increased earnings, which enabled them to send their children to school.

(c) Women empowerment programme in Nepal found that 68 per cent of its members were making decisions on poverty, family planning and daughter's education, and also negotiating their children's marriages.

(d) **Microfinance contributes to improved nutrition, housing and health, especially among women clients. Access to a wide range of financial services can have significant positive effects on a wide variety of manifestations of poverty. The new vision driving the microfinance industry is for a world in which all poor have permanent access to a wide range of financial services, delivered through a variety of convenient mechanisms by different types of institutions. Financial services for the poor includes besides microcredit, other services like savings, money transfers, remittances, and insurance. As in India, these service providers include savings and credit cooperatives, commercial banks, community finance institutions, NGO-MFIs, consumer credit companies, insurance companies,** and other types of institutions including the private sector companies. E-Banking and other emerging technologies offer a huge opportunity in this sector which has resulted in the growing number of commercial financial institutions initiating efforts to serve the low income market.

There are more than 1000 private MFIs operating in the country today. However, not more than 1-2 per cent of these have an outreach of 1, 00,000 microfinance clients. It is estimated that the MFIs share of the total institution-based microcredit portfolio is about 8 per cent. NGO-MFIs are unable to offer a range of financial services and focus primarily on credit. However, many number of NGO-MFIs are transforming into NBFIs to offer wide array of services while others are trying to offer the same through the route of agency agreements with other players in the market like insurance companies. But these services are offered at very high interest rates (12 – 36% p.a). Due to the nature of these services at the village level and lower business volumes, the transaction costs of these services were found to be exorbitant than that of formal banking channels. Most of the MFIs in India have thus far not able to significantly scale up the operations and reach a large population group across different states.

SHG-Bank Linkage

India has the world's extensive banking infrastructure. There are about 60,000 retail credit outlets of the formal banking sector comprising 12,000 branches of district-level cooperative banks, over 14,000 branches of Regional Rural banks and over 30,000 rural and semi-urban branches of commercial banks; in addition to 1,12,000 cooperative credit societies at village level. There is at leat one retail credit outlet on an average for about 5,000 rural people or every 1,000 households. This is an extensive and remarkable network that is present no where in the world and is capable of meeting the financial needs of the entire rural population. However, poor credit-deposit ratios (except in PACSs), unsustainable lending and high levels of NPAs, often cripple much of this infrastructure.

NABARD has been making continuous efforts through its micro-finance programme for improving the access of the rural poor to formal institutional credit. The Self Help Group (SHG) - Bank Linkage Programme was introduced in 1992 as a mechanism to provide the poor in rural areas, at their doorstep, easy and self-managed access to formal financial services on a sustainable basis by enabling them to gain access to banking services in a cost-effective manner. In all, 547 banks (47 commercial banks, 158 RRBs and 342 co-operative banks) are now actively involved in the operation of this programme. As on March 31, 2006, bank loans of Rs.11,398 crore were availed of by 2,238,565 SHGs from the banking system (Table. 1). As on March 31, 2006 the average bank loan per SHG was around Rs.50,917; the programme has enabled nearly 329 lakh poor families in the country to gain access to microfinance facilities from the formal banking system. During 2006-07, as against the target of 3.85 lakh new SHGs, as on December 31, 2006, as many as 2.38 lakh SHGs were credit linked and bank loans of Rs.13,511.86 crore were disbursed. The programme is growing at a pace of about 2.5 million households annually. It is the largest and fastest growing microfinance programme in the world in terms of its outreach and sustainability.

The credit linked rural entrepreneurial development programme of NABARD is gaining in rural Karnataka and has helped promote entrepreneurship, particularly among women. During 2003, of 75000 SHGs that received financial assistance, 3628 have become micro-entrepreneurs (< 5%). Of 3628 micro-entrepreneurs, 2476 were women (68%). Almost all the people involved in various activities were earning over Rs.10,000 per month and had enhanced their business and marketing skills. To provide financial assistance to artisans and small entrepreneurs in investment and working capital requirement,

Table 1

Progress of SHG-Bank Linkage

year	*New SHG financed by banks*			*Bank loan** (Rs. crore)*		
	During the year No.	*Growth (%)*	*Cumulative No.*	*During the year Amount*	*Growth (%)*	*cumulative Amount*
2002-03	**255,882**	29	717, 360	1,022.34	87	2,048. 68.
2003-04	**361,731**	41	1,079,091	1,855.53	81	3,904.21
2004-05	**539,365**	49	1,618,456	2,994.25	62	6,898.46
2005-06	**620,109**	15	2,238,565	4,499.09	50	11,397.55
2006-07*	**237,927**		2,476,492	2,114.31		13,511.86

** Includes repeat loans to existing SHGs.

As on 31. 12. 2006.

***Source* : NABARD.**

NABARD had formulated a special credit card scheme called Swarojgar Credit Card (SCC). Under the scheme, Rs.25000 could be borrowed.

At the end of March 31, 2007, 25.5 lakh self help groups – nearly all of them 'women only' groups – were credit-linked to the banks and have taken bank credit of Rs.14320 crores across the country. Beginning with consumption credit, an overwhelming majority among them has graduated to production credit. These groups borrow amounts up to Rs 200,000 for purposes such as land development, rearing cattle or sheep, poultry, garment making, food processing, manufacture of toys and retail shops. The amount of credit advanced to SHGs at the end of March 2007 was Rs 180 billion. It has been estimated that the SHG bank linkage programme and the MFIs together reached some 17 million families by mid-2006. The graph 1 shows the year on year increase in the number of new SHGs that are linked to the programme.

There is a long way to go and a very conservative estimate suggests that, in India, at most, just 20 per cent of all the eligible low-income people have access to financial services from formal financial institutions, MFIs and other such stakeholders.

Considering the increased competition in micro-credit and the pressure to reduce interest rates, it is time to consider moving beyond group lending. The primary reason for group lending is the inability of the takers to offer collateral, and hence the group mechanism was looked as collateral. The commonly stated advantages of group lending are that the problems of adverse selection, moral hazard and enforcement are sufficiently addressed. In India, there are primarily two group lending models, one the Grameen Bank type and the other the SHG model.

In the case of sparsely populated areas and the areas where groups could not be the formed, individual loans can be offered by taking non-traditional collaterals like the borrower's degree certificate, driving license and such others (Bank Rakyat

Graph 1: Progress of Bank SHG Programme

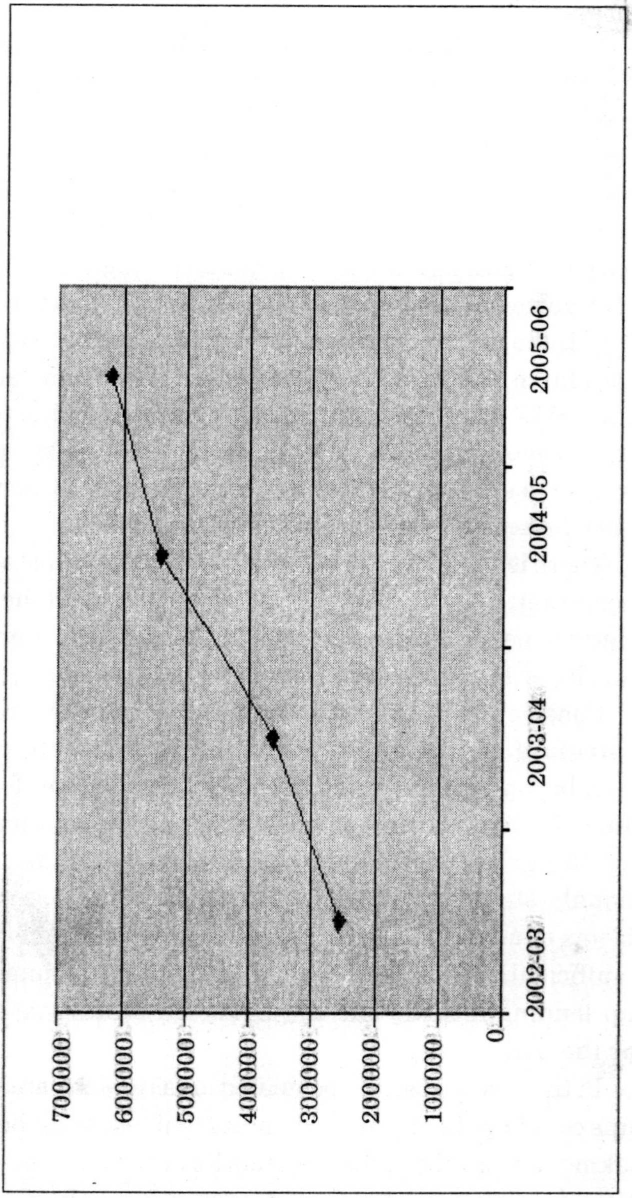

Indonesia, BRI uses this technique effectively). Another way is to insist on the borrowers to demonstrate habitual savings for a certain period before sanctioning the loan (the SHG-Bank linkage model, uses this technique). Other means is to give dynamic incentives and disincentives in the case of repayment. In the Grammen bank, the recent change is removal of joint liability of a group for the loan taken by one member of the group, though the group meeting regimen follows.

Conclusion

There are many studies that provide insights into the impact of micro-credit and/or microfinance on poverty alleviation and the empowerment of women. Some of the notable studies were 'Towards Women's Empowerment and Poverty Reduction: Lessons From Andhra Pradesh, South Asia Poverty Alleviation Programme; Micro-Credit And Women's Empowerment: A Case Study of SHARE Microfinance Limited; Social Mobilisation And Micro-Credit For Women's Empowerment: A Study of the DHAN Foundation; Awareness, Access, Agency: Experiences of Swayam Shikshan Prayog In Micro-Finance And Women's Empowerment; Micro-Credit and Women's Empowerment: The Lokadrusti Case; and Social Mobilisation and Micro-Finance For Women's Empowerment-Lessons From the ASA Trust'. These studies concluded that collective strategies beyond micro-credit to increase the endowments of the poor/women to enhance their outcomes vis-à-vis the family. Markets, state and community, and socio-cultural and political spaces are required for both poverty reduction and women empowerment.

Even though there were many benefits due to micro-finance towards women empowerment and poverty alleviation, there are some concerns. First, these are dependent on the programmatic and institutional strategies adopted by the intermediaries, second, there are limits to how far micro-credit interventions can alone reach the ultra poor, third the extent of positive results varies across household headship, caste and religion and fourth the regulation of both public and private infrastructure in the context of LPG to sustain the benefits of social service providers.

References

1. Neera Burra, Joy Deshmukh-Ranadive and Ranjani K.Murthy, (2005), '*Micro-Credit, Poverty and Empowerment: Linking the triad*', Sage Publications, New Delhi.
2. Jean Dreze and Amartya Sen, (2002), '*India: Development and Participation*', Oxford University Press, New Delhi.
3. K.G.Karmakar (1999), *Rural Credit and Self-Help Groups: Micro-finance Needs and Concepts in India*, Sage Publications, New Delhi.
4. C.K.Prahalad, (2005), *The Fortune at the Bottom of the Pyramid*, Wharton School Publishing.
5. Rasmus Stenbäcken (2005), *Do Self-Sustainable MFI:s Help Alleviate Relative Poverty?*", Department of Economics, Unpublished Ph.D. Thesis, Uppsala University.
6. Robinson, Marguerite S. (2001) The Microfinance Revolution - Sustainable Finance for the Poor, *The World Bank*, Washington, D.C.
7. CGAP, *What is Microfinance?*, http://www.cgap.org/about/faq01.html (2004-10-06).
8. CGAP, *About Microfinance?*, http://www.cgap.org/about/faq01.html (2005-01-26).
9. Ledgerwood, Joanna (1999), *Microfinance Handbook; Sustainable banking with the poor,* The International Bank for Reconstruction and Development/the World Bank, Washington.
10. Morduch Jonathan, (1999) *The Microfinance Promise, Journal of economic Literature*, 37(4): 1609.
11. Anon (2005), *resolution 53 / 197 International year of microcredit*, United Nations.
12. Lincolin Arsyad (2005), "An Assessment of Performance and Sustainability of Microfinance Institutions: A Case Study of Village Credit Institutions in Gianyar, Bali, Indonesia".

13. Anon (2004) 'NABARD Initiatives Turn Rural Women into Entrepreneurs', *The Hindu,* Feb 20, 2004.
14. Anon (2003), 'Where HLL Shakti comes from', *The Hindu Business Line*, May 29, 2003.
15. Anon (2005), 'The Schwab Foundation for Social Entrepreneurship', www.schwabfound.org
16. Anon (2005), 'SHGs help to Promote Women Entrepreneurship' *The Hindu*, Jan 24, 2005.
17. Anon (2005), 'Microfinance: Banking for the Poor and Not Poor Banking', *The Hindu Business Line*, Mar 15, 2005.
18. Anon (2005), 'SHG Movement Takes A Leap Forward', *The Hindu*, September 30, 2005.
19. Anon (2005), 'Gearing up SHGs to Create A 'Silent' Revolution', *The Hindu*, Nov 10, 2005.
20. Anon (2006), 'SHG Women Get Computer Training',*The Hindu*, Nov 18, 2005.
21. Anon (2006). 'Women SHGs Fewer in western India: Expert', *The Financial Express,* Jan 21, 2006.
22. Anon (2006), 'Micro Credit: Looking Beyond Group Lending', *The Hindu Business Line,* April 14, 2006.
23. Anon (2001), ITC Vs HLL, *Business World*, April 25, 2005.
24. www. Csrngo.org
25. http://aardo.org
26. http://indiabudget.nic.in, Economic Survey 2006-2007.
27. http://proxied.changemakers.net
28. www.manndeshi.org
29. Roy Deshmukh-Ranadive (2004), Womenn's Self Help Group in Andhra Pradesh – Participatory Poverty Alleviation in Action, A Case Study, World Bank, Washington.
30. Rathakrishnan L and V P Sriraman (2007), 'Who Says Women Can't Pro-create on Their Own?', *'Empowerment of Women through Entrepreneurship'*, Gyan Publishing House, New Delhi: 76-82.
31. Anon (2008), RBI, Report on Trend and Progress of Banking in India, 2006-07, *"The Basic of Micro Credit;, The Hindu Business Line*, Jan 10, 2008: 8.

16

Development of Rural Women – Role of Self Help Groups

Muthaiyan, P, K. Selvanathan and James Terance Sekar

Abstract

This chapter deals about the role of self-help groups in developing the economic condition of rural women. The chapter stresses the need for self-help groups for enhancement of women's capacities and for creating opportunities to nurture their capacities. It also touches upon the problems faced by the SHGs and the type of support needed for their empowerment.

Introduction

The current economic scenario in the country in terms of growth rate is quite encouraging. The lead economist, World Bank, Lant Pritchett has described India as a rich country in waiting. However, he has cautioned that the economic growth may not guarantee development. The development of rural India needs much attention and therefore the developmental strategies should be oriented towards rural India. Among the rural segment, women population being significant, the development of them needs immediate attention. One such strategy to develop women is by forming Self Help Groups of women in all the villages and supporting these groups in various ways. This chapter deals with the role of Self Help Groups (SHGs) in developing the economic condition of rural women.

The Status of Indian Economy and Paradoxes

If the present gross domestic product growth rate at 8.5 per cent is maintained then India will soon overtake the other countries to become the third largest economy in the world. Its strengths are:

(i) Democracy
(ii) Political continuity
(iii) Elite education
(iv) Open ideology
(v) Large population
(vi) Integrated market
(vii) Surplus food production

However, there are major weaknesses that reveal the existence of paradoxes in the economy. The paradoxes are:

(i) Though the GDP growth rate is higher than what is noticed in developing countries the per capita income is very low.
(ii) Though the growth rate is impressive there is no corresponding growth rate of employment generation especially in rural India.
(iii) Though the food grain stocks are in surplus there is hunger and poverty in rural India.

The economists have pointed out that countries' growth is mostly concentrated in urban India that too in a few cities and the rural areas are far behind. Therefore, the development strategies in the present context of globalisation and liberalisation should be reviewed and altered for the development of rural India, especially of the women folk. A study by women movement against poverty and violence in Tamilnadu brings out the fact that economic reforms in the context of globalisation have aggravated poverty casualisation of womens labour and resulted in the loss of productive entitlements such as land, livestock, water rights and other resources. It is also feared by some economists of the country that globalisation will not create more jobs but it will eventually destabilise the economy. A report by the Mahbub ul Haq, Human Development Centre, in its study on "Human Development in South Asia 2003 : the Employment Challenge" reveals that rural unemployment has increased substantially and India has not benefited from World Trade Organisation (WTO) in employment generation.

Rural Women Development

Out of the rural population 45 per cent are landless labourers and of them nearly 75 per cent are women. Two thirds of women are employed in agriculture or agriculture related activities. They work in various roles such as agricultural labourers, managers of households, etc. They do not have equal opportunities in access to credit and inputs and face discrimination in wages. The present condition of rural women needs urgent attention.

The strategies for the development of the rural women should aim at creation of capabilities of women. Nobel Laureate Amartya Sen's capability approach brings out two inter related aspects. (i) the enhancement of capacities of human beings (ii) the creation of opportunities that people have to nurture and exercise. The rural women's capabilities can be created in terms of education, training etc. and thus empowering them to utilise the opportunities.

The Need for Self Help Groups

Though the Indian cooperative organisations especially in rural India are numerically the largest in the world practically covering all walks of life and all villages of the country they have become weak and inactive barring few exceptions, because of bureaucratisation, excessive government controls and politicalisation of cooperative leadership. The cooperative sector has failed to inculcate two of the very essential values namely self help and member centrality. To supplement the cooperative sector in the development of rural India, the formation of Self Help Groups among women is the need of the hour. To attain the vision of empowerment of women, formation of Self Help Groups is the best strategy.

Current Status of Self Help Groups

Presently all over India 1,31,479 groups have been formed consisting 22,44,985 members. A Self Help Group should consist at least of 5 members and should have been registered under societies registration act as a recognised body to undertake various activities for the benefit of its members.

These Self Help Groups are engaging in various activities for their existence and even produce around 723 products. To mention a few are: making of soaps, detergents and agarbathies, handicrafts, hand woven cloths, cultivating herbal plants, dairy forming and agri- and non-agri related activities.

The Problems Faced by Self Help Groups

The successful functioning of the Self Help Groups depends upon stability, growth, sustainability and self-reliance.

The problems faced by the Self Help Groups can be broadly attributed to the following reasons:

(i) Smallness of the group
(ii) Limited avenues for resource mobilisation
(iii) Non-availability of loans to venture it to viable business activities
(iv) Non-availability of marketing support for the goods produced by the groups

In addition to the above internal factors some external factors also contribute to the nonfunctioning, ineffecting functioning, unsustainability of many of the self help groups culminating into defeating the long term objective of women empowerment.

Problems arise at the formation stage itself due to smallness of the group, groups being formed based on caste lines, lack of proper understanding of long-term objective of women empowerment, social and economical development.

The groups formed with a minimum of 5 members and not more than 20 members mostly function as thrift groups, which can be colloquially called as Chit companies, the members contributing small amounts on monthly basis and lending among them at an normal rate of interest. The groups do not think in terms of long-term sustainability and utilising the resources as capital for income generating activities and asset building.

The groups' stabilisation and growth sustainability and self reliance is achievable only if the group functions with solidarity and a feeling of homogeneity. Lack of education among rural women, the traditional divisions in the rural society compounded by activities of certain vested interested groups to convert the Self Help Groups into political bases have retarded the growth of Self Help Groups as institutions capable of achieving long term objectives for self empowerment.

Normally training is imparted to the groups to undertake income-generating activities. The training is usually confined to soap making, making toilet brushes, preparing juices, making pickles, making papads, etc. However, only in very few cases the training is translated into actions towards self-upliftment. Lack of motivation among the group's non-availability of sufficient funds at reasonable rates of interest and poor channel of marketing of the products are some of the problems.

The members of the self help groups are not adequately trained to make the group a capable unit to handle production with well defined approach accountability and responsibility.

Many of the units started by the Self Help Group have either become sick units or have closed down due to disintegration of the groups.

Liberalisation, globalisation available goods at low cost due to mass production with improved technology by companies with huge share capital and multinational companies which produce products identical to those produced by the Self Help Groups is one of the factors that poses a challenge to the growth and sustainability of income generating activity undertaken by the Self Help Groups.

Aggressive marketing, in other words buying of a product by customers, is an important aspect for the success of the unit / goods produced by the Self Help Groups. In the open market the Self Help Groups are compelled to defend themselves against the onslaught of similar type of goods produced by branded companies. In the absence of any preferential treatment to the goods produced by Self Help Group by way of tax exemptions etc., the survival of Self Help Groups becomes difficult.

Cannibalism is yet another aspect that plagues many of the self help groups. The same product is manufacture by many Self Help Groups thus one group trying to eat into the market share of the toher. The need of the hour is a proper regulating mechanism to ensure that there is diversification in the products produced by the Self Help Groups and no product is produced by more than one Self Help Group in the same region. To achieve this a networking of the Self Help Groups has to be done on a priority basis.

Credit facilities specifically designed for self help groups have to be evolved by the financial institutions. The existing norms for lending loans apart from obtaining credit facilities is a cumbersome process that will dent the stability, growth and sustainability of the Self Help Groups. Specialised institutions in the lines as available for setting up of industries (IDBI), should be formed to exclusively look into the credit needs of units set up by the Self Help Groups.

Conclusion

If the Self Help Groups have to sustain, the Government and its institutions have to extend financial, marketing and infrastructure support. The organisational part of Self Help Groups aspects has been completed and the need of the hour is active support of the Government and its institutions.

17

Promoting Mother and Young Child Friendly Communities Through Health and Nutrition Entrepreneurs

Shahin Sultana, A

Abstract

This chapter is focused on a supportive model, which is both novel and an emerging concept – Health and Nutrition Entrepreneurs (HNEs), which would go had in hand with the governments initiatives. The HNEs can play a significant role in the improvement of the maternal and child health situation in the communities. The paper deals with the need for such enterprises, the areas of their intervention and type of work they may undertake in the community. As the concept of HNEs is new the success depends upon the spirit of the health and nutrition entrepreneurs in the field and the support given by the government and the people.

Introduction

India is one of the most densely child populated country in the world but still the condition of the young children and their mothers is pathetic. There is undoubtedly a great demand for maternal and child health services in many parts of the country in spite of a whole cadre of professionals already serving in the community. The main problems, which stand as a hindrance to the development of the health and nutrition indicators of these target groups are - the outreach of these services, the density of the population it caters to and the number of service providers serving in the community. There is no denial of the fact that the Government has taken intense steps to intervene in this issue but still the condition of these vulnerable groups, the young children (0-6 years) and the mothers are at stake. Moreover, no young child in the age of 0-6 years can be viewed separately from the mother and hence it becomes mandatory for the State and the Community to view them as a single entity and provide holistic services.

At present the reality is that we have reached at such a saturation point that unless and until the community participates, conditions are further going to deteriorate and there can be no accountability for the services delivered in the community. The process of globalisation and privatisation has accentuated it even more. Hence, it is time for all the community members to think of being a part of the process. In this light, this paper would focus on a supportive model, which is both novel and an emerging concept – Health and Nutrition Entrepreneurs, which would go hand in hand with the government initiatives. It would stand as an exemplary community participation initiative in the field of health and nutritional needs in the community. Though there is a whole range of services like ICDS, primary health centres existing in the community besides health personnel like the anganwadi workers, and the Auxiliary Nurse Midwives, still the condition of the young children has not significantly improved. So there is a need for a novel idea to be explored and discussed indepth which is actually the purpose of this chapter and it has specifically limited itself to one single entity – mother and the young child keeping in mind the existing crisis situation in the communities.

Entrepreneur and Entrepreneurship

The word entrepreneur is derived from the French Verb "entreprendre" which means, "to undertake". It can be defined as the ability to create and build something from practically nothing (Swedberg 2000). Any one who is prepared to shoulder responsibility and face challenges can be called a successful entrepreneur. An organisation comes into existence only because of the efforts put in by a person who would be prepared to shoulder responsibility. The person need to have special quality, and that is known as entrepreneurship. It is an economic activity, which emerges and functions in sociological and cultural settings. It could be conceived as an individual's free choice activity, or a social group's action, occupation or profession (Mary 2004).

Entrepreneurship is mainly linked with economic activity. Now to introduce the concept of economic cum social oriented activity for the community's own betterment will work wonders. But a lot of analytical thinking should go into this process as there cannot be an expectation of free services altogether as people's time and efforts certainly matters. Hence, the community has to realise its need in the process so that the so called entrepreneurs are able to carry out their work effectively and then there is a whole lot of support from the community. This process would provide a resource of opportunities for the entrepreneurs and the community members to participate in the betterment of the community's problems.

One of the most difficult tasks in community work in the Indian context is to enlist people's participation. The importance of identifying innovative ways to involve people who are generally apathetic to the conditions around them, and who look upon initiative to better their conditions with skepticism, is obvious. It needs to be emphasised here that a lot of preparation has to go into making it happen. An effective communication system, to generate awareness and to enthuse a sense of confidence and devise adequate mechanisms within the community to encourage discussion, can go a long way in ensuring community participation (Siddiqui 1997).

Health and Nutrition Entrepreneurs

Health and Nutrition Entrepreneurs (HNEs) can play a significant role in the improvement of the maternal and child health situation in the communities. They will certainly go hand in hand with the other health personnel from the government and the local resource people available in the community. These HNE's will be volunteers who will be willing to take up intensive training ranging from 2-3 months, which could be provided by the government free of charge or by any charity organisation or by local non- governmental organisations working in the communities. The HNE's preferably could be women from the community since it would be easier for them to attend the needs of the mothers and children in the community. The concept of 'community' which is often referred to here can be a rural area, an urban settlement or even slum areas where the maternal and child health conditions are drastically poor. The basic educational level of these HNE's could be elementary education sometimes it can be lower or higher depending on the female literacy level of the community. They must be willing to work with a service oriented motive but probably seeing their work and significance the community would come forward to pay some amount to these HNE's. In cases of these HNE'S supported by the charity organisations, Trusts, NGO's they can be paid by them besides providing training, kits and then getting constant feedback from them. These HNE's would be extremely resourceful to the community members where there are no ICDS centres to attend to nor the Primary Health Centres close by. Further, these HNE's will be useful in such a way that once all the needs are identified then with assistance from the NGO's and other local level bodies one can pressurise the government to open up public health services in these areas and monitor them.

Need for Health and Nutrition Entrepreneurs

India is in a much deplorable condition globally as far as maternal and child health and nutritional status is concerned. India stands at 127th position as per the Human Development Report (2005). This situation needs serious introspection. There have been a whole lot of programmes and policies being initiated and implemented at state and national level but still the situation is improving at a snail's pace. In India, there are villages and backward areas where the health services have yet not reached despite fifty nine years of independence.

The basis for organisation of health services in the country through the primary health care approach was developed broadly in line with the recommendations of the Bhore Committee in 1946. The Mukherjee Committee (1965) spelled out the basic components for strengthening the PHCs at the block level. The establishment of the first Primary Health centre in October, 1952 was the major landmark in the development of health care services in India. The PHC occupies a key position in nation's health care system and constitutes the backbone of the present rural health care services in the country (Dutt 1965). But since then there has been a lot of changes in the Indian scenario.

Inadequate public health provision exacerbates vulnerability. Fifteen years after universal childhood immunisation was introduced, national health survey suggests that only 42 per cent of children are fully immunised. Coverage is the lowest in the states with the highest child death rates, and less than 20 per cent in Bihar and Uttar Pradesh. In 2005, the Government of India launched a $1.5 billion National Rural Health Mission, a programme targeting some 3,00,000 villages with an initial focus on the poorest states in the north and north-east. Commitments have been made to raise public health spending from 0.9% of national income to 2.3 per cent (HDR 2005).

In this challenging situation there is an urgent need for service oriented individuals who can come forward, get trained and work for the betterment of the community and can be paid by the government and the community members. Health and Nutrition Entrepreneurs are also needed because every community has its own identity and characteristics and the government cannot really understand their needs and cater to them specifically whereas such entrepreneurs will be fully aware of the needs of the community and can liaise with the government and attend to its needs efficiently. Moreover, corruption could also be checked because the emoluments can be paid as per the target achieved and work done and local bodies can monitor them accordingly and as they are members of the same community they could also be held accountable for any lack of service. Since these entrepreneurs will have their boundaries they will be fully aware of the problems of the community and can reach to them in time of distress, guide them and promote a mother and young child friendly community.

Areas of Intervention

As far as maternal deaths are concerned, sepsis, abortions, hemorrhage, toxemia and anemia account for the large majority of maternal deaths in India and its states. Infective hepatitis and gastro-enteric diseases are also the causes behind high MMR. On the other hand, prenatal and neonatal deaths among infants, too, are related with maternal factors such as health and nutritional status of the mother, ante and intranatal care, place of delivery and educational level of the mother. More specifically, prematurity, very low birth weight, bacterial infection (mostly tetanus), respiratory infections, diarrhea, and cord infection are the common causes behind IMR. This pattern of high maternal and infant mortality in India is the result of series of social, cultural and economic circumstances, which can be traced to the low status of women occupying relative to men, and its seeds are sown long before the occurrence of pregnancy (Tapan 2000).

Keeping all this in mind the Health and Nutrition Entrepreneurs at large can be trained in attending to:

- Maternal Mortality and Infant Mortality rate
- Breastfeeding practices
- Supplementary food for the children
- Child rearing Practices
- Immunisation schedules
- Tetanus, Diptheria, Whooping Cough, Measles, Small Pox, Diarrhea etc.
- Best Sanitation practices
- Water usage, preservation and methods
- Nutritional foods, calories, preservation, amount to prevent malnutrition
- Getting rid of illogical and dangerous practices at home
- Family planning procedures
- Ante-natal, and post – natal care
- Dehydration in children and ORS
- Family participation in maternal and child care

Training Programme

Training is an essential component in this programme because it need not be necessary that the HNEs have good knowledge on the health and nutrition components to be delivered to the community members. There should be a core team of professionals who would help the HNE to understand the maternal and child health problems besides handling them at various levels. It should be remembered that the HNEs main role is only to deliver preventive and curative services.

The HNEs must be trained appropriately by the gynecologist as to how to identify the problems, conduct tests, and have a proper record of various details relating to the mother and the child; in cases of emergency how to handle her clients and receive medical assistance immediately, what are the measures she should follow and how often she should visit the gynecologist, how to have a check on the developments of the child, frequency of vaccination etc.

The pediatrician must also provide the HNEs with adequate tips on symptoms to identify the problems of the child. What needs to be regularly assessed, what are the common problems which could occur during the first six years, ways to handle the problem, common ailments and treatment procedures, simple tests, which could be conducted without medical supervision, check height and weight of the child, other common problems etc.

The nutritionist could provide valuable tips for the HNE because they would know appropriately what is ideal for the pregnant and lactating mothers and the young child. The frequency of intake, blends possible, form of intake, hygienic practices, easily available foods, nutritious foods, calories in it, amount of intake needed, reducing high cholesterol foods, oils recommended and dietary patterns.

The social worker can provide her the valuable tips of how to handle the clients and what strategies can be used to reach out to the family members on the well being of the mother and the child. The social worker could encourage the HNE to understand the problems her clients would be facing during the entire pregnancy process, the pressure of work at home and at work place, economic problems, adjustmental problems with the family members, the labour pains, caring of the young child amidst all other responsibilities and the mental health problems she could face during this entire process. The HNE has to be cautious that the mother could be forced to undergo abortion once sex determination is done and hence should help the mother understand that it is a serious offence. Besides, the sex determination clinics in the community should be shut down with the community's participation and further sensitise the mothers on the repercussions of gender bias.

The Role of the Health and Nutrition Entrepreneurs

The Health and Nutrition Entrepreneurs have a challenging role to play in the community. Once their training is over they would start their work simultaneously with the pregnant women and the young children and their mothers. Their work related to the pregnant women would be:

- Know about the period of pregnancy and enquire about the medical procedures attended.
- Perform all the tests like blood pressure, diabetes, check weight, and ensure if vaccination and HIV/AIDS test has been done and other information's.
- Provide her with details to keep in check during the entire pregnancy.
- Counsel her to take appropriate food in terms of adequate calories and include vegetables, greens, liver, milk, nuts, etc.
- Counsel the family members to participate in her care and to ensure that she takes adequate rest.
- Meet her frequently to have a check on the child's growth and other requirements.
- Encourage her for hospital deliveries and not by untrained quacks.
- Provide her referral services to the nearby public health dispensaries and if needed assist her for getting prescriptions on iron intakes, vitamin tablets etc.
- Encourage her for family planning in future after two kids.
- Sensitise her on the need to be clean and use proper sanitation places to avoid risks and infections.
- Explain to her the entire developments in the pregnancy process so that she understands and expresses her apprehensions accordingly.

Mothers and the Young Child

- Encourage the mother to breastfeed exclusively for six months right from the time of delivery including the colostrums (first secretion of the mother's milk).

- Clarify the mother that no matter what type of delivery (normal or caesarean) she has to breastfeed the child immediately.
- Orient on the appropriate method of breastfeeding and the frequency in an elaborate manner.
- Sensitise on the adequate intake of nutritious food for breastfeeding the child.
- Ensure that the child immunisation is done at the right intervals.
- Provide orientation on dehydration and ORS mixtures.
- Since the child is very sensitive in the initial periods methods of preventive care should be clearly explained.
- Time of supplementary food and various combinations need to be clearly explained.
- Bottle feeding should be strictly not recommended.
- Whenever assistance from the doctor is required immediate attention should be taken, and
- The mother should be explained about the significance of the Early Childhood Care and Development (0-6 years) and its long lasting effects on the child.

Besides all these basic roles the health and nutrition entrepreneurs could encourage all the mothers to meet once in a month and address some common issues like how they are benefiting:

(a) If they are taking care of their and child's health and nutritional needs.

(b) How much money they are saving by breastfeeding the child instead of bottle feeding.

(c) How much money they are going to save if they attend to the child in the first six years.

(d) In what way the child's developments are faster when attended to rather than neglected.

(e) How a child's disabilities can be identified at an early stage.

(f) How they can demand more public health services if they come together.

(g) How the whole community benefits if their health and nutritional needs are taken care of.
(h) How the community is being empowered if the members are healthy.
(i) How disastrous it would be for the mother to constantly have abortions.
(j) How family planning can influence family and nations' economy and progress.

It would be a mutual sharing experience for all the members and seeing the successful models of some mothers and children each one would get motivated and inspired to do the same. Moreover, in such sessions fathers could also be made to speak and share their feelings so that there is a sense of involvement from their side and that the child is not the sole responsibility of the mother but the father also has a role to play. In this process the mothers will also feel empowered because maternity is a very arduous task for every mother and unless and until the mother and the child are taken care of the maternal mortality rate and the infant mortality rate and other complications will never go down. Community pressure can make the government monitor and upgrade the public health services available in the community regularly.

Health and Nutrition Entrepreneurs – An Experimental Model

To improve the health care outreach in villages, an experiment was carried out in five non-ICDS villages (total population 4400) of the Narsapur Mandal of Medak district of Andhra Pradesh. Local women (one per village) with an educational level equivalent to seventh grade were trained in aspects of preventive and curative health care, and nutrition. These women advise the community, particularly women, on health, nutrition, sanitation and family planning. They register all pregnant women; ensure antenatal check-up, compliance with taking of iron folic tablets, record blood pressure, identity at-risk pregnant women and treat minor ailments for which the community pays them. Records of deaths with age and cause, and births with birth weight (wherever possible) are maintained. 'Dais' (traditional birth attendants) are also being trained so that both groups of women can work in tandem. While no monthly stipend is paid, a daily wage is given for days of training and small incentive money of Rs.5/- for each vital event reported. The positive outcome after three years were: remarkable improvement in mother's knowledge of nutrition, and practices related to maternal diet, and child feeding; increase in institutional deliveries; reduction in prenatal and neonatal mortality, (infant mortality also declined after three years), and reduction in morbidity and in the incidence of Vitamin A deficiency (Bitot's spots) in preschool children. There was only marginal improvement in child nutrition, and no improvement in the incidence of low birth weight which was around 20 per cent (Bamji et. al. 2004).

This model gives a learning that a lot of planning and systematic work goes into making the nutrition and health entrepreneurs' model successful. Moreover, since they become so much recognised in the community there are no hindrances as far as their family members are concerned because every neighborhood receives their service. Since everything is at the doorstep the community members also find it very convenient and acceptable. There is no discrimination on the basis of caste, creed or religion. Everyone will be attended to and the child and the mother are taken due care of. In cases where there is absolute poverty there can be serious problems in terms of nutrition and in such instances the HNE will clearly identify the below poverty line family and can also build a community pressure on the Public Distribution system to attend to the needs of these families regularly and effectively without any delay or less supply, poor quality, etc. Since availability of the exact profile of the community in terms of maternal and child health is available with the HNE, which actually is the problem of the government. Many problems can be attended to effectively at various levels with the community members with these data.

Process for Ground work

- Areas need to be identified in the communities where there are no public health services.
- Local level representatives have to take initiatives in this regard with the help of any charitable trust or NGO working in the community.
- Exact number of the population needs to be identified and also the population of the mother and young children in particular.
- Depending on the number of mother and young children the Health and Nutrition Entrepreneurs needs to be decided.
- Identification of the appropriate individuals fluent in the local language and preferably women willing to do service oriented work needs to be done.
- There need not be any prescribed timings for them since the more flexible it would be the more comfortable women can perform.
- Training has to be provided with a stipend and then an assessment can be done and necessary kits could be provided free of charge.
- The HNE needs to be provided with a minimum stipend every time a case is attended to by the NGO/Trust/ Government and the community leaders should facilitate this.
- Discussion with the community mothers once in a month could be encouraged to receive a feedback for improvisation in the services.
- Subsequent training programmes on innovative methods could be provided by the NGO/Trust/Government and the community leaders should facilitate this.
- An evaluation needs to be done once in three months or once in six months by the local people in the community

and based on feedback further strategies can be worked on.

- The community could contribute to these entrepreneurs in any form like small incentive, free housing facility or any other provision they could provide with.

The Health and Nutrition entrepreneurs can be easily identified by the community and they will be also willing to work, but the main problem is the finance/budget for this model. With the rising unemployment such strategies would enable many of the community members to work dedicatedly to the community but some incentive is mandatory. Either the local NGO's or charitable trusts can adopt this model and liaise with the government for the need to fund such model and the entire responsibility can be taken by the appropriate body (identification of HNE's, training, providing emoluments, research, evaluation and feedback) or the model could also be adopted by the NGO's and carried forth with funds available. But since it is the duty of the state to provide adequate and accessible public health care services the trusts and NGO's can play a supportive role to the Government in improving the standards of the community. The HNE's could be paid a monthly stipend or incentive based on cases identified or attended, so that the work is carried out seriously and monitored by the local bodies. The emoluments can be worked on relating to various factors like density of the population needed to be catered to, number of mothers and young children, absence of public health service in the vicinity, and severity of the problems etc.

Conclusion

"The slow improvement in the health status of our people has been a matter of great concern. We have paid inadequate attention to public health".

- Manmohan Singh, April 2005.

Government has been put to alert on the existing situation in the nation by several surveys. At present the problems of maternal and child health are very severe in nature and it needs a massive task force to attend to them with great care and attention. The slow progress in the health and nutrition condition as an impact of the government programmes also slows down gradually due to lack of community participation. Hence introducing the concept of Health and Nutrition Entrepreneurs is a trial method and there is no assurances that there will be intense progress at one stretch. But with this there will be a greater check on the problems of the community and the spirit of the entrepreneur will be highly motivated as she has to genuinely attend to the problem to receive her emoluments. Moreover, the community will realise that they all can play a pivotal role in the needs of the community starting from health and nutrition to other needs in the community like water, electricity, schools, PDS shops, crèches etc. As a sapling grows out of a seed let this very idea be considered a seed, which has to be germinated and be grown into a sapling to reap benefits but it has to be watered adequately.

References

1. Bamji, S.M., Murthy, PVVS, Rao, V.M., Dangoria, D (2004), "Impact of Women Health and Nutrition Entrepreneurs and Mobilisers on Health and Nutrition of Rural Children and Mothers' Knowledge and Health-related Practices", **Regional Health Forum**, WHO, South-East Region, 8(1).
2. Dutt (1965), *Rural Health Services in India: Primary Health Centers*, Central Health Education Bureau, DGHS, Ministry of Health, GOI, New Delhi.
3. Anon (2005), *Human Development Report (2005)*: United Nations Development Programme.
4. Mary, L.M (2004), "Social Entrepreneur in Stanley" in **Social Problems in India – Perspectives for Intervention**, Allied Publishers, New Delhi.
5. Siddiqui, H.Y (1997), **Working with Communities,** Hira Publications, New Delhi.

6. Swedberg, Richard (2000), **Social Science View of Entrepreneurship,** Oxford University Press, New York.
7. Tapan, N (2000), **Need for Women Empowerment,** Rawat Publications, Jaipur.

18

An Analytical Study of Women Empowerment Through Entrepreneurship Development Policies : A Case of Chhattisgarh

Sambit Kumar Mishra

Abstract

Women entrepreneurship in economic development of any nation has been documented for its significant contribution. This means that the neglect of women in the development process constitutes a human waste. The increased role of women in economic development had spurred the government in developing policies on women development. However, several studies have discovered that women performance was still low specifically in the small and micro scale industries. Problems like low productivity, high rates of business failures, and no access to credit among others had hindered their growth. In the light of this, the study examined the policy implementation of the two programmes created to mobilise women on entrepreneurship development. It attempted to determine if the programmes have succeeded in empowering women economically. It also aimed to uncover the possible implementation gap problems and determine the extent of which these gaps have affected the effectiveness of the policy implementation. The study was carried out in Chaattisgarh State, India. The samples were selected by random sampling method. A total of one hundred fifty respondents were interviewed with the aid of predetermined questions. The questionnaire was designed to ferret information using the Women Equality Empowerment Framework. This was to determine the level of development impacted by the programmes. Statements were developed to operationalised development into welfare, access, conscientisation, participation, and control. These were measured by a 5-point scale method. The variables were described and highlighted using descriptive analysis. The results showed that despite some constraints in the implementation due to implementation gap, there was an average impact of the programmes on women development. Welfare like housing, clothing and food were average. Access to land was also average, but access to credit and services were low. However, the respondents had high access to their own labour. It was further revealed that the programmes had impacted highly on the ability of the respondents to relate themselves with the society and that their participations to group activities had increased. Although a high result was revealed in conscientisation level, their low level of control over the resources might affect their involvement because of the gap that exists between efforts and rewards. It is therefore imperative that overcoming gender inequality must be a high priority in policy development concerning women.

Introduction

One of the key factors in determining the success of development is the status and position of women in the society.

This means that the neglect of women in the development process of any country constitutes a human resource waste. In this premise, it will be a disservice for any country to ignore its women population in its development efforts. The task before any government, therefore, should be that of moving steadily and firmly in the direction of economic development by involving women. Faleye (1999) stressed that women's development is not nearly about reducing poverty by increasing productivity, but also about women's liberation and empowerment. True development means the development in three categories for a woman. These are individual, social, and economic development (Rodney, 1972). Individual development means increased skills and capability, greater freedom, creativity, self-discipline, responsibility and material well being. Increasing capacity connotes social development, while economic development is determined by the increased capacity of the members of a society in dealing with their environment. This emphasis means that development at the individual stage subsumes both the social and economic categories of development. Development is dynamic and therefore assumes a continuous transformation process and a movement towards better and improved conditions, locally and internationally. For a meaningful development to take place, women development must not be overlooked.

In India, women actively played a meaningful role in the industrialisation process of the country in 21st Century . The role of women in social and economic development specifically in the small and micro enterprises was found to primal in the economic development of their communities. Their potentials have spurred the government in devising policies to stimulate the industrial sector specifically in the development of indigenous technology. Accordingly, the government has developed trade and industrial policies that will foster industrial development and increase production of manufactured goods in the country. Majority of these policies were created for the informal sector.

For instance, the government has formulated policies introducing the National Rural Employment Guarantee Act (NREGA) to improve the conditions of the rural women and Swarnajayanti Gram Swarozgar Yojna (SGSY) to improve the fortune of the family and the condition of women in general. This chapter is devoted towards this end.

Problem Statement

The National Rural Employment Guarantee Act came into existence in 2006 and later was launched in all states and local areas of the nation aimed at mobilising women for resource productivity. The primal objective of this programme was to sensitise the government and indeed private organisations to the useful role that women could play in national development. It gave insight into the conception of the Swarnajayanti Gram Swarozgar Yojna , which was predominantly in favour of women in the rural area. This programme aimed to improve and sustain family cohesion through promotion of social and economic well being of the Indian family. The programmes were introduced with the purpose of stimulating and motivating women towards achieving a better life and higher standard of living and good family life of women specifically the entrepreneurs in the small and micro scale industries. In line with these programmes, the policy is supported with other fiscal and monetary policies geared to making efficient use of resources, mobilising domestic savings for investment, and utilisation of raw materials among others.

However, observation showed that the fortune of women in India has not been considerably improved inspite of these programmes. According to a recent survey, there have been complaints about the implementation of the two projects. Some social scientists in their study concluded that the NREGA and SGSY programmes had not really accomplished much. They referred to the programme as merely publicity –grabbing gimmick, which is better known for its manner than for its matter.

This had been predicated by some social scientists who in their study pointed out the weaknesses in the programmes. They revealed that the rural women and the family unit did not feel the impact of the programmes despite the propaganda through mass media. This is not to say that nothing positive came out of the programme. Some reported an increase in the number of women cooperatives and also highlighted the social awareness among rural women through intensive public enlightenment campaigns organised by the programmes. Several studies discovered further that women engaged in the small and micro scale of the industrial sector were still striving to grow and were still bombarded with problems.

The problems include high rates of business failures, low productivity, no access to capital, credit, and labour among others. It was also noted that the policies introduced for economic enhancement programmes were gender-blind. It was also observed that women were not explicitly included in the programmes. Although it was evident that women were found to have been engaged in small-scale business, a lot of constraints have hindered their economic participation. In the light of this, the study investigated and evaluated the implementation of the programmes to determine their impact on women entrepreneurship development, that is, how far the programmes have succeeded in achieving their primal objectives of empowering the women involved in the programmes, both economically and socially. It attempted to uncover the possible causes for the gap, problems and determine the extent to which these gaps have affected the effectiveness of the policy implementation.

Framework for Analysis

Policy implementation is mainly the activities that are carried out in the light of established polices. Egonmwan (1991) was of the view that implementation refers to the process of converting inputs such as financial, material, technical, human into outputs – goods and services. He further described it as the stage where the earlier preparation and designs, plans and analyses are tested in the harsh light of reality. Policy implementation has been described as one major problem confronting developing countries such as India. The implementation problem in developing countries is the problem of a widening gap between intentions and results. A manifestation of implementation gap is the phenomenon of the rich getting richer while the poor are getting poorer in spite of the avowed stated policy goal of elimination of poverty and equality of access to the basic needs of life. Implementation gap also manifests in the widening of the distance between stated policy goal and the realisation of such planned goals (Egonmwan 1991).

Boserup (1970) opined that development programmes in developing countries tended not to be effectual or productive because planners had failed to understand gender inequalities. Development can be viewed as empowerment, the liberation of women. Development is not complete without the reduction of poverty through increasing productivity. However, to achieve a high level of empowerment, structural inequality in the society should be addressed. Therefore, for the empowerment of women, there must be women's collective mobilisation to overcome particular instances of institutionalised gender discrimination. Empowerment is a process aimed at consolidating, maintaining or changing the nature and distribution of power in a particular cultural context. The process is rarely linear because it takes twists and turns. It includes both resistance and consent, and ebbs and flows as groups with different relations to the structures and sources of power come into conflict (Morgen and Bookman 1988). Smith (1996) considers empowerment to be a process that can only begin in a climate in which there are high expectations and where everyone's feelings should be respected and valued. The concept of empowerment ranges from encouraging people to play a more active role in their work through involving them in taking responsibility to enabling them to make more and bigger decisions without having to refer to someone higher in position. Similarly, empowerment is seen as an expansion of freedom of choice and actions, which means an increase in one's authority and control over the resources and decisions that affect one's life (World Bank 2003). In other words, focusing on how women have to be empowered economically and socially, policy implementation must stem from the framework on the Women's Equality and Empowerment Framework (WEEF), which looks at all levels of equality from the perspectives of welfare, access, conscientisation, participation, and control (Ostrom 1974).

Women's Equality and empowerment are ladders of equality identifying the five levels of empowerment for women to advance towards equal status with men. The higher the levels of equality automatically mean high levels of development and empowerment. The lowest level is the welfare level, while the highest is the control level. Welfare is the level of material resources that females have relative to males in such areas like nutritional status, food supply, and income. Women are seen here more as passive recipients of welfare benefits. The gender gap can be identified through the disparity between males and females on indicators of nutritional status, mortality rates among others. Women's empowerment cannot highly take place at this level because an attempt to improve welfare level will entail access to resources. Access is the restricted access to the resources of production available in the society that results in women's lower level of productivity. These include land, credit, labor, and services.

Empowerment means that women are made aware of the differential situation and encouraged to take actions for gaining access to their fair and equal share of the various resources made available within the household and within the wider system of state provision. When there is an attempt by women to overcome the obstacles to access, it means that they have confronted the systematic discrimination, which can be addressed only through the empowerment process to conscientisation. Conscientisation refers to the gender gap as a belief gap. The belief that women's lower socio-economic position, and the traditional gender division of labour is a part of natural order. So empowering women, therefore, implies the sensitisation to such beliefs and practices and their rejection. It also means that women's subordination is not part of the natural order of things but is imposed by a system of discrimination, which is socially constructed and which can be altered.

The realisation by women that their problems do not derive so much from their own personal inadequacies, but rather by institutionalised discrimination against women and girls helps to bridge the gender gap caused by inequality. Participation refers to the participation of women in various positions. However, women participation in the developing countries is very marginal. In terms of gender gap, women's participation is the visible and obvious phenomenon. Participation means that women equally with men, are actively involved in the development process. This includes equal participation in the decision making process as well as in development projects; particularly the projects that affected their direct community. This could mean that women would be adequately represented in a development project in the area of needs assessment, project planning, management, implementation, and evaluation. Equality of participation means involving women from the community affected by the project and involving them in the same proportion in decision making as their proportion in the community at large. The need to effectively involve the target beneficiaries in the direct projects can be likened to the belief of the public choice theorists, which give room for polycentric structure of administration by which people will be able to contribute to decisions that affect their lives.

Control means a balance of power between men and women, so that neither is in a position to dominate. It means that women have power alongside men to influence their destiny and that of the society. Women's increased participation at the decision making level can only be said to lead to their increased development and empowerment, if such participation enables them to achieve increased control over factors of production, access to resources and the distribution of benefits. In a situation where the wife makes the effort but the husband collects the benefits, there is a serious gender gap between effort and reward. Following the above premise, at what level can one say then that a woman is empowered. Using the analytic framework for evaluation, the issue of women empowerment from the perspective of the process overcoming gender inequality through the five levels (ladders) of equality would show that the lowest level of women empowerment is attained when equality gap between man and woman is bridged at the level of welfare. Access, which is the next level, implies access to land, loan facilities, labor services, opportunities, and to use own labour. In this case, there is no doubt that empowerment will improve or better still, guarantee better and steady income.

In conscientisation, the woman is being conscious of her environment, which cannot be done without the individual socialising with the people in the environment. In the participation level, women equally with men, are actively involved in the development process and when there is increased control over the factors of production and when there is a balance of power between women and men, so that neither a position of dominance. This level of empowerment enables women to actualise themselves. Self-actualisation produces such satisfaction as power, prestige, status, and self-confidence. It is at this level at which women needs fulfilled.

Methodology

The study was carried out in Chhattisgarh-State, India. The state comprised three senatorial Districts, namely Bastar, Dantewada, and Rajnandgaon. The subjects of the study were selected from each of the senatorial districts using the random sampling technique. The selected communities were Scheduled Caste, Scheduled Tribe, and Other Backward classes. One hundred and fifty women respondents that participated in the programmes were identified in the three communities with the assistance of local people in the state that were stationed in the various local government as project officers.

The study used both primary and secondary sources of data. Structured interview with the aid of predetermined set of questions were used to collect the pertinent primary information. The interview schedule was supported by focus group discussion among the selected fifty women groups that participated in the two programmes using the double sampling technique. There were three focus group discussions held in each of the three communities. Selection of groups was based on age and education level. The focus group discussion was carried out before the interview schedule as an interactive measure apart from eliciting deeper issues relevant to the variables of the study.

The dependent variable development of women entrepreneurs was operationalised using women's equality and empowerment framework from the perspectives of welfare, access, conscientisation, participation and control. Statements were developed in each category addressing the objectives of the programmes to measure the success of implementation employing the five point scaling method. The independent variables, which were the two programmes, were measured using the objectives set for the policies by liker scale method. Data collected were analysed using descriptive statistics to describe and highlight the variables of the study.

Results and Discussion

Demographic Characteristics of the Respondents

The results in Table 1 show that majority (42 per cent) of the respondents were between 30 and 39 years of age. About 23 per cent were above 50 years of age and about 17 per cent were between 40 and 49 years. The results also show that majority (89 per cent) of the respondents were married and about 51 per cent of them had more than four children, while 26 per cent had 3 children. It can can be inferred that the respondents are still at the working age and the married status of the respondents

Table 1: Distribution of Respondents on Demographic Characteristics

Variable		*Frequency*	*%*
Age :	Below 3o years	22	14.7
	30-39 Years	64	42.7
	40-49 years	32	21.3
	Above 5o years	32	21.3
Total		150	100
Martial Status :			
	Single	4	2.6
	Married	133	88.7
	Divorced	6	4.0
	Widow	7	4.7
Total		150	100
Number Of Children :			
	One	3	2.0
	Two	25	16.6
	Three	46	30.7
	More than four	76	50.7
Total		150	100
Educational Level :			
	Primary	35	23.3
	Modern	31	20.7
	Secondary	28	18.7
	Others	56	37.3
Total		150	100

Source: Field Survey - 2006.

Table-2: Distribution of Respondents on the Perceived Impact of the Programmes on Welfare

Scores	*5*		*4*		*3*		*2*		*1*		
Variables	*Very High*		*High*		*Average*		*Quite a bit*		*Not at all*		*Mean Score*
	F	*%*	*F*	*%*	*F*	*%*	*F*	*%*	*F*	*%*	
Food Intake	12	8.0	79	52.7	21	14.0	30	20.0	8	5.3	3.380
Clothing	20	30.3	67	44.7	31	20.7	29	19.3	3	2.0	3.480
Housing	15	6.0	45	30.0	36	24.0	35	23.3	19	12.7	3.013
Income	9	6.0	51	34.0	40	26.7	21	14.0	29	19.3	2.993
Health	43	28.7	54	36.0	42	28.0	8	5.3	3	2.0	3.840
Grand Mean Score											3.341

***Source :** Field Survey - 2006*

connotes high level of responsibility. Having more than four children indicates the necessity of having additional income. This explains the need in participating in the programmes. The data also revealed that 37 per cent had attained higher than secondary level of education, while primary was the lowest level attained by the respondents, which shows that the programmes were not left to the illiterates alone, neither left in the hands of those with only certificates.

Assessment of Programmes on Welfare

The programmes aim was to enhance the economic standards of women entrepreneurs in the small and micro scale industries and empower them economically. The results in Table 2 reveal that the programmes had average impact on their welfare with a grand mean score of 3.329. Furthermore, the programmes had made positive impact on the women health care with an average mean score of 3.840. The data also showed that nutritional status, clothing, and housing were affected averagely with mean scores of 3.380, 3.480, and 3.013 respectively. It is further revealed that income had low mean score (2.933). In fact, it is revealed that 19 per cent of the respondents indicated that they did not feel the impact of the programmes on their income at all. Also, about 13 per cent indicated the same that in housing the programmes did not have impact at all.

Assessment of Programmes on Access

Access means facilities to land, credit, labour, services and utilisation of own labor. The results in Table 3 show that the respondents had an average access to facilities with a grand mean score of 3.136. The results further show that the respondents had high access to own labour (4.020), and average access on service (3.140). The access to land (2.78), credit (2,860), and labor (2.880) were revealed to have quite a bit impacted by the programmes. These are important resources in the process

Table-3: Distribution of Respondents on the Perceived Impact of the Programmes on Access

Scores *Variables*	*5 Very High*		*4 High*		*3 Average*		*2 Quite a bit*		*1 Not at all*		*Mean Score*
	F	*%*	*F*	*%*	*F*	*%*	*F*	*%*	*F*	*%*	
Improved Access To Land	19	12.6	25	16.7	26	17.3	64	42.7	16	10.7	2.780
Improved Access To Credit Facilities	1	0.7	56	44.0	22	14.6	33	22.0	28	18.7	2.860
Improved Access To Labour	7	4.7	45	34.0	27	18.0	43	31.3	18	12.0	2.880
Improved Access To Services	21	14.0	48	32.0	28	18.7	37	14.7	16	10.7	3.140
Improved Opportunities To Utilise Own Labour For Own Benefit	49	32.7	39	26.0	28	18.7	24	16.0	10	6.6	4.020
Grand Mean Score											3.136

Source : Field Survey - 2006

Table 4: Distribution of Respondents on the Perceived Impact of the Programmes on Concsientisation

Score	*5*		*4*		*3*		*2*		*1.*		
Variables	*Very High*		*High*		*Average*		*Quite a bit*		*Not at all*		*Mean Score*
	F	*%*	*F*	*%*	*F*	*%*	*F*	*%*			
Being Conscious of The Beliefs & Practices Injurious to Development	50	33.3	54	36.0	34	22.7	9	6.0	3	2.0	3.927
Rejection Of The Negative Beliefs & Practices Against Women	55	36.7	42	28.0	43	28.7	6	4.0	4	2.6	3.920
Improvement attitude to Self	78	52.0	45	30.0	19	12.7	5	3.3	3	2.0	4.267
Grand Mean Score											4.038

Source: Field Survey -2006

of production and the absence of these resources has a significant effect on the capacity of the women to contribute economically. It is revealed that 19 per cent of the respondents had the opinion that credit facility did not affect their capacity to contribute economically. The results can also be inferred as, if these facilities were available to them, they could positively contribute socially and economically, hence they have the access to their own labour. However, the lack of access by some of the respondents was due to the low level in some of the variables in the welfare level of development like the housing and the income.

Assessment of Programmes on Conscientisation

The data in Table 4 reveal that there was high awareness of the respondents on their environment. This is indicated by the grand mean score of 4. 038. This result indicates that the programmes had high (4.267) influence on the improvement of their attitude toward self. The respondents were also conscious on the beliefs and practices injurious to their development as well as the understanding on the negative beliefs and practices. Women indicated this by almost high mean scores of 3.297 and 3.920 respectively. It can be inferred from these results that the programmes had sensitised and improved their level of awareness about their selves and that of the environment, which are significant to the development of personality. Once women have the realisation of their problems especially the discrimination against women, this will help to bridge the gender gap caused by inequality. It can be inferred that there would be a high level of development among women once the programmes are modified specifically on variables that concern overcoming gender inequality; hence development starts from the personality of an individual.

Assessment of Programmes on Participation

The data reveal the participation of women was enhanced, indicated by the grand mean score of 4.028, which is high. The

Table 5: Distribution of Respondents on the Perceived Impact of the Programmes on Participation

Score *Variables*	*5* *Very High*		*4* *High*		*3* *Average*		*2* *Quite a bit*		*1* *Not at all*		*Mean Score*
	F	*%*	*F*	*%*	*F*	*%*	*F*	*%*			
To What Extent Have The Programmes Encouraged Your Economic Participation	70	46.6	40	26.7	33	22.1	4	2.6	3	2.0	4.133
To What Extent Did You Enjoy The support Of Your Husband as regards to Economic Participation	60	40.0	44	29.3	34	22.7	10	6.7	2	1.3	4.000

(Contd.)

(Contd. Table 5)

Score *Variables*	*5 Very High*		*4 High*		*3 Average*		*2 Quite a bit*		*1 Not at all*		*Mean Score*
	F	*%*	*F*	*%*	*F*	*%*	*F*	*%*			
To What Extent Did You Enjoy The support Of Your Father as regards to Economic Participation	43	28.7	42	28.0	52	34.6	7	7.4	6	4.0	3.272
Since Your Participation In the NREGA & SGSY Programmes , To what extent have you taken Part In Community Activities	70	46.4	51	34.0	27	18.0	1	0.7	1	0.7	4.253
Grand Mean Score											3.914

Source : Field Survey-2006.

Table 6: Distribution of Respondents on the Perceived Impact of the Programmes on Control

Score *Variables*	*5* *Very High*		*4* *High*		*3* *Average*		*2* *Quite a bit*		*1* *Not at all*		*Mean Score*
	F	*%*	*F*	*%*	*F*	*%*	*F*	*%*			
To What Extent does your Husband not Control Your Labour	22	14.7	55	36.7	45	30.0	18	12.0	10	6.6	3.407
To What Extent Has Your Cash Income Increased Lately As A Result Of NREGA & SGSY Programs	19	12.7	60	40.0	35	23.3	27	18.0	9	6.0	3.353
To What Extent Does Your Husband Not Control Your Increased Finance	17	11.4	54	36.0	36	24.0	32	21.3	11	7.3	3.227

(Contd.)

(Contd. Table 6)

Score *Variables*	*5 Very High*		*4 High*		*3 Average*		*2 Quite a bit*		*1 Not at all*		*Mean Score*
	F	*%*	*F*	*%*	*F*	*%*	*F*	*%*			
To What Extent Has Your Standard Of Living & That Of Your Children Improved as a Result of Increased Cash Income	21	14.0	78	52.0	30	20.0	14	9.3	7	4.7	3.613
To What Extent Do You Feel Not Dominated By your Husband	22	14.7	42	28.0	64	42.7	11	7.3	11	7.3	3.400 3.380
Grand Mean Score											3.396

Source : Field Survey-2006.

participation of women means involving themselves into any development process in the community. It could be in decision making or in development projects. Their involvement has to do with the extent of encouragement by their male counterparts like the husband or the father. The support of the male figure in the family influences their participation. This is shown in Table 5, indicating high (4.000) encouragement by the husband. Hence, the evaluation scale used indicates that once conscientisation level is high, the understanding of environment is also high. If this happens, there is gender equality at home. This means that women would be able to gain the understanding of the husbands, which implies that men are not an impediment to their participation. This would build self-confidence among women to face the challenges of the environment.

Assessment of Programmes on Control

Development will not take place, neither empowerment through policies and programmes if one has no control over resources. An empowerment that is devoid of control cannot be tagged real empowerment. The study revealed that control over possession was averagely (3.396) influenced as shown in Table 6. The control over their labour recorded an average mean score of 3.407. Certainly, even if the respondents have high access over their own labour but do not have control over it, development will not take place. Equality of control means a balance of power between man and woman, so that neither is in a position to dominate. It means women have power alongside men to influence their destiny and that of the society. There is an increase in development and empowerment if such participation enables them to achieve increased control over the factors of production, access to resources and the distribution of benefits.

Constrains of Policy Implementation

In the focus group discussion held, it was revealed that sound policies were formulated but failed at the level of implementation. Problems like inadequate definition of goals, overambitious policy goals, choice of inappropriate organisational structure in implementation of policies, lack of continuity in commitment to policy, lack of monitoring process, inadequate manpower planning, and non-inclusion of the target groups in the determination of policy were revealed to have contributed to the failure of policy implementation.

Corruption was also revealed to be one of these problems. Inadequate definition of goals makes a policy lack clarity, internal consistency and compatibility with other policy goals. The successful implementation of a policy filled with inadequacies becomes problematic.

Over ambitious policy goals in policy formulation are muddled in ideological context that may confuse the actual problems involved in implementing them. Due to scope and comprehensiveness such policies may experience implementation bottlenecks arising from any or combination of the lack of appropriate technology for implementation; inadequate human and material resources; over-stretching of available resources for maximum visibility and impact at the end of which nothing concrete may be achieved. The lack of continuity in commitment to policy, usually when there is instability in government results in unstable priorities particularly in India where change of executive power always resulted to change of priorities and objectives. A serious problem is that of bribery and corruption which has contributed greatly to the failure of policy implementation. When huge amounts of money get stolen by officers in charge of implementation, the problem is bound to arise.

Conclusion and Recommendation

Although the programmes had some constraints in the implementation due to implementation gap arising from problems like inadequate monitoring process, inadequate manpower planning, corruption and non inclusion of target groups in the determination of projects to be established for them, the two programmes have succeeded averagely in empowering women in all the five areas under the equality/ empowerment framework. The women who participated in the programmes were empowered economically because they were able to control their financial resources strengthening their income standing.

The programmes have impacted more on their involvement in many activities and had exposed them to the environment, which have great magnitude of changing their abilities to understand their selves as well as their relations to the society. The programmes had motivated women to develop positive attitude forwards themselves. They had been sensitised to the injurious beliefs and practices against the development of women. In spite of the inadequacies the programmes have succeeded in achieving their objective of primarily to sensitise women economically. However, despite the high conscientisation level of the women, their average control level over the resources could significantly retard their motivation in engaging themselves to group and societal issues around them because of a gap that exists between efforts and rewards. It is therefore imperative that any aim of developing policy addressing women, there exists a need to significantly consider overcoming gender inequality so that women will have power alongside men to influence their society.

References

- Boserup, Ester (1970), *Women's Role in Economic Development,* St. Martins Press, New York.
- Egonmwan, J.A. (1991), *Public Policy Analysis: Concepts and Applications*, S.M.O Aka and Brothers Press, Benin City.
- Faleye, G.O. (1999), *Women and Accountability: A case study of the Family support,* Kogan Press Ltd., London.

- Morgen, S. and Bookman, A. (1988), "Rethinking Women and Politics: An Introductory Essay" in *Women and the Politics of Empowerment*, Temple University Press, Philadelphia, USA.
- Ostrom. Vincent (1974), The intellectual crisis is American public Administration, The University of Alabama press, Alabama.
- World Bank (2003), "What is Empowerment? World Bank Poverty Net", www.worldbank.org/poverty/empowerment.

Part – V Small and Medium Enterprises: Challenges and Opportunities

Part – V Small and Medium Enterprises: Challenges and Opportunities

19

Small and Medium Enterprises in India under Globalisation: Challenges and Opportunities

M. Sabesh Manikandan

Abstract

Global economic activity recorded robust growth in the first-half of 2004, before encountering some slackening of pace in the second-half of the year and in the first half of 2005. Global growth reached a 28 year peak in 2004, and world trade volumes as well as net capital flows to developing economies returned to 1997 (pre-east Asian crisis) levels. Indian economy recorded one of the highest growth rates in the world in 2004-05, despite some setbacks arising from insufficient monsoon and sporadic supply side pressures on inflation. Macro economic performance during the period was marked by an improvement investment climate and pick-up in the industry and services, emergence of buoyant exports as a driver of demand in a large spectrum in industries; a modest consolidation in the fiscal position; a successful management of liquidity in the backdrop of continuing capital flows; a health investor confidence, and finally, foreign exchange reserves to the tune of US $141.5 billion at the end of March 2005. Industrial globalisation refers to an evolving pattern of cross-border enterprises activities. These can include international investment, trade, strategic alliances for product development, production sourcing, and marketing. International activities enable firms to enter into new markets, to exploit their technological and organisational advantages, and to reduce business costs and risks. At this juncture it is pertinent to mention that globalisation of economic activity affects SMEs mainly in two ways. For some businesses, it opens up new opportunities for outward expansion and growth; for a much larger group of SMEs, inward globalisation poses new competitive challenges and threats from abroad. In this regard, the present paper made an attempt to analyse the development of the SMEs in India.

Introduction

Small and Medium Enterprises (SMEs) occupy an important and strategic place in economic growth and equitable development in all countries, which constitutes as high as 90 per cent of enterprises in most countries worldwide. SMEs are the driving force behind a large number of innovations and contribute to the growth of the national economy through employment creation, investments and exports. Its contribution to the poverty reduction and wider distribution of wealth in developing economies cannot be underrated. India is one of the fastest developing countries in the world. The SMEs occupy a place of strategic importance in the Indian economy as well. Furthermore, it accounts for around 95 per cent of the industrial units, 40 per cent of the value added in the manufacturing sector output and 33 per cent of exports, provides the direct employment to 26 million persons in around 3.5 million registered SSI units and contributes to about 7 per cent of GDP in 2002-03 during globalisation.

Industrial globalisation refers to an evolving pattern of cross–border enterprise activities. These can include international investment, trade, and strategic alliances for product development, production, sourcing, and marketing. International activities enable firms to enter into new markets, to exploit their technological and organizational advantages, and to reduce business costs and risks. Now it is pertinent to mention that globalisation of economic activity affects SMEs mainly in two ways. For some businesses, it opens up new opportunities for outward expansion and growth; for a much larger group of SMEs, inward globalisation poses new competitive challenges and threats from abroad. In this regard, this chapter attempts to analyse the current opportunities and challenges in the development of the SMEs in India.

Operational Definition of SMEs

The basic definition of SMEs differs widely across countries. For instance, SMEs are defined differently across the world in terms of employment, assets, shareholders' funds, sales and even paid up cappital (Table 1). Thus, depending on the criterion selected, the same firm may be classified as "small" under one criterion and as "medium" under another criteria. As such, broad comparisons of SMEs across different countries may not be entirely appropriate because of the varied operational definitions employed. In highlighting these differences, it must be noted that the definitions adopted by countries do not in practice fundamentally affect the important issues facing and surrounding SMEs. Although the definitions vary, they have one thing in common that the vast majority of SMEs are relatively small and most SMEs employs less than 100 people. This permits broad comparisons across economists despite internal differences among them.

As there is no uniform definition of a SMEs in the global economy, different countries have defined SMEs in different ways. In Japan, an SME in the manufacturing sector is defined

Table 1: Definition of SMEs in Selected Countries

S. No.	*Country/ Region*	*Number of Employees*	*Other conditions*	*Source*
1	Argentina	Up to 300	Annual Sales: Up to US$ 18 millions Productive Assets Up to US$ 10 millions	Ministerio de Economia Resolution (2003)
2	Australia	< 500 (small: up to 100)	-	Australian Bureau of Statistics (2003)
3	Chile	< 200 (micro: less than 10)	Annual Sales : Up to 50,000 UF (about US $ 1.6 millions Micro: Less than 2.400 UF	General Definition (No Standard Definition) 2003
4	China	101–500 persons for Medium and 50–100 persons for small enterprises	-	REPSE Project (2005)

(Contd.)

(Contd. Table 1)

S. No.	Country/ Region	Number of Employees	Other conditions	Source
6	Italy	Up to 500 (small: 11-50, artigiano: less than 10)	Capital: less than lire 3 billions	Government Law (2003)
7	Japan	Up to 300	Capital: up to ¥100 millions	Small medium Enterprises Basic Law (2003)
8	Korea	Up to 300	-	Small and Medium Industry Promotion Corporation (2003)
9	Malaysia	<150 person	-	REPSE Project (2005)
10	Mexico	Up to 250 (micro: less than 15)	Annual sales Subject to the classification of micro, small and Medium	Government Circular (2003)

(Contd.)

(Contd. Table 1)

S. No.	Country/ Region	Number of Employees	Other conditions	Source
11	Philippines	Up to 199 (small: less than 100 and Cottage: less than 10)	Capital $287.9 to $1.15 million ($0 to $28.8 and 28.8 t o287.9 thousands for cottage and small industry respectively)	REPSE Project (2005)
12	Singapore	< 200 person (100 for Manufacturing)	Capital: Less than $ 0.8 million	REPSE project (2005)
13	Thailand	<200 persons (less than 50 for small)	Capital: Less than $4.67 millions (less than $1.17 millions for small enterprises)	REPSE Project (2005)
14	U.S.A	Up to 500	-	U.S. Small Business Administration (2003)
15	Vietnam	< 200 persons (less than 30 per sons for small enterprises)	Capital: Less than $260 thousand (less than $65 thousand fro small enterprises)	REPSE Project (2005)

in terms of upper limit of paid-up capital of 300 million Yen or 300 employees (Small & Medium Enterprise Agency 2004). In Korea, SMEs are defined as firms, which are independently owned and employ less than 300 persons in the manufacturing, mining, transportation, and construction sectors. In the European Union, SMEs are defined in terms of employment and turnover/balance sheet total. To classify the SMEs, an enterprise must satisfy the criteria for the number of employees and one of the two financial criteria, that is, either the turnover total or the balance sheet total. In addition, it must be independent.

SMEs in the Context of Indian Economy

In India, industries are segmented into 'factory sector' large scale units, small-scale units; village and small industries (VSI), cover a wide range of units that differ from one another in terms of nature of products manufactured, techniques used, scale of production, location, etc., The VSI sector comprises of (a) modern small–scale industries; and b) traditional industries. Small – scale industries (both factory and non- factory sector) and power loom units are covered under modern small-scale industries.

The office of the Development Commission, Small Industries Development Organization (SIDO), prepares estimates of annual by registered Small Scale Industries (SSI) which takes into account that the residual industrial units are not covered by any assistance programme of the sector-specific statutory bodies, viz., handicrafts, handlooms, sericulture, coir etc.,. Some of the units under Khadi and Village Industries Commission (KVIC) are registered with the State Directorate of Industries, as SIDO units.

Another prominent categorisation is based on level of organization; the classification of units in the organised and unorganised sectors is based on the criteria of employment, in combination with use / non–use of electricity. The units in the factory sector, which registered under the Factories Act, 1948, are termed as organised sector whereas the segment of SSI sector units, not covered under the Factories Act, 1948, are treated as the unorganised sector. In addition to that, such units are also classified based on work force employed in terms of units- less than 20 workers (if power is not used) or less than 10 workers (if the unit is using power). The crucial categories which provide comprehensive overview of the industrial sector of India are (i) the Directory Manufacturing Establishments (DME) -Employing less than ten, but more than five workers, of whom at least one is hired; (ii) non-Directory manufacturing Establishments (NDME) - employing between one and five workers, of whom at least one is hired; and Own-Account Enterprises (OAE) not employing any paid workers.

In addition to this statistical definition, SMEs have been also defined on the basis of time and the administrative angle as well. Under this circumstance, the present definitions are as follows:

Small Scale Industrial Undertakings: The industrial undertakings with investment in fixed assets (in plant and machinery), whether held on ownership terms or lease, or on hire purchase basis, and which do not exceed Rs. 10 millions.

Ancillary Industrial undertakings: Industrial undertakings which are engaged in, or proposed to be engaged in, the manufacture or production, rendering of services, supplies, or renders or proposes to supply or render not less than 50 per cent of its production or services, (as the case may be) to one or more other industrial undertakings, and whose investment in fixed assets in plant and machinery, whether held on ownership terms or on lease, or on hire – purchase, do not exceed Rs. 10 millions.

Tiny enterprises: Those having investment limit in plant and machinery upto Rs. 2.5 millions irrespective of location of the unit.

***Women Enterprises*:** Small-scale industrial units/ industry-related services or business enterprises managed by one or more women entrepreneurs in proprietary concerns, or in which she / they individually or jointly have a share capital of not less than 51 per cent as partners / shareholders/ directors of a private limited company members of cooperative society.

Small-scale Service and Business (industry-related) Enterprises (SSBE): industry-related service/business enterprises with investment up to Rs. 1 millions in fixed assets, (excluding land an building) are called Small Scale Service/ Business Enterprises (SSBEs), (subject to the condition that the unit is not vowed, controlled or is subsidiary of any other industrial undertaking)

Contributions of SMEs to Indian Economy

In India, about 3 million SMEs account for 50 per cent industrial output and 42 per cent of India's total export. They constitute the most important employment generating sector and an effective tool for balanced regional development. They account for 50 per cent of private sector employment and 30-40 per cent of value addition in manufacturing. Over the years, the SSI sector in India has continued to remain an important sector of the economy with its noteworthy contribution to the gross domestic product, industrial production, employment generation and exports. As per the Third All India Census of SSIs (2001-02), there were 10.52 million SSI units in the country, of which 1.37 were registered and 9.15 unregistered units. For the year that ended in March 2004, the said number increased to 11.52 million, providing employment to 27.40 million persons and contributing an output of over Rs.3,480 billion in 2004.

Performance of SSIs in India

The numbers of small-scale units have grown from 18.20 lakhs in 1990-91 to 35.20 lakhs in 2002-03 (Fig.1). During the same period of 13 years, employment has grown from 15.83 million to 26.01 million. Production per employee has increased from Rs. 54 thousands to Rs. 81 thousands (Fig. 2).

The average annual growth rate of employment in the small-scale sector for the period 1995-96 to 1999-2000 works out to be 2.97 per cent, that of the production per employee to be 3.94 per cent (Fig. 3). Whereas the growth rate of employment is commendable and strengthens the belief that the absorption of surplus labour can really take place in the small-scale sector, the growth rate of 3.94 per cent exaggerates the achievement since figures of production are at current prices and thus they conceal the inflationary rise in production per employee. At 1993-94 prices, production per employee of the small-scale sector grew from Rs. 54 thousand in 1994-95 to Rs. 81 thousands in 2002-03, giving and annual average growth of 3.17 per cent. However, for the 3-years price (2000-01 to 2002-03), employment of the small-scale sector further increased from 32.30 to 35.20 – increasing at an average growth rate of 2.85 per cent (Fig. 1) per year.

Export Performance of the SSIs in India

The substantial increase in exports were observed in the case of ready-made garments, canned and processed fish, leather sandals and chappals, food products, hosiery and marine products, etc. The value of exports increased to Rs. 9,664 crores in 1990-91 to a record high figure of Rs. 86,013 crores in 2002-03. A very significant feature of exports from the small-scale sector is their share in non-traditional exports. The share of exports from the small-scale sector representing about 34.29 per cent of total exports in 2000-01 decreased to 33.71 per cent in 2002-03 at -0.57 per cent of annual growth rate (Fig. 4).

The global economic activity recorded robust growth in the first-half of 2004, before encountering some slackening of pace in the second half of the year and in the first half of 2005. Global growth reached a 28-year peak in 2004, and world trade volumes as well as net capital flows to developing economies returned to 1997 (pre–east Asian crisis) levels.

Table 2: Performance of SSIs in India

Year	*No. of Units (lakh nos.)*	*Employment (million)*	*Production Per employee (Rs.'000s at 1993-94 prices)*	*SSI exports (Rs. In Crores)*	*Total Export (Rs. In Crores)*	*SSI share in Export*
1990-91	18.20	15.83	54.00	9664.00	32557.63	29.68
1991-92	19.50	16.60	53.00	13883.00	44041.81	31.52
1992-93	20.80	17.48	53.00	17784.00	53688.25	33.12
1993-94	22.50	18.26	54.00	25307.00	69751.39	36.28
1994-95	23.90	19.14	57.00	29068.00	82674.11	35.16
1995-96	25.70	19.79	61.00	36470.00	106353.34	34.29
1996-97	27.20	20.59	66.00	39248.00	118817.08	33.03
1997-98	28.60	21.32	69.00	44442.00	130100.64	34.16
1998-99	30.10	22.06	71.00	48979.00	139753.14	35.05

(Contd.)

(Contd. Table 2)

Year	*No. of Units (lakh nos.)*	*Employment (million)*	*Production Per employee (Rs.'000s at 1993-94 prices)*	*SSI exports (Rs. In Crores)*	*Total Export (Rs. In Crores)*	*SSI share in Export*
1999-00	31.20	22.91	74.00	54200.00	159561.39	33.97
2000-01	32.30	23.91	77.00	69797.00	203571.01	34.29
2001-02	33.72	24.91	79.00	71244.00	209017.97	34.09
2002-03	35.20	26.01	81.00	86013.00	255137.28	33.71
Average annual Growth Rate						
1990-91 to 1994-95	3.23	3.87	1.09	24.64	20.49	3.45
1995-96 to 1999-00	3.26	2.97	3.94	8.25	8.45	-0.19
2000-01 to 2002-03	2.70	2.85	1.70	7.21	7.82	-0.57

Fig. 1.
No. of SSI units (in lakhs)

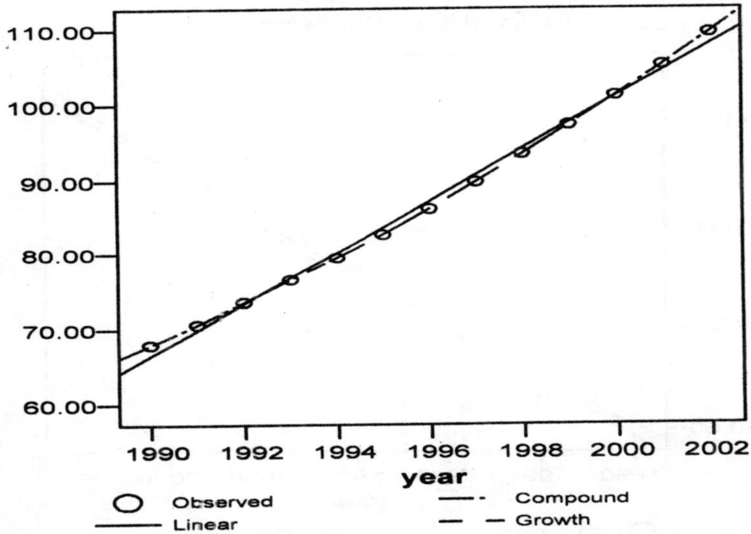

Fig. 2.
Employment Generated through SSI sectors (inlakhs)

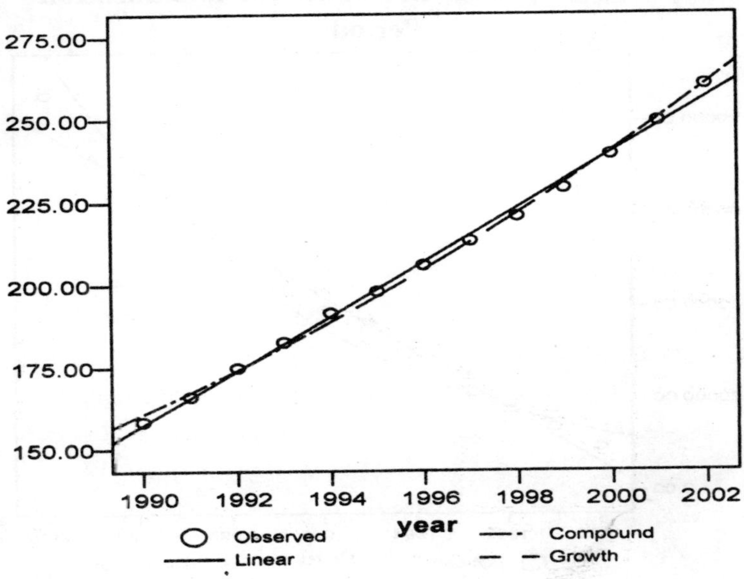

Fig. 3.
Production per employee
(in Rs. '000 at 1993-94 prices)

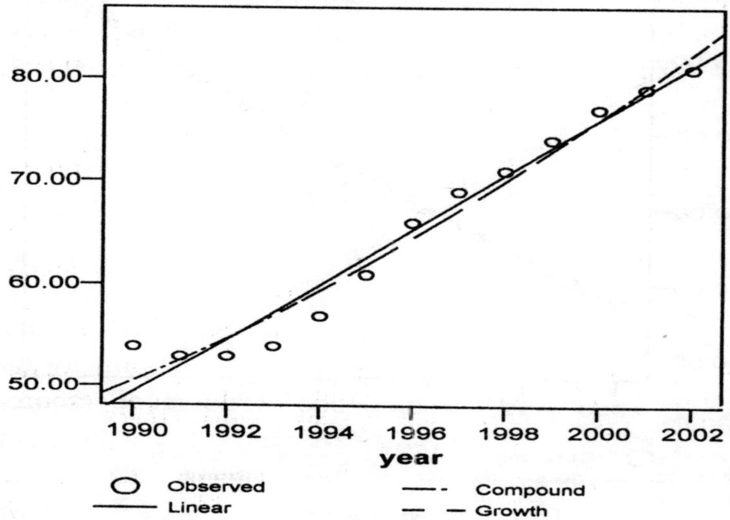

Fig. 4.
Export of the SSI sector under the Globalisation Period

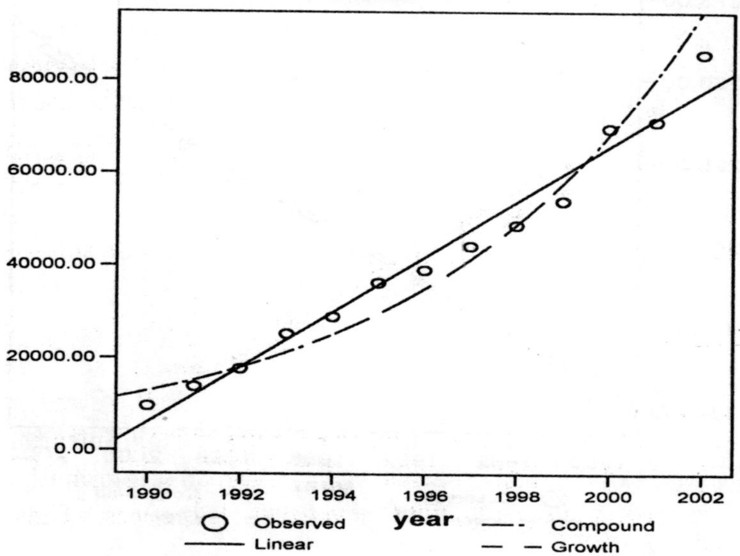

SMEs under Globalisation

Globalisation is usually seen as the conversion of the world into a single economic space, one macro-economy, or perhaps mega-economy, and as a result, into a single seamless society and culture (Sutcliffe 1998). Globalisation as the process of continuing integration of the countries in the world – is strongly underway in all parts of the globe. While the movement of goods, services, ideas, capital and technology across national borders is not a new phenomenon, its process since the past decade marks a qualitative break with the past. Globalisation has exposed national economies to much more intense competition than ever before (Mrak, 2000). This process is characterised by national governments across the world moving towards more open and market-oriented regimes, with greater reliance on private business and less direction of resource allocation. Protective barriers are being lowered, restrictions to Foreign Direct Investment (FDI) removed, and the private sector allowed into areas previously reserved for public enterprises (Lall 1995). During 1990-2003, the number of countries that have introduced changes in their investment regimes has more or less steadily increased from 35 in 1991 to 82 in 2003 and the number of regulatory changes introduced favouring FDI increased from 80 in 1991 to 220 in 2003 (UNCTAD 2001 & 2004). As a result, there was a remarkable increase in FDI inflows: it increased from US $209 billion in 1990 to US $ 560 billion in 2003 (UNCTAD 2001 & 2004). Of course, in the last three years, there has been a consistent decline in global FDI inflows, which was caused by economic decline in developed countries, particularly the US, Latin American and Caribbean countries (UNCTAD, 2004). The setting up of the World Trade Organisation in 1995 and the subsequent dilution of tariff and non-tariff barriers have given a fillip to the growth of international trade. The Information and Communication Technology (ICT) revolution has made the spread of information and communication easy, fast, and virtually costless. These have contributed immensely to the accelerating process of globalisation.

Table 3: Performance of Foreign Direct Investment

(in billion)

Item	*1990*	*2000*	*2001*	*2002*	*2003*
FDI inflows	209	1 388	818	679	560
FDI outflows	243	1 189	722	596	612

As a result, globalisation affects almost every economy, favourably or adversely. Even, the Indian economy is perhaps no exception. The Indian manufacturing industry comprised about 18.20 manufacturing SMEs with an employment of 15.83 million in 1990-91, which increased to about 35.20 with an employment of 2.601 million in 2002-03. By 1990s the share of SMEs' export to the total export gradually increased about 36.28 per cent in 1993-94 but employment increased to 18.26 million. The export performance of the SMEs declined to 33.7 per cent from 35.16 per cent in 1994-95 to the total exports from India. It was registered a high share in 1998-99 as 35.05 per cent.

Opportunities for SMEs under Globalisation in India

Major policy reforms aimed at substantially deregulating industrial sector and liberalising foreign investment as well as technology imports, have been the most significant development in India since 1991. The post-liberalisation era in the Indian economy has enhanced opportunities and challenges for the small industries sector. The following factors strengths coupled with opportunities work in favour of Indian SMEs

(i) High contribution to domestic production

(ii) Significant export earnings

(iii) Low investment requirements

(iv) Operational flexibility

(v) Location wise mobility

(vi) Low intensive imports
(vii) Capacities to develop appropriate indigenous technology
(viii) Import substitution
(ix) Contribution towards defense production
(x) Technology – oriented industries
(xi) Competitiveness in domestic and export markets

By the very nature of their operations, industrial units in the small-scale sector enjoy certain inherent advantages over their larger counterparts. The free economy ushers in accessibility to bigger markets, greater linkages for SMEs with larger companies and marketing outfits, improved manufacturing techniques and processes. Various measures adopted by Government of India, Reserve Bank of India and SIDBI have attempted to alleviate the problems of SME sector. These initiatives coupled with other developments in the economic environment will enhance the prospects of SMEs.

With increasing globalization and entry of multinationals, immense opportunities have been created for outsourcing, sub-contracting, and ancillarisation of the products manufactured by corporates particularly in non-core sectors like automobiles, engineering and consumer electronics. A vibrant SMEs sector can derive maximum benefit of these developments.

By its less capital intensive and high labour absorption nature, SMEs sector will make significant contributions to employment generation and to rural industrialisation. This sector is ideally suited to build on the strengths of the traditional skills and knowledge, by infusion of technologies, capital, and innovative marketing practices. This is the opportune time to set up projects in the small-scale sector. This expectation is based on an essential feature of the Indian industry and the demand structures. The diversity in production systems and demand structures will ensure long-term co-existence of many layers of demand for consumer products/ technologies/ processes. There will be flourishing and well grounded markets for the same product/ process, differentiated by quality, value added and sophistication. These characteristics of the Indian economy will allow complementary existence for various diverse types of units.

However, the SMEs in India continue to be in technological backwaters vis-à-vis advances in science and technology. They suffer from problems of sub-optimal scales of operations and technological obsolescence, while most of the large companies, even in developing countries, have financial as well as technical capacity to identify technological sources and evaluate alternate technologies for their requirements. Unfortunately, this capacity is conspicuously missing in most of the SMEs. It is these features of SMEs that make them an ideal target for technological upgradation through technological cooperation with larger enterprises, with R&D institutions, academic institutions, and centres of technology development.

As the countries merge into a global village, these SMEs will have to respond accordingly and thus deserve special attention. To enable SMEs to mitigate problems of technological backwardness and enhance their access to new technologies, it is imperative to give them a conducive environment, which in the present context of globalisation, calls for redefining approaches with knowledge (Innovation, Technology, Entrepreneurship, Advancements in ICT) playing a predominant role.

Challenges for SMEs under Globalisation in India

Under the globalization the developing countries look into new approaches to strengthen them effectively by understanding the limitations of SMEs, that are: i) Low Capital base, ii) Concentration of management functions in one / two persons, iii) Inadequate exposure to international environment, iv) Inability to face impact of WTO regime, v) Inadequate R & D and vi) Lack of professionalism. Besides these, the most formidable problem gripping the SMEs has been in accessing technology and maintaining competitiveness. The reasons for the inability of SMEs to identify their technology needs appear to be:

(i) Poor financial situations and low levels of R&D

(ii) Poor adaptability to changing trade trends

(iii) Desire to avoid risk, non-availability of technically trained human resources, emphasis on production and not on production costs

(iv) Lack of management skills

(v) Lack of access to technological information and consultancy services

(vi) Isolation from technology hubs

Under this circumstances the developing countries, including India face lot of threats to compete with international market regime. Of these, some of the problems/ challenges the SMEs facing are as follows:

- Unable to capture market opportunities, which require large production facilities and thus could not achieve economies of scale, homogenous standards and regular supply,
- Having trouble in purchase of inputs such as raw materials, machinery, and equipments, finance, consulting services, new technology, highly skilled labor etc.
- Small size hinders the internalisation of functions such as market research, market intelligence, supply chain, technology innovation, training, and division of labour that impedes productivity,
- Emphasis to preserve narrow profit margins makes the SMEs myopic about the innovative improvements to their product and processes and to capture new markets,
- Unable to compete with big players in terms of product quality, range of products, marketing abilities and cost,
- Absence of a wide range of financing and other services that are available to raise money and sustain the business,
- Absence of infrastructure, quality labour, business acumen and limited options / opportunities to widen the business,

Poor IT and Knowledge infrastructure.

Conclusion

Globalisation has been affecting every economic activity in almost every country across the world. Indian SMEs are no exception. As a result of globalisation and liberalisation, coupled with WTO regime, Indian SMEs have been passing through a transitional period. With slowing down of economy in India and abroad, particularly USA and European Union and enhanced competition from China and a few low cost centers of production from abroad many units have been facing a tough time. Those SMEs who have strong technological base, international business outlook, competitive spirit, and willingness to restructure themselves shall withstand the present challenges and come out with shining colours to make their own contribution to the Indian economy. The performance of SMEs has declined in the Indian economy in terms of number of units, employment, export, and percentage of contribution to the total export, due to the characteriation of the Indian SMEs. To sum up, SMEs are not able to achieve self-sustainable competitiveness and reap the fruits of globalisation for their own growth and the growth of the Indian economy. In order to enable SMEs overcome the above problems, it is imperative to give them a conducive environment, such as i) Formulation of appropriate national policies and programmes; ii) Building up technological capacity; iii) Knowledge flows and technology databases; and iv) R&D and inter-firm linkages.

References

European Commission (2000) "The European Observatory of SMEs"– *Sixth Report*, European Commission, Luxembourg.

Government of India (1992), "Report on the Second All-India Census of Small-Scale Industrial Units," Development Commissioner, Small Scale Industries, Ministry of Small Scale Industries, Govt. of India, New Delhi.

Government of India (1997), "Report of the Expert Committee on Small Enterprises," Ministry of Industry, Government of India, New Delhi.

Government of India (2001), "Reports of the Study Group on Development of Small Enterprises," Planning Commission, Government of India, New Delhi.

Government of India (2004), "Final Results: Third All –India Census of Small-Scale Industries, 2001-2002," Development Commissioner, Small Scale Industries, Government of India, Min. of Small Scale Industries, New Delhi.

Government of India (2005) "The Khadi and Village Industries Commission (Amendment) Bill, 2005," Ministry of ARI, Government of India, New Delhi.

Government of India (2005) "The Small and Medium Enterprises Development Bill, 2005 (As Introduced in Lok Sabha)", Min. of Small-scale Industries and Agro and Rural Industries, Government of India, New Delhi.

ISED (2005), State of Small and Medium Enterprises in India (2005), Cochin : ISED.

Michibradt, A. O and Mary McVay (2004) "Developing Commercial Markets for Business Development Services," ILO, Turin.

Reserve Bank of India (1997), "Globalisation and Small and Medium Enterprises," OECD, Paries.

Reserve Bank of India (2003), "State Frances: A Study of Budgets of 2003-04,RBI, Mumbai.

Reserve Bank of India (2005), "Annual Report-2004-2005,"RBI, Mumbai.

Reserve Bank of India (2005), "Report on Currency and finance-2004-2005,"RBI, Mumbai.

RIS (2003) "World Trade and Development Report-2003," RIS, New Delhi.

The United States Small Business Administration (1996), "The State of Small Business: A Report of the President," USSBA, Washington.

20

Challenges for Small Scale Industries in the Era of Globalisation

Thiripurasundari, K and V.Gurumoorthy

Abstract

In most developing countries, Small and Medium Enterprises (SMEs) constitute the bulk of the industrial base and contribute significantly to their exports as well as to their GDP or GNP. Their contribution to regional development, their complementary role to support the large sector, and as a basis for technological innovations and adaptation are widely acknowledged. SMEs in most countries make up the majority of businesses and account for the highest proportion of employment. SMEs account for a considerable share of industrial enterprises, employment and production and therefore, occupy a place of strategic importance in Indian economy as well. India has nearly three million SMEs, which account for 50 per cent industrial output and 42 per cent of India's total exports. These account for 50 per cent of private sector employment and 30-40 per cent of value addition in manufacturing. They produce a diverse range of producs (about 8000), including consumer items, capital and intermediate goods. SMEs in India constitute more than 80 per cent of the total number of industrial enterprises and form the backbone of industrial development. However, since the early 1990s, SMEs have been exposed to intense competition due to the accelerated process of globalisation and therefore, their survival as well as growth is under strain. Against the above background, this chapter attempts to analyse the challenges faced by the SMEs. The chapter further suggests some measures to face these challenges.

Introduction

In most developing countries, Small and Medium Enterprises (SMEs) constitute the bulk of the industrial base and contribute significantly to their exports as well as to their GDP or GNP. Their contribution to regional development, their complementary role to support the large sector, and as basis for technological innovations and adaptations are widely acknowledged. SMEs, in most counties, make up the majority of businesses and account for the highest proportion of employment. SMEs account for a considerable share of industrial enterprises, employment and production and therefore, occupy a place of strategic importance in Indian economy as well. India has nearly three million SMEs, which account for almost 50 per cent of Industrial output and 42 per cent of India's total exports. These account for 50 per cent of private sector employment and 30-40 per cent of value addition in manufacturing. It produces a diverse range of products (about 8000 items produced), including consumer items, capital and intermediate goods. SMEs in India constitute more than 80 per cent of the total number of industrial enterprises and form the backbone of industrial development. However, since the early 1990s, SMEs have been exposed to intense competition due to the accelerated process of globalisation and therefore, their survival as well as growth is under strain.

The government of India announced the policy towards small sector on 6th August 1991. The main thrust of the policy is on liberalisation, privatisation and globalisation. With the result, the small scale units have to compete with large scale units and multinationals manufacturing similar products. Globalisation has become a big blow to the SSI units, which have already been struggling to exist. The transition from an era of protection to an era of globalisation has posed threats and also challenges for the small-scale sectors in India. The threat is to be taken as a challenge and it must be converted into an opportunity for sustained development making major contribution to domestic output, employment, better distribution of income and more even distribution of industries in urban and rural areas. Hence, this chapter attempts to analyse the challenges faced by the SMEs in the era of globalisation. Further, this chapter suggests some measures to face these challenges.

Research in six developing countries shows that, collectively small establishments account for most industrial employment. Particularly in less developed countries (LDCs), much manufacturing employment is found in rural areas. Japan is the outstanding example of those who have achieved rapid industrialisation through the small and medium industries.

Like wise Taiwan has produced 90 per cent of its industrial output through small scale industries. SSIs sector plays a pivotal role in the Indian economy in terms of employment since independence inspite of stiff competition faced by them from large sectors. It is an accepted truth that the comprehensive balanced growth mainly depends upon two major sectors, such as, Agriculture and Industry. In the industrial sector, the SSIs constitutes a very important segment. The predominance of SSIs sector in the Indian economy is very clear, when we look to its contribution to different aspects of the economy – such as – total output, export and employment.

According to the CSO, manufacturing Enterprises Survey (1994-95), one fifth of the SSI units (19.8%) are engaged in wood products, 16.5 per cent in food products and 15.1 per cent in repair services. These three industries account for 51.4 per cent of the total number of SSI units. Cotton textiles, hosiery, chemical and garments are another major group accounting for 13.1 per cent, followed by beverages and tobacco products for 9.8 per cent. Besides this SSI units are engaged in wool, silk and synthetic fibre, jute textiles, paper products and printing

Table -1: Industry wise Distribution in SSI units (1994-95)

S.No	*Industries Type*	*Enterprises*	*% to total*
1.	Wood products	28.73	19.8
2.	Food products	23.94	16.5
3.	Repair services	21.87	15.1
4.	Beverage & Tobacco products	14.27	9.8
5.	Misc. manufacturing industries	11.59	8.0
6.	Hosiery & garments	10.94	7.5
7.	Cotton textiles	8.19	.5.6
8.	Others	28.57	11.8
	Total	**145.04**	**100.0**

Source: Banking Finance 19(7) July 2006: 5.

Table -2: Growth pattern of SSIs (Before liberalisation 1980-81 to 1990-91)

Year	*No. of units (No. in Lakhs)*	*Production (Rs. in crores)*	*Employment (No. in lakhs)*	*Export (Rs. in crores)*
1980-81	8.74	28060	71.0	1643
1981-82	9.62	32600	75.0	2071
1982-83	10.59	35000	79.0	2045
1983-84	11.55	41620	84.15	2164
1984-85	12.40	50520	90.0	2541
1985-86	13.53	61228	96.0	2769
1986-87	14.62	72250	101.40	3643
1987-88	15.83	87300	107.0	4372
1988-89	17.12	106400	113.0	5489
1989-90	18.23	132320	119.60	7625
1990-91	19.48	155340	125.30	9664

and leather products, metal products, machinery (electrical and non-electrical) and transport equipment etc.

Table 3: Growth Pattern of SSIs (After liberalisation 1991-92 to 2002-03)

Year	*No. of units (No. in Lakhs)*	*Production (Rs. in crores)*	*Employment (No. in lakhs)*	*Export (Rs. in crores)*
1991-92	20.82	178699	129.80	13883
1992-93	22.86	209300	134.06	17785
1993-94	23.81	241678	139.38	25307
1994-95	25.71	293990	146.56	29068
1995-96	27.24	356213	152.61	36470
1996-97	28.57	412636	160.0	39249
1997-98	30.14	465171	167.20	44437
1998-99	31.21	527515	171.58	49481
1999-00	32.25	578470	177.30	54200
2000-01	33.7	639024	185.64	6979
2001-02	34.64	690522	192.23	71244
2002-03	35.1	824363	200.79	86103

Source: Southern Economist, 45(7) August1, 2006: 12.

Table 2 shows that the changes took place from 1991-92 to 2002-03 in number of units, production, employment and exports, the variation appear to be positive. The rate of growth is not as required in certain aspects. The tables throw a clear light on the pre and post liberalisation periods. In the post liberalisation period, the decline in the different aspect of contribution of SSI to the economy is very sharp. The condition of the SSI sector is mainly due to the problems faced by SSIs in the present situation.

Globalisation and Performance of SSI

The overall performance and contribution of small scale industry to the Indian economy is generally described in terms of its absolute growth in units, employment, production and exports. Thus, the growth performance of small-scale industries can be evaluated by comparing the growth rates of units, employment, output and exports of small industry before liberalisation with that of after liberalisation.

Among other things, the main objective of reforms was to place India on a high growth path. In particular industrial liberalisation and globalisation unleashed hopes of healthy and competitive industrial expansion, but contrary to general expectations of business and industry, the post-reforms industrial performance has not been robust; atleast in quantitative terms. Indeed during the pre-reform period spanning over a decade (1981-92) industry scored an average growth rate of 6.3 per cent per annum. In the post-reform period of over nine years (1992-2001), the average growth rate has just been marginally higher at 6.5 per cent. In short, the general perception is that reforms have not provided any impetus to the growth momentum of Indian industry particularly SSIs.

Challenges of SSIs

Small enterprises in India, with their dynamism, flexibility and innovative drive are increasingly focusing on improved production methods, penetrative marketing strategies and modern scientific management capabilities to sustain and strengthen their operations. They are poised for global partnership and have the potential to absorb latest technologies in diverse industrial fields. They deserve special attention as they play a pivotal role in a country's socio-economic development. The problems faced by the SMEs, particularly in accessing technology and maintaining competitiveness have been formidable. The reasons for the inability of SMES to identify their technology needs are:

- Poor financial situations and low levels of R&D;
- Poor adaptability to changing trade trends.
- Desire to avoid risk;
- Non-availability of technically trained human resources;
- Emphasis on production and not on production costs;
- Lack of management skills;

- Lack of access to technological information and consultancy services;
- Isolation from technology hubs;

To enable SMEs to mitigate the above problems and enhance their access to new technologies for increasing their competitiveness in the international market, it is imperative to give them a conducive environment which includes:

- Formulation of appropriate national policies and programmes;
- Building up technological capacity;
- Knowledge flows and technology databases;
- R&D and inter-firm linkages.

Formulation of Policies and Programmes

Conducive policy environment is a pre-requisite. Major policy reforms aimed at substantially deregulating industrial sector and liberalising foreign investment as well as technology imports, have been the most significant developments since 1991. The Post-liberalisation era in the Indian economy has enhanced opportunities and challenges for the small industries sector. The ultimate objective of promotional policies is to enhance SMEs capacity to grow so that they become viable units. The national policies and programmes may be oriented to:

- Setting up Industrial Districts / technology parks / clusters to promote sourcing of new technology, innovation and effective transfer;
- Organising local level information services, data banks and seminars in collaboration with professional bodies;
- Sending experts to SMEs to assist them with the introduction of new technologies;
- Establishing training centres for human resource development for SMEs;
- Establishing business centres
- Promoting strategic alliances with R&D institutions, universities and other enterprises at national, regional and international levels.

This calls for promoting indigenous industrialisation with emphasis on self reliance, through use and creation of local resources and at the same time adoption, absorption and diffusion of the imported technologies. This strategy involves an expanded role of SMEs, which can alleviate high levels of unemployment and income inequality.

Building up Technological Capacity

Access to advanced technologies and assistance in its adoption is crucial to buildup Indigenous Technological Capacity (ITC) to face international competition. In the present scenario of globalisation, knowledge of and access to latest advances hold the key to international competition. In this venture the industrial sectors, which are able to identify their technology needs and adopt in time, will benefit the most. In India, the traditional sector which has shown this remarkable ability to adapt to technological change is leather. Central Leather Research Institute (CLRI), Chennai, has successfully introduced microprocessor control in tannery wet operations at industrial level and promoted cleaner processing, quality consistency and international equivalence. Anticipating the impact potential of computer – aided techniques in foot-wear and garment design, CLRI alerted and prepared the industry so well that CAD is today widely employed by export manufacturers of footwear and garments.

Some of the notable examples are design and development of 10 TPD modern oil expeller, sugarcane harvester, electric cloth cutting machine, high speed overlock machine, leather shaving machine, flat bed and post bed leather sewing machines, button hole attachment for domestic sewing machine, wool knitting machine, friction welding machine, etc. The technologies developed by Mechanical Engineering Research and Development Organisation (MERADO) have benefited not only the SMEs in the state, but also in other states like West Bengal, Haryana and UP. It also caters to major testing facilities for the SMEs in Ludhiana.

However, in the present scenario of globalisation and liberalisation, stronger linkages still need to be promoted not only between technology support institutions and SMEs, but also between SMEs for horizontal transfer of technologies. In this direction human resource development in the technology support institution is one area of crucial importance, which needs attention. Similarly, other SMEs sectors, which need to be technologically upgraded are electrical and electronics, light engineering, food processing, building materials, chemicals, drugs and pharmaceutical, ceramics and telecommunication. In this direction, a number of efforts are being made by the Indian government. For example, the National Small Industries Corporation (NSIC) has pioneered several schemes for the growth and development of the small scale sector. In the initial stages of development of the small-scale industries after independence, it was the innovative and novel schemes of the NSIC such as government purchase, hire purchase, development of prototypes, technical training, etc. which led to the establishment of new enterprises, development of appropriate manufacturing technologies and creation of a strong first generation entrepreneurial base. These schemes of the corporation acted as a catalyst for this sector. It has helped the small units in identification, adoption, absorption and transfer of technology, entrepreneurial and technical training, common production facilities, marketing and financial support.

With the successful implementation of NSIC schemes, a number of financial institutions and banks have also come forward to assist this sector, thus creating an important constituent of the Indian economy. Further, Council of Scientific and Industrial Research (CSIR) is also an important technology generator in the country and has a lot of S&T inputs to offer to the small-scale sector. To further invigorate this sector, the NSIC, CSIR and Asia and Pacific Center for Transfer of Technology (APCTT) have pooled their resources and have formed a strategic alliance to help upgrade technology in the small-scale sector.

Knowledge Flows and Technology Databases

The SMEs should have capabilities for generating, accessing and diffusing knowledge and also have openness to external sources of knowledge, including new technology databases. For this, efficient national information services and networks are essential. In developing countries, most of the SMEs do not have access to well-researched technology databases that provide information pro-actively on a regular basis. The information usually remains in the banks untapped, while the purveyors of the information wait for the targeted beneficiaries to request it. In India, an important technology information databank is the National Research and Development Corporation (NRDC), which serves as an important link between research and SMEs. NRDC acquires, evaluates, develops and transfers all worth while technologies generated at the various national laboratories.

The technologies available with NRDC for commercial exploitation cover a wide range of products, namely drugs and pharmaceuticals, pesticides and herbicides, plasticisers, resins, electro-chemical products, metals, paints and varnishes, leather chemicals and auxiliaries, electrical and electronic goods, building materials, etc. It provides a comprehensive international patent search and also has a few renowned international databases on-line for carrying out the search. Through the Ministry of Science and Technology, the Government of India has also established information centres in specific areas for assisting academic institutions and industry under the scheme called National Information System for Science and Technology (NISSAT). There are information banks on food, leather, drugs and pharmaceutical, machine tools and aeronautics. SME units can approach them for assistance, especially with regard to the latest developments in the field of technology.

R&D and Inter-firm Linkages

At present, there are 2900 R&D institutions in India, of which 1350 are in the private sector. Out of these, over 1250 are in house R&D units, employing over 45,000 scientific and technical, personnel and incurring an expenditure of the order of seven billion rupees per annum.

However, the small scale sector is largely devoid of such facilities and is mainly supported by public R&D for acquisition of new technologies. In general ,SMEs are encouraged to invest in localised technological development. As most SMEs lack financial resources, the best way is to enter into linkages and partnerships with other enterprises, academia and R&D institutions.

Learning by interaction' is an important feature of technological upgradation and can only happen when firms cooperate and interact through strategic alliances and other forms of linkages. For this to happen, the most viable systems are the clusters, which offer good opportunities for interaction and industrial upgrading. The common feature of these new forms lies in the sharing of knowledge in technological capabilities and in co-operative intentions, which may or may not include government incentives. The diverse forms of alliances include:

- Long-term multi-project partnerships that pool the production, research and marketing divisions in a single country or across several countries to accomplish strategic goals;
- Flexible networking mechanisms that promote research consortia at the pre competitive and development phases. Such partnerships have technical education, training and retraining, innovation and sustainability as inherent features.

Networking /Industrial Districts/ Clusters

The approach encompassed by the concept of industrial districts /technology parks/ clusters, offers new insights into the potential role of SMEs in enhancing their access to new technology. Sector specific and geographically bound clusters seem to be a common phenomenon for small scale manufacturing in developing countries. Most of them have been very successful, which are primarily based on tacit and accumulated knowledge through learning by doing and learning by interaction. For example, in India there have been a large number of 'spatial clusters' of small firms engaged in specialised industries such as: locks in Aligarh, leather footwear in Agra and Kanpur; cotton polishing in Kolkota and Delhi; blankets in Panipat; power looms at Bhiwadi; diamond polishing in Surat. Space-bound `dense clusters', related to a specialized industry are even more pronounced in Punjab with woolen garments, bicycle and bicycle parts, sewing machine parts and machine tools in Ludhiana; printing and printing goods, water pipes and bathroom fixtures in Jallandhar; foundries in Batala ,etc. Lundhiana clusters make 95 per cent of the country's woollen knitwear: 85 per cent of the sewing machines and 60 per cent of the bicycle and bicycle parts.

The knitwear clusters in Tiruppur, Tamil Nadu is responsible for 85 per cent of Indian market and its export earnings have expanded from US$25 Million in 19?6 to US $636 Million in 1997. What is interesting about the Tiruppur cluster is that it is organised in a web of small work places through which the entire town works like a living industrial organisation.

Characteristics of a successful industrial district mentioned by various researchers are: inter firm co-operation, co-operation blended with competition, the importance of local value systems, flexibility and innovative capacity, geographic proximity, sectoral specialisation, the provisions of a local pool of skilled labour and the presence of a large number of firms. It also includes willingness to work together to resolve potential clashes of interest, wide-spread entrepreneurial spirit and ability, promotion of a social compromise, etc.

The institutional capacity of industrial districts is to learn, adjust and improve their economic performance continuously. The above characteristics, more or less, are inherent in the

Indian clusters. These clusters form a kind of knowledge network which works like a honey beehive, where there is constant sharing of knowledge and the benefits. It links not only people, but both formal and informal science, i.e, tacit knowledge. The innovative atmosphere and entrepreneurial dynamism are part of the secret of success of these districts.

Role of Financial Institutions

The availability of financial resources on affordable terms and in a non-bureaucratic manner is yet another problem the SMEs confront, hindering access to new technologies. It is imperative, therefore, to influence the existing financial networks and, if need be, to set-up a separate mechanism for funding smaller enterprises, especially those categorised as micro enterprises. One of the important ways to promote access to new technologies among SMEs in developing countries is to provide venture capital, which in a way helps in indigenous development of technologies. Financial institutions such as Industrial Development Bank of India (IDBI), Industrial Credit and Investment Corporation of India (ICICI), Industrial Finance Corporation of India (IFCI), and other banks are providing assistance for commercialisation of indigenously developed technologies and adoption of imported technologies for wider domestic applications through venture capital companies. A large number of small innovations are also being supported by SRISTI venture capital fund.

One of the main factors of the success of knit wear cluster at Tiruppur is the state intervention in the supply of short term credit to facilitate networked production. In order to create a business environment, with adoption and assimilation of new technologies that are resource efficient and have little waste output, the supportive infrastructure also needs to be strengthened in many developing countries. There is a need for such institutions to deal exclusively with the myriad problems that SMEs face in their day –to-day work. In India Department of Scientific and Industrial Research (DSIR)is one such institution. It is engaged in technology promotion, development, utilisation and transfer activities. The department has launched several initiatives to encourage increased utilisation of locally available R&D options through its major schemes, viz. Programme Aimed at Technology (SEETOT). Technology Bureau for Small Enterprises a result of collaboration between APCTT and Small Industries Development Bank of India (SIDBI), represents under one roof, synergy of technology and finance, which facilitates capability building and identifying market channels.

Conclusions

In conclusion, any effective technological capacity-building exercise to enhance competitiveness of SMEs will have to address issues that can be broadly classified under the generic heads of a conductive policy frame-work, knowledge acquisition and dissemination, new technology demonstration and networking, and financing and institutional support systems. In each of the above categories, the barriers must be clearly identified and enabling strategies developed so that the technological capacity building process in SMEs becomes meaningful, in terms not only of international trade and business or of the environment, but also of making it responsive to the needs of the people.

Indian small-scale industry faces challenges of globalisation. The issue is of great importance in the post-WTO scenario. Undoubtedly global market offers opportunities for all, but opportunities do not guarantee the desired results. For high performing Asian economies as well as for China, the benefit of globalisation is clearly reflected in the rising ratio of their trade (imports, exports) to GDP, which is currently hovering around 40 to 45 per cent. But in case of India even granting the fact that our trade to GDP ratio has increased in the post-reform period from about 13 per cent of GDP in early

90s to about 20 per cent of GDP at present, but we have a long way to catch up with the level achieved by Asian Tigers.

References

- Best, M.H. (1990), *The New Competition, Institutions of Industrial Restructuring,* Harvard University Press, Cambridge.
- Cooley, M. (1991), *Architect or Bee? The Human price of Technology*, The Hogarth Press, London.
- Juneja, J.S. (1998), Small and Medium Enterprises Challenges and Opportunities, *All India Management Association,* New Delhi.
- Knorringa P and Meyer-Stamer, J. (1998), *New Approaches to Science and Technology and Capacity Building*, UNCTAD, New York.
- Ruddar Datt and KPM Sundaram (2006), *Indian Economy*, S. Chand and Co., Ltd., New Delhi.
- www.icai.org/icaiwot/publications/complimentary/cajournal.sept.05/421-427.pdf.
- http//www.i.a.s.ac.in/currsci/feb10/2001/343.pdf.

Index

A

Advanced Technologies, 339
Africa, 40
Agreement on Agriculture (AOA), 222
Agro and Rural Industry (ies), 47, 78
Agro-Based
  Country, 70
  Industry, 188
All India
  Congress Committee, 74
  Spinners Association (AISA), 74
  Village Industrial Association (AIVA), 74
Amutha Lakshmi Traders, Micro Enterprise, 114
Andhra Pradesh Wind Power Potential, 176
Anganwadi Workers, 270
Animal Husbandry Development, 187
Asia and Pacific Centre for Transfer of Technology (APCTT), 100, 340, 345
Asian Development Bank (ADB), 251
ASSOCHAM, 47
Association for Social Advancement (ASA), Bangladesh, 246
Auxiliary Nurse Midwives, 270

B

Bactojugation Technology, 204
Bamboo
  Basket Weaving Industry, 146
  Consumption Pattern, 144, 145
  Craft, 145
  Industries Characteristics, 144
  Products, 151
  Sector, 144

Sector Micro Enterprise, 146
Banco Solidarion Bolivia, 246
BancoSol, 249
Bangladesh and India, 235
Bank Rakyat Indonesia, 246
Banking System, 238
Basked
Weavers, 142, 144
Weaving Occupation, 146
Biological Diversity, 156
BIS (Bureau of Indian Standard), 227
Brazil and Vietnam, 211
Break Even Output, 197-198
BRI Unit Desa System, 249
BRIC Report, 91
Buffalo Population, 200, 201
Business Opportunities in
Exporting, (BOE), 120
Flowers, 120
Fruits, 120
Vegetables, 120

C

Cannibalism, 267
Cashew
Factories in Kerala, 210
Industry, Highly Profitable, 210
Kernals Exports, 211
Kernals Major Markets, 214
Processing Industries,
Characteristics, 210
Problems, 215
Processing Industry, 208-216
In India, 206-216
Exploitation of Women, 216
Cashew Demand in-, 208
America, 208
Europe, 208
South and Far East Asia and Africa, 208
Cashew Exports to
African Zone, 213
America Zone, 212
Asia, 213
European Zone, 212
South East/Far East, 213
West Asian Zone, 213
West Europe, 212
Centre for Bhartiya Marketing Development (CBMD), 245
Certification, 227
CGAP (Consultation Group to Assist the Poorest), 250, 251
Charity Organizations, 270
Cheap Labour, 113, 118
Chemicals and Pharmaceuticals, 53
Chhatisgarh Study, 285-307
Child Health Ratio, 273
Bihar, 273
Uttar Pradesh, 273
China, 45, 330
and Brazil, 210
and India, 90
Chingleput, 243
CII (Confederation of Indian Industries), 47, 99, 100
Clean Development Mechanism (CDM), 87, 88, 89, 98, 102

Projects, 87, 100
Cleaner Technology, 100, 101
Promotion, 88, 90
Promotion in India, 99
Commercial Imports and Exports, 201
Community Development, 251
Compound Annual Growth Rate (CAGR), 51
Computerization and Automation, 222
Consumer Goods, 28
Contaminated Water Bodies, (CWB), 88, 79
Cooperative
Movement, 228
Societies, 78, 145
Thrift and Credit Societies, 153
Corruption, 306
Cottage
and Traditional Industries, 144
and Village Handicrafts Industries, 144
Industries (CI), 45, 70, 121-140, 151, 209
Cross Border Enterprise Activities, 313

D

Dairy, 187, 188
Business and Trade, 221
Cooperative (s), 231
Marketing Business Organization (DCMBO), 218-232
Marketing Organization, Essential Strategy, 229
Milk Organizations, 221
Credit States, 223
UP, Punjab, Andhra Pradesh, TN, 223
Development, 189
Enterprises India, 189
Farming, 187, 188
Industry, 202, 203, 210
Markets, 222
Producers, 222
Trade and Commerce, 219
Dairying, 187, 199
Dairying in Madurai, 190
Decision Making Process, 237
Defence Production, 44
Degradation of Environment, 88, 89
De-Licensing Policies of Government, 223
Demographic Characteristics of Respondents, 294
Dermatological Problems, 215, 216
Developing
Countries, 42, 70, 89, 155, 227, 228, 237, 290
Economies, 311, 312
Small Scale Industries, 62
Development
And Infrastructure, 95
Commission, 317

Of Communication Strategy, 101
Dindigul
District Spinning Mills, 109
Major Centre of Tamato Production, 150
Distribution Management System, 220
District
Dindigul, 109, 112, 113, 115, 118, 119, 120, 146, 150, 152
Kanyakumari 210
Madurai, 187-199
Medak, 279
Nalgonda, 244
Domestic Economic Reforms, 36
Drugs—Building Materials, 341

E

E-Banking, 254
Economic
Change, 41
Crisis, 63
Development, 42, 60, 61, 219
Empowerment, 167
Environment, 219
Growth, 92, 262
Liberalization, 219, 224
Policies of Nations, 88, 90
Program, 122
Reforms, 264
Economy (ies), 42, 54, 65, 76, 89, 223, 319, 336
Capital Scarce, 28
Developed/Developing Transitional-, 156
Global, 91
Globalized, 57, 123
Household, 237
Indian, 28, 43, 48, 62, 63, 74, 91, 144, 159, 160, 317, 330, 338
International, 94
National, 60, 76, 312
Neo-Classical, 65
Planned, 43, 159
Rural, 70, 72, 223
Tamil Nadu, 27, 35
Urban, 70, 72
Economy's Largest Industry, 110
Educational Qualifications of Respondents, 148
Electro-Medical Equipment, 28
Electronic Control System, 28
Emission Reducing Projects, 89
Employment
Generation, 43, 61, 159
In Small and Medium Enterprises, 49
Of Working Women, 119
Opportunities, 74, 110
Energy Conservation Program, 101
Engineering Goods, 53
Entrepreneurship Development Policies, 285
Environmental
Control, 101

Damage, 88
Impact, 98
Problems, 88, 96, 97, 102, 181, 102
Standard, 103
European
Commission, 158
Union, 224, 317, 330, 355
Union Markets, 227
Exhibitions and Government Melas, 153
Export
Markets, 44
Of Quality Yarn, 118

F

Family Planning, 246
Federation of
All India Small Scale Industries (FASSI), 47
Small and Medium Industries (FOSMI), 47
FICCI (Federation of Indian Chamber of Commerce and Industries), 47
Financial
Crisis, 68
Management Practices, 122
Services, 252
FINCA (Foundation for International Community Assistance), 249
First World War, 41
Five Year Plan (6th), 76
Fixed Price Policy, 115
Food and
Agriculture Organization (FAO), 227
Beverages—Forgings, 53
Social Security, 187
Foreign
Direct Investment (FDI), 36, 57, 171, 325
Performance, 326
Exchange, 43, 110, 144, 159
Exchange Control, 62
Forest Based
Employment, 156, 165
Industry, 78
Forest Protection Committees, (FPC), 166
FTAs (Free Tree Agreements), 56

G

Gandhi, Mahatma, 74
Gandhian Ideology, 122
Gender Division of Labour, 237
Global
Dairy Market, 228
Dairy Trade, 221
Economic Activity, 311
Economic Dynamism, 90
Environmental
Impact, 92
Quality, 92
Markets, 221
Globalization, 40, 41, 56, 87-91, 103, 110, 111, 112, 115, 119, 208-216, 224, 264, 311, 312,

325, 330, 333 334, 339, 340, 346
And Liberalization, 45, 263, 267
And Privatization, 270
And Small and Medium Enterprises, 42, 48
Benefits of-, 109
Challenges of-, 88, 90
Direct Benefits, 113
Era, 113, 332-341
Impacts of-, 200
Of Trade, 225
Globalized Markets Environment, (GME), 218, 222, 226, 227
Government Promotional Framework, 45
Grameen Bank in Bangladesh, 235, 238, 249
Green
House Gases (GHG), 89
Revolution, 188
Ground Water, Over Exploitation of-, 89
Growth
And Resource, 27
Model, 27
Of Employment, 29
Of Employment—Units, 27
Rate of Production and Employment, 27
Gujarat, 174
and Karnataka, 181
Cooperative Milk Marketing Association (AMUL), 226
Gulf Crisis, 63

H

Health and Nutrition Entrepreneurs (HNE), 269, 270, 272, 273, 274-276, 279-283
Training in-, 275
Health Care System, 273
Household Economy, 237

I

Integrated Child Development Scheme (ICDS), 270, 272
ICMAT (International Centre for Advanced Manufacturing Technology), 100
IMF, 225
Immunization, 273, 278
Impact of
Liberalization, Privatization and Globalization, 223
Micricredit, 259
Import
License, 62
Licensing, 41
Of Raw Cashew Nuts, 214, 215
Substitution, 44
Importation of Textile Machinery, 114
Imported Machines, 110
Improved Technology Adoption, 222
Infant Mortality Rate (IMR), 274, 275

Income
- Distribution, 70
- General, 110

India and
- Bangladesh, 239
- China, 98

India's
- Growth, 40

Industrial Production, 94
- Largest Producer of Milk, 201
- Manufacturing Exports, 54
- Small and Medium Enterprises, 42
- Textile Industry, 110
- Textile Industry, Second to China, 111
- Wind Power Generation, 180
- Wind Power Potential, 172

Indian
- Agriculture, 188
- Cashew Kernals, Major Markets, 214
- Companies, 67, 68
- Cooperative Dairying, 223
- Cooperative Organizations, 264
- Council of Small Industries, (ICSI), 47
- Dairy Association (IDA), 226
- in India, 219

Industry, 189
- Sector, 227
- Dairying Enterprise, Features, 189, 190
- Economy, Status of-, 263

Industrialization, 42
- Markets, 36, 67
- Small and Medium Enterprises (SMEs), 45, 54, 326
- Small Scale Industries under Globalization, 87
- Small Scale Industries (SSI), 67, 346
- Spinning and Weaving Industries, 111

Indian Industries, (II), 45, 160, 163
- Agricultural Inputs, 45, 160
- Bio Engineering, 45
- Chemical and Pharmaceuticals, 45, 160
- Computer Softwares, 45
- Electrical and Electronics, 160
- Electro-Medical Equipments, 45
- Electronics, 45
- Engineering, 45
- Food Processing, 45, 160
- Gems and Jewelry, 160
- Leather, 45
- Medical/Surgical Equipment, 160
- Plastic Products, 45
- Sports Goods, 45
- Textile, 45
- Textile and Garments, 160

Indigenous Technology, 44
Industrial Clusters, 113
  Brass Metal Products, 113
  Coir and Coir Products, 113
Iron Scraps, 113
  Leather and Leather Tanneries, 113
  Lock Industry, 113
  Rice Mills, 113
Industrial
  Development, 41, 54, 70, 73, 144, 333
  Districts, 338
  Globalization, 313
  Growth, 48
Infrastructure, 45
  Policies, 159, 287
  Policy Resolution (1956), 74, 76
  Policy Resolutions, 41
  Policy, 41
  Policy, 1956, 28
  Policy, 1980, 76
  Structure, 72
  Units, 88, 114
Industrialization, 60, 73, 96, 102, 334
Industrialized Countries, 89
Industries, 88, 89, 98, 144
  And Commerce, 30
  Forest Based, 145
  Large Scale, 160
  Wood Based, 145
Inflation, 63
Information Technology and Modern Communication (ICT), 222, 325, 328
Information, Communication and Technology (ICT), 58
Infrastructure, 95, 172
  Facilities, 113, 118
Institutional Year of Micro Finance, 249, 253
Insurance Companies, 254
Inter-Group Borrowing, 242
International
  Emission Trading (IET), 89
  Markets, 111
  Year of Micro Credit, 250, 253
Internationalization of Production, Distribution and Marketing, 91

J

Japan, 313
Japan, Korea, Taiwan, Italy and USA, 118
Joint Forest Management Program (JFM), 166
Joint Implementation (JI), 89
Judiciary System, 89

K

Kamusime Memorial Rural Development, 167
Kanyakumari, 172
Kerala, MP, Maharashtra and Andhra Pradesh, 181
Khadi, 77, 78, 81
  Boards, 122

Commission, 74
Program, 74
Yarn, 122
Khadi and Village
Industries (KVI), 48, 74, 81, 84, 122
Boards, 78, 80, 81, 122
Commissions, 74, 78-80, 122, 123, 317
Act, 78
Employment, 84
Industries, Role of NGO, 122
Producers, 140
Products, 121, 139
Programmes, 78
Training and Products/ Sales
Centres, 122
Industries Commission (KVIC), 74
Industry Units, 123
Korea, 317
Kyoto Protocol (KP), 87, 102, 88-90, 98, 100

L

Labour
Intensive Industry, 208
Standards, 92
Landless Labourers, 264
Large Scale Employment, 28
Latin America, 40
Least Developed Countries, 334
Liberalization, 27, 29, 33, 36, 62, 67, 92, 340
And Globalization, 58
Policy (ies), 43, 219
Policy Impact, 223
Privatization Globalization, 334
Liberalized
Economic Framework, 45
Regime, 60
Limited Liability Partnership, 48
Literacy and Nunerary, 246
Low Cost of Labor, 111

M

Macro-Economy, 325
Madurai and Thirumangalam, 187
Mahavir Prasad, Minister for Small Scale Industries, 47
Major Policy Reforms, 338
Malaysia, Small Scale Industries in-, 61
Mandal (s), 243
Samakhya in AP, 240
Mann Deshi Mahila Sah Bank, (Maharashtra), 244
Marine Product, 51, 53
Market Segmentation, 95
Marketing System, 220
Maternal
And Child Health Services, (MCHS), 270, 272, 273
Mortality Rate, 274, 275

Mechanical Engineering
Research and Development
Org. (MERADO), 339
Medicinal Plants Harvesting, 164
Mega-Economy, 325
Micro and Small Scale
Enterprises, 246
Growth and Development, 246, 250
Micro Enterprises, (ME), 111, 112, 114
In Tamil Nadu, 112
Micro Finance Institutions, 252, 254
Micro, Small and Medium
Enterprises Development
Act, 48
Micro-Credit
Lending (MCL), 238
Program, 250
Micro-Economic Stability and
Policy, 40
Micro-Enterprise in Bamboo
Based Industry, 142-153
Micro-Finance (MF), 235-260
And Women Empowerment, 251
Program, 251, 252
Middle East, 118, 119
Middle East and Asian
Markets, 202
Milk
Processing, 201
Producer Group, 200
Product Techniques, 204
Production
Cost, 194, 195
States, 220
System, 200
Millennium Development Goals
(MDGs), 167, 235, 245, 252, 253
Mineral Based Industry, 78
Ministry of
Environment and Forest, 100
Environment and Forests, 89
Non-Conventional Energy
Sources, 172, 174
MMPA (Milk and Milk Products
Association), 226
Modern
Machinery, 111
Spinning Mills, 111
Monopolistic Practices of
Production and Marketing, 43
Mozambique, 210
Muhammad Yunus,
(Bangladesh), 238
Multinational Corporations,
(MNCs), 36, 42, 58, 201, 220
Mutually Aided Cooperative
Society (MACS), 242

N

NABARD, 255, 257
Narsapur Mandal, 279

National
- Commission, 29
- Common Enterprises, 95
- Common Minimum
  - Program, (NCMP), 48
- Dairy Development Board
  - (NDDB), 231
- Economic Policies, 28
- Emissions Reduction, 89
- Policies and Programs, 338
- Policy on Cooperative, 219
- Productivity Council, 101
- Quality Standard, 204
- Research and Development
  - Corp (NRDC), 341
- Rural Employment
  - Guarantee Act, 288
- Rural Health Mission
  - (NRHM), 273
- Small Industries Corp
  - (NSIC), 340
- New Economic Policy,
  - (NEP), 41
- And Small and Medium
  - Enterprises, 45

New Technology, 103

NGO (Non-Governmental Organizations), 122, 165, 253, 254, 270
- Micro Finance Institutions, 254
- Services, 122

Non-Availability of
- Raw Materials, 68
- Trained/Skilled Labour, 68

Non-Farm Sector, 142

Non-Governmental Promotion Structure, 47

Non-Timber Forest Products (NTFP), 155-169
- Based on SMEs, 165
- In Madhya Pradesh, 166

O

OECD Countries, 98

On Farm Tea Planting, 166

Open Market Economy, 219, 224

Operating Project
- Expenses Ratio, 131
- Ratio (OPR), 129

Operation Flood, 201
- World Largest Dairy
  - Program, 201

Out Reach Countries (Middle East), 227

Outsourcing, 56

P

Palam Hills, 146

Palghat Pass, 172

Patriarchal System of Society, 237

PDS (Public Distribution System), Shops, 283

Plant and Machinery, 44

Plastic Products, 53

PMRY (PM Rozgar Yojna), 48

Policy
- And Programs for Textile
  - Industry by Govt., 113

And Strategy for Milk Supply System, 204, 205
Implementation Constraints, 305
Measures, 113
Of Liberalization and Globalization, 159
Reforms, 111
Political Institutions, 63
Pollution, 88, 96, 97
Air, 89
Control Board (PCB), 89
Control Techniques, 97
Industrial, 87, 89, 101
Polymer and Chemicals Based Industry, 78
Poverty
Alleviation, 155, 259
Alleviation Program, 242
Eradication, 70
Reduction, 144, 312
Power Subsidy, 114
PRB (Regional Rural Banks), 254, 255
Prevention of Food Adulteration (PFA), 227
Pricing Policy, 204
Primary Health Centres (PHCs), 270, 273
Processed Products/Byproducts, 223
Australia, New Zealand, 223
European Union, USA, 223
Processing
And Marketing System, 155, 157
System, 220
Production Technology, 123
Productivity Enhancement Program, 202
Profit and Sales, 128
Profitability
Analysis, 124
Analysis Ratio, 125
Programs
Aimed at Technology, 346
On Women Development, 286
Project Shakti, 244
Promotional Package, 47
PTAs (Preferential Trade Agreements), 56

Q

Quality Wooden Packing, 118

R

Raw Cashew Nuts, 211
Largest Producer India, 211
Production, 211
Regional Development, 319, 333
Renewable Energy Technology, 181
Role of Financial Institutions, 342
Rural
Development, 70
Employment
Generation Program, 48
Opportunities, 156

Engineering and Bio Technology, 78
Enterprises, 70
Entrepreneurial Development Program of NABARD, 255
Entrepreneurs, 144
Health Care Services, 273
Industrialization, 73, 74, 76, 327
Industries, 72, 73
Program, 76
Projects, 76
Labour Force, 157
Markets, 164
Population, 73
Poverty, 155, 165
Women, 236, 237, 244, 245, 262-268
Development of-, 262-268
Role of Self-Help Groups, 262-268
Social Education Centre (RUWSEC), 243
Workers, 119

S

Sanitation and Photo Sanitary Measures, (SPSM), 91
Sarvodaya Sangham (SS), 121-140
Sector,
Agriculture and Dairy, 228
Cooperation, 219
Dairy, 188, 190, 200-202, 205, 221
Dairy Cooperative, 224
Indian Dairy, 204
Indian Manufacturing, 53
Industrial, 48, 60, 72, 160, 287, 338
Khadi, 84
Khadi and Village Industry, 70, 77, 79, 81, 83-85, 122
Leather and Textile, 53
Small
Enterprises, 95
Scale, 41, 48, 66, 72
And Medium Enterprises, (SMEs), 165
Scale Industry (SSI), 28, 29, 33, 36, 45, 51, 53, 94, 96, 334
Village and Small Industries, 317
Self-Help Groups, (SHGs), 235, 236, 240, 242-245, 251, 255, 267, 268
Bank Linkages, 254, 255, 257, 259
Current Status, 265
Federation, 240, 242
Of ICICI Bank, 236, 238
Problems, 265, 266
Structure, 240
Sen, Amartya, Economist and Nobel Laureate, 264
SEWA 244
Shri Mahila Griha Udyog Lajjat Pappad, 244

SIDO (Small Industries
Development Organization), 317
Skills Training, 246
Small
Enterprises in Dairying, 187-199
Industries Development Bank of India (SIDBI), 45, 69, 96, 100
Report, 94
Industries, 96, 97
Industry
Technology Development, 69
Units, 29
Scale Enterprises, (SMEs), 29, 40, 42, 43, 54
Scale Forest
Based Enterprises, 156
Products, 164
Scale Industrial Undertakings, 318
Scale Industries Exports, 53
Scale Industries
in India, 27, 28, 32
in Tamil Nadu, 27
Scale Industries Units (SSIU), 27, 28, 29, 30, 32, 33, 35, 36
Employment Generation Capacity, 34
In Tamil Nadu, 33, 36
Scale Sectors in India, 334
Scale Service and Business Enterprises, (SSSBE), 43, 319
SMED Act, 160
SMEs (Small and Medium Enterprises), 44, 45, 47, 48, 109, 111, 155, 54-57, 96, 155-160, 163, 165-169, 225, 327-330, 332, 333, 337, 339-342, 344-346
And Economic Development, 42
Associations, 166
Challenges for-, 328, 329
Classification, 160
Contribution to Indian Economy, 319
Defined, 43, 157
Development Act, 44
Development Constraints, 163-164
In India, 40, 43, 54, 159, 311-330
In Uganda, 168
Major Industries, 163
Objectives, 44
Operation Definition, 313
Role in Economic Development, 42
Technology Needs, 329, 337
Under Globalization, 325
Social
Development Organization, 167
Transformation, 235
Workers, 276
Socio-Economic
Development, 190
Policies, 43
Programs and Schemes, 219

Revolution, 199
Security, 188
Soil Erosion, 209
Spinning Mills (SMs), 109, 110, 112, 113, 114
SSI (Small Scale Industries), 41, 43, 43, 44, 45, 51, 60-62, 64, 65, 68, 88, 94, 98, 101, 102, 159, 160, 317, 332-346, 340
Export Perspective, 320
In India, 80, 90, 92, 319
In Industrialization, 66-68
Performance, 41
Products, 66
Units, 53, 55, 95, 96, 312, 334, 335
Challenges, 337
Growth Pattern, 336
Performance, 336
Illegal Discharges, 89
Problems, 67
Standard of Living, 146
Strategic Alliances, 313
Sugar Mills at, 114, 115, 119
Coimbatore, 114
Dindigul, 114
Rajapalayam, 114
Supply Chain Management, 221
Swaranjyanti Gram Swarojgar Yojna, (SGSY), 288
Swarojgar Credit Card, (SCC), 256
SWOT analysis, 142, 151
Synthetic
Industry, 152
Raw Materials, 111

T

Tamil Nadu, 27, 29, 33, 34
Best Windy State, 176
Economy, 27
Electricity Board (RNEB), 176-178
Electricity Board, Power Generation, 178
Small Scale Industries Units, 33, 36
Wind Power Generation, 176
Wind Power Potential, 176
Tanzania, 210
TBT (Technical Barrier to Trade), 224
Techniques of Manufacturing Wooden Frames, 119
Technological
Change, 42
Development, 45, 163
Exports, 163
Innovations, 333
Technology (ies), 68, 91, 92, 103, 111, 115, 145, 152, 164, 306
And Management, 72
Bureau for Small Enterprises, 346
Foreign, 57
New, 103
Parks, 342
Strategy, 57
Support Institutions, 340
Traditional, 51
Up-gradation, 29, 95, 96

Textile
- Industry, 114
- Policy, 111

Timber Plantations, 167
Trade, 313
Trade Outlets, 61
Traditional
- Financing System, 250
- Industries/Skills, 73

Training Program, 275
Transfer of
- Cleaner Technology, 98
- Technology, 222, 340

TRIMS, 91
TRIPS (Trade Related Intellection Property), 91, 222
Trusts, 270

U

UK, 61
United Nations (UN), 250, 251
- Commission on Status of Women, 236
- Convention on Climate Change (UNFCCC), 87, 88
- Development Programmes, 235
- General Assembly, 250
- Industrial Development Organization (UNIDO), 98, 99, 100, 104

UPA Government, 29
Uruguay Round
- Agreement on Agriculture, (URAA), 201
- Of Multilateral Trade Negotiation, 222

US, 45, 91, 330
- Small Scale Industries in-, 61

V

Village
- And Small Industries, (VSI), 317
- Banking Model, 249
- Industries, 74, 78, 122
- Organization, 240, 242

VLCC Systems, 204

W

Waste Minimized Circle (WMCS), 101
Water
- Pollution Problems, 97
- Rights, 264
- Treatment System, 97

Western Technological System, 97
White Revolution, 220
Wind Power
- Generation, 171, 179
- Of Various States, 179-181
- Tamil Nadu, 179, 180
- Industry, (WPI), 171
- Industry In Tamil Nadu, 171

Installation Capacity, 174
In India, 174
In TN, 174
Women
Development, 286, 287
Empowerment, 235-239, 259, 291, 285-307
Enterprises, 318
Entrepreneurs, 238
Entrepreneurship (WES), 235-260
Equality Empowerment Framework, 286
Forums, 243
In Social and Economic Development, 287
Labour, 122, 264
Liberalization and Empowerment, 287
Role in Industrialization Process in India, 287
Self-Help Groups, 239
Status and Position in Society, 286
Workers, 110, 216
Women's Equality and Empowerment, 291
Woolen Garments, 53
Working Women Forums, 244
World
Assembly of Small and Medium Enterprises (WASME), 47
Health Organization (WHO), 227
Milk Production, 200
World Trade Organization (WTO), 91, 94, 103, 222, 223, 224, 225, 226, 231, 232, 264
Agreements, 228, 232
Regime, 42, 45, 222, 227, 328, 330

Y

Yarn for Export, 117